PRAISE FOR
PARTISAN SONG

"Full of real-life heroes...a stirring tribute to the courage of Jewish partisans. Grymes has written a stunning tale of resistance and bravery—a real page-turner."
—HEATHER DUNE MACADAM, AUTHOR OF *999*

"A vivid, compelling, and unblinking account, beautifully researched and written. Grymes illustrates that Jews did not go 'like sheep to the slaughter,' but, rather, fought back and exacted revenge. Highly recommended."
—SUSAN J. EISCHEID, AUTHOR OF *MISTRESS OF LIFE AND DEATH*

"Award-winning author James A. Grymes honors both the resilience of one man and the strength of a people who refuse to be silenced."
—MIKE CROISSANT, AUTHOR OF *BOMBING HITLER'S HOMETOWN*

"A must read...a riveting story that needs to be heard to teach future generations. History buffs and Holocaust educators should add this well-researched account to their libraries."
—BARBARA GOLDSTEIN, EXECUTIVE DIRECTOR, HOLOCAUST EDUCATION RESOURCE COUNCIL

"An extremely important contribution to the history of the genocide that was conducted against the Jews...a deeply researched and essential account."
—LEAH GARRETT, AUTHOR OF *X TROOP: THE SECRET JEWISH COMMANDOS OF WORLD WAR II*

"A remarkable book...a compelling and inspiring narrative on the brave and ingenious Jewish partisan leader 'Uncle Misha' in the forests of Nazi-occupied Ukraine."
—DAVID E. FISHMAN, AUTHOR OF *THE BOOK SMUGGLERS*, WINNER OF THE NATIONAL JEWISH BOOK AWARD

ALSO BY JAMES A. GRYMES

Violins of Hope: Violins of the Holocaust—Instruments of Hope and Liberation in Mankind's Darkest Hour
(Winner, National Jewish Book Award)

PARTISAN SONG

A HOLOCAUST STORY OF RESILIENCE, RESISTANCE, AND REVENGE

JAMES A. GRYMES

CITADEL PRESS
Kensington Publishing Corp.
kensingtonbooks.com

CITADEL PRESS BOOKS are published by

Kensington Publishing Corp.
900 Third Avenue
New York, NY 10022

All Kensington titles, imprints, and distributed lines are available at special quantity discounts for bulk purchases for sales promotions, premiums, fund-raising, educational, or institutional use. Special book excerpts or customized printings can also be created to fit specific needs. For details, write or phone the office of the Kensington sales manager: Kensington Publishing Corp., 900 Third Avenue, New York, NY 10022, attn Sales Department; phone 1-800-221-2647.

CITADEL PRESS and the Citadel logo are Reg. U.S. Pat. & TM Off.

10 9 8 7 6 5 4 3 2 1

First Citadel hardcover printing: February 2026

Printed in the United States of America

ISBN: 978-0-8065-4345-1

ISBN: 978-0-8065-4347-5 (e-book)

Library of Congress Control Number: 2025945763

The authorized representative in the EU for product safety and compliance
is eucomply OU, Parnu mnt 139b-14, Apt 123,
Tallinn, Berlin 11317; hello@eucompliancepartner.com

To Amnon Weinstein (1939–2024),
who introduced me to this story, and so many others.

Contents

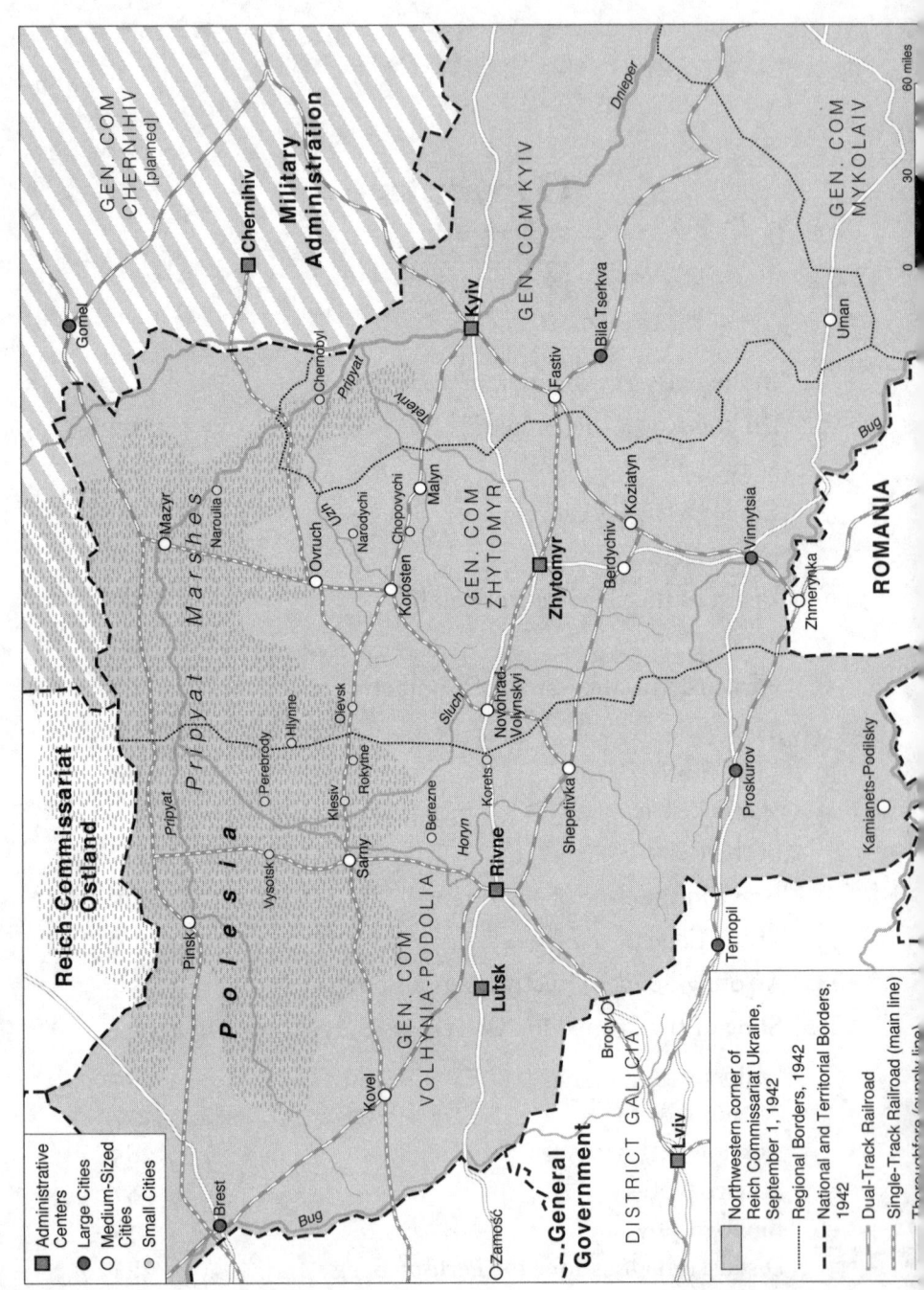

GEN. COM CHERNIHIV [planned]

Chernihiv ■

Military Administration

Gomel ⬤

GEN. COM KYIV

Kyiv ■

Dnieper

GEN. COM MYKOLAIV

Chernobyl ○

Pripyat

Teteriv

Fastiv ○

Bila Tserkva ⬤

Uman ○

Mazyr ○

Naroulia ○

Ovruch ○

Uzh

Narodychi ○

Chopovychi ○

Malyn ○

GEN. COM ZHYTOMYR

Koziatyn ⬤

Berdychiv ○

Vinnytsia ⬤

ROMANIA

Pripyat Marshes

Korosten ○

Zhytomyr ■

Zhmerynka ○

Bug

Hlynne ○

Olevsk ○

Sluch

NovOhrad-Volynskyi ○

Pererebrody ○

Klesiv ○

Rokytne ○

Korets ○

Berezne ○

Shepetivka ○

Proskurov ⬤

Reich Commissariat Ostland

Pripyat

Wysotsk ○

Sarny ○

Horyn

Rivne ■

Kamianets-Podilsky ○

Pinsk ○

Polesia

GEN. COM VOLHYNIA-PODOLIA

Lutsk ■

Ternopil ⬤

Kovel ○

Brody ○

DISTRICT GALICIA

General Government

Brest ⬤

Bug

Zamość ○

Lviv ■

Legend:

Administrative Centers ■

Large Cities ⬤

Medium-Sized Cities ○

Small Cities ○

■ Northwestern corner of Reich Commissariat Ukraine, September 1, 1942

⋯⋯⋯⋯ Regional Borders, 1942

– – – National and Territorial Borders, 1942

═══ Dual-Track Railroad

━━━ Single-Track Railroad (main line)

Throughfare (supply line)

60 miles

30

0

© Peter Palm, Berlin, Germany

CHAPTER 1

"In the Salty Sea of Human Tears"

In the salty sea of human tears,
There is a terrible abyss.
It could not be darker, it could not be deeper,
It is marked with a bloody tide.

The abyss has been carved out over thousands of years
By faith, hatred, and pain.
And for thousands of years, drop by drop,
It has filled with tears.

> —S. ANSKY, "IN THE SALTY SEA"
> (JOSEPH GLADSTEIN, *FREEDOM'S SONGS*, P. 61)

WHEN MOSHE GILDENMAN RETURNED TO his hometown of Korets, Ukraine, after helping to defeat the Nazis, he was heartbroken not by what he saw, but by what he could not see. The proud Jewish community into which he had been born, where he had grown up, and where he had raised his own family, was gone. The Jewish homes and businesses had been reduced to rubble, and the Jews themselves had been murdered.

1

Jews had been living in Korets as far back as the sixteenth century, when its region of Volhynia was annexed from the Grand Duchy of Lithuania to the Crown of the Kingdom of Poland. By the early seventeenth century, there were eight synagogues and a Jewish hospital in the town. That community was all but wiped out during the Cossack–Polish War, when Cossacks massacred tens of thousands of Jews throughout Volhynia. By 1655, there were only ten houses in Korets that were owned by Jews.

But the Jewish community recovered quickly. Volhynia was on the trade route from the Black Sea to Western Europe, and the Jews developed not only local trade, but also importing and exporting. They moved furs and hides from Russia to the West, along with silk, spices, and rugs from Turkey. They sold gold, textiles, and leather goods from western countries to the East. There were more mass atrocities, specifically during successive invasions by the Cossacks, Swedes, Russians, and Poles in the early eighteenth century, but the Jews persevered.

By 1765, there were 937 Jews living in Korets, and the town had developed into an important site for the Hasidic spiritual revival movement. Rabbi Pinchas Shapiro, a disciple of the founder of Hasidism, settled in Korets in 1760. He became a prominent voice in the growing Hasidic movement, and attracted many of his own disciples to Korets. In 1776, a prominent Hebrew publisher of texts on Hasidism and the Jewish mystical tradition of Kabbalah moved its printshop to Korets. They printed twenty books between 1776 and 1781, when they sold the shop to a Polish printing magnate. The new owner published eighty-eight Hasidic and Kabbalist texts between 1782 and 1787, all while employing Jews as printers, typesetters, and proofreaders. With a second Jewish printshop opening in 1780, and a third in 1794, Korets established itself as a major center of Jewish publishing.

The industrialization of Korets began in earnest in the 1780s, when Prince Józef Klemens Czartoryski started to develop the town. He restored the fourteenth-century castle, which had been destroyed by a fire, transforming the fortress into a residential palace. He cleaned up Korets and paved its roads with cobblestones. In 1786, he opened a textile mill with ten workshops, two of which were managed and staffed by Jews. Within five years, sixty Jews were working at the mill, and a rabbi had opened a second textile mill that only employed Jews. Czartoryski also established a porcelain factory, a ceramics factory, a belt factory, and a brewery. The porcelain and belt factories, in particular, were renowned for the quality of their products throughout Poland and beyond.

The internationalization of Korets's industries came to a sudden end in 1795, when Volhynia was annexed by the Russian Empire. Korets and the other towns in Volhynia found themselves cut off from their economic partners in Poland. Nevertheless, Korets and its Jewish community continued to grow, with most of the Jews making a living from small commerce and various trades. The community received a boost in the 1860s, when wealthy Hasidic rabbi and forester Yaakov Yosef Horenstein moved to Korets. Horenstein built a lumber mill and a sugar factory, initiating another brief period of economic stability. Many Jews were able to find employment in the timber and grain trades, as well as in four Jewish-owned tanneries.

The Jewish community suffered another disaster on the morning of June 29, 1881, when a massive fire broke out. It started with the straw roof of a small house at the edge of town and spread quickly. Within three hours, all of the stores and thirteen synagogues were destroyed, including one that had dated back to the seventeenth century. Twenty Jews perished in the fire, and hundreds of others lost their homes. But the Jews again bounced back. They rebuilt the town and most of its houses of worship, including six Hasidic synagogues.

The Jewish community continued to grow over the next four decades, largely thanks to the leadership of Crown Rabbi Nehemiah Hershenhorn. In 1886, Hershenhorn founded a Talmud

Torah—a school that provided free elementary education in Hebrew, the Torah, and the Talmud to underprivileged children. In the years that followed, there was a new school for young boys that also offered Hebrew courses for adults in the evenings, as well as a Jewish hospital and a home for the elderly. In 1902, Hershenhorn established a library, stocking the shelves with philosophical tomes, classic literature, and even pulp fiction in Russian, Hebrew, and Yiddish. The library quickly became a hub of intellectual activity for young Jewish men and women, who gathered there to debate journalism, literature, and politics.

By the time Moshe was born in Korets on May 13, 1898, the town was home to a vibrant community of over four thousand Jews. He left Korets to attend secondary school in Rivne and then studied engineering at the polytechnic school in Novozybkov, but returned to his hometown after completing his education. He assumed the role of town engineer, and quickly became a leader in the professional community. In 1922, Moshe helped organize an Artisans Association to support fellow Jewish craftsmen. When the association established an executive committee in 1935, they elected Moshe to serve not only as a member of the committee, but as its chair. By then, Moshe had founded a concrete plant in Korets. Although the construction business slowed during the winter, the half of the year that the plant was able to fully operate provided Moshe with a quiet, comfortable life as he and his wife, Golda, raised their family in a beautiful house in the nice part of town. He was a content and peaceful man who had never even held a weapon. That is, not until the Nazis came and murdered Golda and their thirteen-year-old daughter, Feigela.

STANDING IN KORETS'S market square after the Holocaust, Moshe looked around in disbelief. All that was left of the rows of stone storefronts that had once surrounded the square was a pile of rubble. In his mind's eye, Moshe could still see a busy day at the market. The Jewish storeowners would stand at the thresholds of their stores, touting their goods in broken Russian to everyone passing by. The street merchants known as *shotimayeshnikes*—from the Ukrainian *"shcho ty maiesh,"* or "what do you have?"—would wander through the crowd looking for things to trade. In a mixture of Yiddish, Polish, and Russian, peasants would sell chickens and eggs from their woven baskets. For hundreds of years, the market square had been filled with the sounds of the hustle and bustle of Jewish life. Now there was only silence.

Moshe was saddened, but also angry. "Where are you, poor, hardworking Jews? Why did you leave this place that your fathers and grandparents left you as their legacy? Why didn't you, strong Jews whom the gentiles feared, strangle at least one German with your bare hands?" he asked. "Why didn't you resist? Why didn't you physically respond? Why did you let them lead you like sheep to the slaughter without fighting back?" There was nobody to answer.

Moshe headed down Kościuszko Street. It had been along this main thoroughfare that the majority of businesses and shops had been located. Their Jewish owners had waited anxiously inside, hoping that a customer would stop by. It had been difficult for Jews to succeed as shopkeepers ever since 1921, when Poland had reclaimed Korets, along with two-thirds of Volhynia, at the end of the Polish–Soviet War. The severing of the economic ties with Russia that had been in place for over a hundred years had been devastating for Korets businessmen. The impact had been especially hard on the 3,888 Jews living in Korets, who by that time comprised 78 percent of the town's population.

The four Jewish-owned tanneries that had employed large numbers of Jewish workers had gone out of business in 1925. Aside from a small cotton mill that catered to the local community, the only working-class jobs that had been available to Jews were in small Jewish-owned businesses, like the local flour mill. Chaim Sapir's textile mill, which had produced thick fabric for the peasants' winter coats, had only employed two workers. The sugar industry had continued to thrive, but by then, there were no Jews among the hundreds of workers in the sugar factory at the edge of town.

Jews had also been excluded from much of the agricultural industry. The fields that produced sugar beets and other vegetables were all owned by rich Ukrainian farmers or the owners of neighboring estates. Jewish workers had, however, purchased fruit from local orchards to sell locally and all over Poland. They had also gathered onions from surrounding villages, becoming so prolific at selling them throughout the country and abroad that the Jewish community of Korets had become synonymous with the phrase "bushel of onions."

Even after Poles had opened their own stores and had convinced the other gentiles in town to boycott the Jewish shops, some Jewish storeowners had managed to continue carving out livings by selling clothing and footwear to members of the local Jewish community, a rather small market, given how destitute that population had become. The tiny garment market in Korets had also provided a few local jobs sewing clothes for the Jewish shops.

But those Jewish workers and businesses had been annihilated during the Holocaust. As Moshe continued down Kościuszko Street, he watched a group of Ukrainian shoemakers working in a building that had once housed a Jewish store. Their long hair slicked back, the young cobblers were singing a song while flapping the leather soles of the shoes they were making. He continued past a house that had once been a Jewish haberdashery and walked by a Jewish iron shop that had since been turned into a state cooperative.

MOSHE HEADED TOWARD Synagogue Street, where four Jewish houses of worship had once stood. By the early twentieth century, Korets had been home to eighteen synagogues, along with three houses of study and worship, known as *kloyzes*, and a number of study halls, or *beth midrashes*. The Jewish community had been diverse, and each sector of the population had its own sacred space where they could gather in times of joy, as well as in times of danger. There had been two synagogues for the Jewish leaders, a synagogue and a *kloyz* for the wealthier Jews, and one synagogue each for the merchants, the tanners, the hatmakers, the tailors, the shoemakers, the porters, and the musicians. There had also been several synagogues and *kloyzes* for the various Hasidic dynasties.

As Moshe turned onto Synagogue Street, he wondered if he was in the right place. It certainly did not look like the same street where he and his Jewish friends had grown up together. On the Sabbath and during Rosh Hashanah and Yom Kippur, light had emanated from behind white curtains in the windows of the simple one-story wooden houses that had once lined the street. The families who lived in them had filled the neighborhood and the brightly lit synagogues by the hundreds. Nothing remained of that neighborhood except piles of stone blocks and charred wood. Scorched and warped remnants of iron beds jutted from the rubble. In the debris, Moshe noticed a torn Torah, opened to the book of Exodus. The thought of the Holy Scriptures being trampled by human feet added to his anger.

Moshe could barely make out the lots where Jewish houses had once stood. He found the property of the Jewish apple merchant and remembered smelling the apples from blocks away whenever they were being loaded onto wagons to be sent by train to Rivne. Nearby had stood a small house of prayer that had been run by an old Jewish merchant who had limped around selling candles, tassels, amulets, and calendars. Across the street from the apple merchant had been a row of four connected houses where the Jewish tailor had lived next to the shoemaker's workshop. As a boy, Moshe had visited both for some of his first clothes and shoes.

Moshe paused for a moment at the site where a Jewish miller's house had once stood. When the Nazis had established a ghetto in Korets, Moshe had lived in this house with his nineteen-year-old son, Simcha, along with the baker Moshe Krasnostavski, Krasnostavski's son, and several other survivors. It was in this house that Moshe and Simcha had secretly met with a small group of young men who were preparing to take up arms against the Nazis. Under the stairs, Moshe had hidden the revolver that he had later taken with him when he, Simcha, and ten other Jews had escaped from the ghetto. Only a concrete porch with two stairs remained.

Near the end of the street, Moshe reached the Great Synagogue. Once the most beautiful house of worship in town, the synagogue had housed an ornately carved Torah ark. Above the heavy doors that had housed the Torah scrolls, there had been an inscription in gold of Psalms 118:20: *This is the gate of the Lord, through which the righteous may enter.* That inscription had been torn down by the Germans on July 2, 1941, the day they invaded Korets.

Within two hours of entering Korets, the Germans had gathered all of the town's rabbis in the Great Synagogue and marched them in small groups to the other synagogues. The rabbis were forced to take the Torah scrolls and other sacred texts into the streets, douse them with gasoline, and set them on fire. Those who refused were beaten and shot. The rest were photographed with the burning Torahs in the background. The rabbis were then forced to cut off each other's beards. When they were done humiliating the rabbis, the Germans burned down the Great Synagogue and several *beth midrashes*. Jews from neighboring houses ran to the synagogue with buckets of water, only to be turned back by hails of gunfire. By the end of the day, all that was left were the stone walls of the synagogue's basement.

At the very end of Synagogue Street was the lot where the Jewish library had once stood. While Korets had been reclaimed by Poland in 1921, its easterly neighbor Novohrad-Volynskyi had remained in the Soviet Union. Rabbi Yoel Shurin had moved a yeshiva—a school for the advanced study of rabbinic literature—from Novohrad-Volynskyi to Korets, housing it alongside the Talmud Torah on the library's second floor. The yeshiva had trained generations of Jewish scholars, and its students had taught the children in the Talmud Torah until 1939, when the Soviets had shut it down. Moshe remembered hearing the bustle of the children in the school, and how the yeshiva students would call from the second-floor windows, conveying the latest news or greeting a Torah reader on his way to celebrate Rosh Hashanah or to observe Yom Kippur. Now the only sound he could hear was the whining of a dog in the backyard of the perfectly preserved churchyard that bordered the former Talmud Torah.

MOSHE WALKED DOWN a set of stairs to the left of where the library and the Talmud Torah had been. The "bridge of the dead" that had once led to the Jewish cemetery had been replaced with two boards. Moshe could not help but think about the final generation of Korets Jews, who had made their last journeys through other roads and bridges as they were marched four miles north, to a forest near the village of Kozak. On May 21, 1942, over 2,200 of them, including Moshe's wife and daughter, had been taken to Kozak, shot, and buried in mass graves. New pits had been dug that September for the Jews who had remained in Korets, with the exception of the few who, like Moshe, had managed to escape.

Moshe reflected on how the path leading to the cemetery had looked before. This was where the poorer Jews had lived, in squat wooden shacks covered with straw or thin strips of wood that they had built into the cemetery wall. Generations of working-class Jews had raised their families there. Moshe vividly recalled the children with dark, intelligent eyes who were always playing in the middle of the street, laughing, dancing, and watching all of the pedestrians. On May 21, 1942, while the Nazis were rounding up the Jews and marching most of them toward Kozak, the Jews' former neighbors had ransacked Jewish homes throughout the town, and had torn down the shacks for wood. The local Ukrainians had also demolished the moss-covered wall that had once surrounded the Jewish cemetery, using its large stones and red bricks to pave their streets.

Moshe stepped into the Jewish cemetery. Rabbi Yaakov Yosef Horenstein's marble tombstone had been destroyed. All that was left were a few pieces of white stone, one still bearing a portion of the gilded inscription. Also gone were the two rows of *ohels*— mausoleum-style structures that had been built around the graves of prominent Jewish figures. Every year, hundreds of believers had made pilgrimages to the *ohels*, inserting into small windows slips of paper onto which they had written prayers. After the Ukrainians had dismantled the *ohels* and used their stone blocks to build ovens and stoves, the slips of paper had flown over the town like birds whose nests had been crushed by pranksters. There had been no place of refuge for the prayer notes, just as there had been none for those who had written them.

Moshe climbed up the narrow, grass-covered path to the top of the hill that the Jews of Korets had chosen centuries earlier as their place of eternal rest. To his right was the Korchyk River, which had been the namesake of the original Lithuanian village of Korchesk in the twelfth century. The Korchyk River flows from the Pripyat basin into the Sluch River, winding through Korets along the way and separating the Old Town, where the Jews had lived, from the New Town, where the gentiles had moved after the great fire of 1881.

The river had held a special place in the Jewish community, especially among the youth. In the winter, groups of boys and girls had sled down the sloped riverbank and skated on the ice. In the spring, children had traipsed through the mud to find the flowers' first blooms. In the warmth of summer, they had spent their mornings bathing in the river, their days playing on the adjacent playgrounds and athletic fields, and their evenings relaxing on blankets along the riverbed. Jews of all ages visited the river at the end of the autumnal Festival of Sukkot, looking for willow branches to beat on the ground to symbolize the elimination of sin. They returned again during Rosh Hashanah to symbolically cast off their sins.

Looking across the river at the New Town, Moshe could see white brick houses surrounded by idyllic gardens. On the riverbank, a group of Ukrainians was singing while tying large tobacco leaves to a rope. Two peasants were standing in a tanner's yard, hanging fleece out to dry. An old peasant was fishing on a rock in the middle of the river. The gentiles were peacefully engaged in their daily chores, as if nothing out of the ordinary had transpired just a few years earlier. They were living their lives exactly as they had before, showing no remorse for the atrocities in which they had eagerly participated.

Moshe stared at their hands. The same hands that had plundered Jewish property and which would be forever stained with the blood of innocent Jews were calmly reaching for tobacco, drying fleece, and catching fish. During the day, the Ukrainians wore the bloody clothes they had stripped from Jewish bodies. They wore embroidered silk aprons sewn from Jewish prayer shawls, cinched their pants with belts made of tefillin straps, and wrapped fish in pages torn from Torahs. Young Ukrainians wore engagement rings they had slipped from severed fingers, and mothers carried fruit from their gardens in the baby carriages of Jewish infants they had smothered with their bare hands. At night, they slept peacefully on pillows stuffed with feathers that Jewish mothers had cleaned during long winter nights, preparing them as dowries for their daughters.

DISGUSTED AND BITTER, Moshe turned back toward the cemetery. Now that he could see the full extent of the damage, he shivered at the desecration. What had once been a proud cemetery dotted with ancient trees was now an open field littered with rubble. The Ukrainians had chopped down the trees and overturned the gravestones, taking some away to serve as whetstones, millstones, and cellar walls. Other gravestones had been rolled down the hill toward the river. Those that had made it to the bottom intact were now being used as stepping stones for Ukrainian women washing their laundry. One could still read the inscriptions on the stones in the river and the fragmented rubble that remained behind in the field.

"How much effort, how much time, how much energy did they expend shattering these sandstone, granite, and concrete gravestones?" Moshe wondered. "How much unbridled ruthlessness and limitless hatred did they have to possess to do such bestial work?"

He went searching for the graves of relatives and friends who had been allowed the privilege of dying in their own beds and being buried in sacred ground rather than in the mass graves that peppered the roads and fields of Ukraine.

There were 6 million Jews killed during the Holocaust. Approximately 2.7 million were murdered in the killing centers of Auschwitz-Birkenau, Belzec, Chełmno, Sobibor, and Treblinka. Up to 1 million more were killed in ghettos, labor camps, and concentration camps, and at least 250,000 Jews were killed in acts of violence that took place outside of the camps and ghettos. The remaining 2 million were massacred in mass shootings throughout Eastern Europe. This method of genocide—mass murders committed not by transporting Jews by train to killing centers, but by marching them just outside of their hometowns and shooting them at close range—is often referred to as the "Holocaust by Bullets."

An hour later, Moshe was still wandering around the cemetery ruins, unable to find anything among the piles of broken headstones and open graves. Mentally and physically exhausted, he sat on the trunk of a felled tree. More memories of his child-hood came flooding back. He and his friends had climbed that very tree on the fasting day of Tisha B'Av, picking pears while hiding from the gravedigger. Moshe remembered a woman they had called the dancing mourner. A short, bespectacled woman with a perpetual smile on her face, she would greet those who had come to visit the graves of their relatives. "Who are you, Jews, and who are you looking for?" she would ask, leaning on her cane. Moshe desperately wished that the dancing mourner was with him on that day, to help him find his mother's grave be-fore he left the cemetery forever.

A group of gentile boys led a herd of cattle and horses into the cemetery to graze. They looked at Moshe with curiosity. *What are you doing in our pasture, lousy Jew?* the surprised looks on their faces seemed to ask. *Didn't Hitler promise to kill you all?*

DEPRESSED AND DAZED, Moshe started walking back into town. Gone were the families of the grain traders who had once carried heavy sacks of wheat and corn through the Jewish streets, along with the Jews who had traded with the gentiles and loaned them money. Every house along the narrow street reminded him of people he had once known. He walked past the houses where a wagoner, a wheelwright, a miller, and a klez-mer musician had once lived. He passed Chaim Sapir's textile mill. Smoke still rose from the chimney, but now the mill was run by Ukrainians.

Piles of broken stone marked the lot where the craftsmen's synagogue had once stood. The building had survived the great fire of 1881, but not the Holocaust. The synagogue was the site of some of Moshe's earliest memories. Moshe thought back to Simchat Torah, the Jewish holiday that celebrates the end of the annual cycle of public Torah readings. As a small child, he had stood on a bench, holding a flag topped with a candle stuck into a red apple. He had watched excitedly as the celebrants had

taken out the Torah scrolls and filled the synagogue with singing and dancing.

As Moshe walked past the Old Marketplace, on the other
side of the street from the textile mill, he once again noted how
empty and eerily quiet everything was. Once or twice a month,
the Old Marketplace had been a hub of activity as it had hosted
market days that had provided many Jews with their primary
sources of income. Merchants from Korets, as well as dozens of
farmers and vendors from nearby towns, had packed the Old
Marketplace with stalls loaded with goods that they had hoped
to sell to the thousands of peasants who had flocked to the town
looking for deals. The quality of the merchandise had been
cheap, and the prices had been so low that they had barely
yielded any profit. Because of the fierce competition, the shopkeepers had continually lowered the costs of their products, forcing them even further into poverty.

Moshe had been very involved in the charitable organizations that the Jewish community had established to care for
those in need. In connection with his longstanding leadership
of the Artisans Association, he had helped lead Korets's Cooperative Bank. As with its counterparts in other Jewish communities throughout Eastern Europe, the Cooperative Bank
served not just as a financial institution, but also as a charity, extending payment dates when necessary and even disbursing out-
right donations.

Moshe had also been a leader in the local chapters of two of
the most important Jewish aid organizations in Poland: the Society for Safeguarding the Health of the Jewish Population and the
Central Society for the Care of Orphans, which had been known
by their Polish acronyms, TOZ and CENTOS. TOZ had provided
medical care and nourishment for Jews whose health was suffering because of the destitute economic conditions. In addition to
providing a medical clinic, a pharmacy, a dental clinic, and
health education to the adults, the Korets branch of TOZ had

cared for the children. In the winters, they had provided in-school medical care and hot lunches. In the summers, they had hosted two-month summer camps that they called "colonies," so that poor children who lived in unlit, overcrowded, and unsanitary apartments and cellars could enjoy three meals a day while exercising in the sunshine and fresh air. CENTOS had focused on assisting children who had lost their parents in the catastrophic aftermath of World War I. Moshe had even sat on the board of CENTOS's orphanage, a building on Kościuszko Street that had provided shelter, food, clothing, and education to around seventy Jewish orphans at a time.

As Moshe continued his tour of postwar Korets, he again noted how easily the Jewish community had been replaced. Ukrainian peasants sat comfortably on the porches of perfectly preserved Jewish homes. Three houses and the fire station had been destroyed by a bomb, and their lots were now serving as a potato field. In the northern part of town, the Berezne synagogue and the Trisker *kloyz* still stood, but both had been converted into grain warehouses.

On his way out of town, Moshe crossed the bridge and passed the beautiful houses where the Jewish tannery owners had once lived. Ukrainians watched out of the windows. Moshe imagined them being unhappy with the "debris," as they referred to the remnants of the Jewish survivors, walking down "their" streets, looking into "their" homes.

MOSHE'S CONTRIBUTIONS TO the Jewish community of Korets had not been limited to philanthropy. He had also played a leading role in cultural life. Korets had been a very musical town that had taken great pride in the vocal abilities of the cantors in its various synagogues, as well as in the virtuosity of the klezmer musicians who had played dance tunes at weddings and other celebrations. As many as half of its Jewish residents had sung or played instruments. Many of them had received their earliest musical training from Moshe, who had conducted the choir and the orchestra, along with a mandolin ensemble that he had founded, at the Tarbut school—one of many secular Hebrew-language schools that had been established by Zionist groups throughout Eastern Europe after World War I.

Moshe had also been a leader in the Jewish Drama Lovers' Circle, an amateur theater troupe of which the town had been quite proud. The drama circle had put on plays, melodramas, and operettas in Russian and Yiddish, accompanied by a choir and an orchestra. Each production would start with the orchestra playing a series of joyful melodies, and then the curtains would open and the play would begin. Packed into a three-hundred-seat theater, the Jewish audience members could forget about their financial problems and other everyday woes, if only for the evening. At the end of each performance, the orchestra would play dance tunes, and the attendees would dance into the wee hours of the morning. The proceeds from the plays and reading parties that the drama circle hosted went to TOZ.

Moshe had been a member of the drama circle since its founding in 1917, originally playing in its orchestra and later becoming the troupe's director. He was not only an actor and musician, but also a gifted playwright and composer. He had enjoyed particular success with his play *The King of the Schnorrers*, for which he had written both the script and the music. Nearly a hundred cast members performed, along with a large choir. Years later, a survivor who had sung in *The King of the Schnorrers* still remembered the humorous title song that Moshe had composed for the production. As always, the proceeds were donated to support the orphans and the poor.

There had been few philanthropic or cultural events in Korets to which Moshe had not lent his considerable talents. One survivor later described him as "a friend and a companion, a vibrant man, and a talented musician who brought the joy of life everywhere he came. He invested his mental strength in our

town, Korets, and loved its people, especially the young generation. His home and his heart were open to all in need. His energy,
his time, and his talents were sacred to all."

As with many Jewish communities in Central and Eastern Europe, Korets had been home to a number of organizations asso-
ciated with Zionism, a secular movement based on the belief that
Jews would never be free from persecution until they left Europe
and returned to their ancestral home in the Land of Israel. It was
Poale Zion, the Socialist-Zionist Jewish workers party, that had
spearheaded the creation of the Artisans Association that Moshe
had led. Moshe had also organized a choir for members of the
Poale Zion party and its youth movement, Freedom.

Although Moshe had been one of the most active members
of Zionist organizations in Korets dating as far back as 1917, he
was actually a Bundist. Bundism was a relatively small Socialist-
Jewish movement that arose at the end of the nineteenth century from the General Union—or *Bund*—of Jewish Workers in
Lithuania, Poland, and Russia. While Zionists encouraged their
fellow Jews to start new lives in Palestine, Bundists advocated
for staying in Europe and working to improve conditions there,
specifically for the working class. Given Moshe's attachment to
his hometown, it is not surprising that he would gravitate toward an ideology that envisioned a multiethnic Eastern European society in which Poles, Lithuanians, and Jews coexisted
peacefully, and where each culture was allowed to thrive, side
by side, with the others.

One of Moshe's most prized possessions was his copy of Joseph Gladstein's *Freedom's Songs*, a collection of thirty Yiddish-
language songs that was published in Warsaw in 1919. The first
song is a translation of "The Internationale," the socialist anthem
that had become the national anthem of the Soviet Union in 1918.
Some of the songs are settings of socialist texts by popular Yiddish poets. Others are specifically Bundist, including S. Ansky's
"The Oath," which was the official anthem of the Bund. Moshe's

copy of *Freedom's Songs* includes several of his own markings, suggesting that he used the book while leading performances.

In addition to "The Oath," *Freedom's Songs* includes Ansky's ten-stanza poem "In the Salty Sea," which is also known by its alternate title, "To the Bund." The text of "In the Salty Sea" promises that the Bund would liberate the Jewish worker from millennia of suffering and show him the path to freedom, brotherhood, equality, and peace. The poem is critical of the Jewish establishment, specifically wealthy Jews, who continued to oppress their workers, and Zionists, who are accused of creating a permanent ghetto for Jews in Palestine. The first two lines of the ninth stanza were so controversial that Gladstein omitted them from *Freedom's Songs*, printing only ellipses where the text would have gone. Moshe added those contentious lines back by hand: *Messiah and Jewry are both dead. A new Messiah is on his way.* According to "In the Salty Sea," it would be the newly liberated Jewish worker who would free and heal the world.

THE BEGINNING OF the end of Jewish life in Korets arrived on August 23, 1939, when the Soviet Union and Nazi Germany signed a peace treaty. Officially titled the "Treaty of Non-Aggression between Germany and the Union of Soviet Socialist Republics," the accord is often referred to as the Molotov–Ribbentrop Pact, after the Soviet and German foreign ministers who negotiated it. In addition to pledging that they would not go to war against each other, the two countries agreed that neither would lend support to the other's enemies.

Appended to the pact was a secret protocol, the existence of which would not be confirmed until after Germany's defeat in 1945. The addendum specified that Poland, along with the Romanian region of Bessarabia to the south, and Lithuania, Latvia, Estonia, and Finland to the north, would be portioned into Soviet and German "spheres of influence." The Soviets would exert influence over their neighbors in Bessarabia, Latvia, Estonia, and

Finland, while Germany would have Lithuania. Poland was divided roughly in half between the Soviet sphere to the east and the German sphere to the west.

On September 1, 1939, one week after signing the pact, Germany invaded Poland. Attacking from three directions with a massive force that introduced the world to the word blitzkrieg, or "lightning war," the German forces quickly overwhelmed the Polish Army. On September 10, Polish officials and Jewish refugees fleeing eastward swarmed into Korets and other towns throughout Volhynia, bringing with them stories of the horrific atrocities they had witnessed. Within a week, there were one hundred thousand Jewish evacuees in Korets alone, mostly from Warsaw, Lviv, and Kraków. Although the arrival of so many refugees stirred panic among the Jews of Korets, they provided them with food and shelter. Moshe welcomed fifty of them into his home.

As the German Army continued to quickly fight its way eastward, Moshe and his Jewish neighbors grew increasingly fearful. On September 17, when they were awakened by the sounds of tanks firing nearby and airplanes flying overhead, they were convinced that the Germans had arrived to kill them all. To their great astonishment and joy, they discovered that it was not the Germans who were approaching, but the Soviets. The Red Army entered Korets that night, and were in control of the city by the morning.

Believing that the Soviets had arrived to help Poland fight the Germans, the Polish peasants cheered, "To our aid! To our aid!" But the Red Army had come not to liberate eastern Poland, but to occupy it. Germany had advanced farther into Poland than had been agreed in the Molotov–Ribbentrop Pact, but compensated the Soviet Union by giving up most of Lithuania. The western border of Volhynia was now the western border of Soviet-occupied Poland.

The Polish government officials, policemen, and soldiers quickly disappeared and were replaced by Soviet officials and

soldiers. The Polish mayor was arrested and replaced with a tri-
umvirate of Soviet appointees. By the end of October, the Soviets had orchestrated elections to a National Assembly of
Western Ukraine, which quickly convened and requested that
Volhynia be returned to the Ukrainian Soviet Republic. On November 29, the Soviet Union granted citizenship to everyone living in the occupied territories. Korets, which had been annexed
by the Kingdom of Poland in 1569, claimed by the Russian Empire in 1795, and then reclaimed by Poland in 1921, was now part
of the Soviet Union.

Moshe was very suspicious of the Soviets. He feared that
their occupation of Korets would bring with it the antisemitic violence that had terrorized the Jews in the Soviet Union. Moshe's
concerns for his physical safety proved to be unfounded—at least
at first—but the implementation of communism would result in
the dismantling of many of the Jewish institutions in Korets.

The library was shuttered, but a few members of the Jewish
community managed to hide some of the Hebrew books to preserve their proud traditions. The Tarbut school was closed, and
the children were placed in state-run general and vocational
schools. There was also an order to shut down the Zionist youth
organizations. Young Jews were recruited—sometimes through
intimidation—into the Komsomol, the All-Union Leninist Young
Communist League. Although the Jewish youth were not ideo-
logically aligned with communism, they slowly integrated into
the new economy and social order through the conversion of
their schools and youth organizations into Soviet models, combined with the prospects of government jobs. The Jewish youth
of military age were drafted into the Red Army and never heard
from again.

The Sovietization also disrupted the economy. Private businesses were abolished and replaced with state-run cooperatives.
The Jews who had owned factories and stores found themselves
out of work. But they adapted and started to identify new liveli-

hoods, becoming government officials or working in state institutions and cooperatives. Those who were physically strong
found jobs as construction workers six months into the occupation, when the Soviets initiated a large construction project.

The Soviets decided to build an asphalt highway that would
connect Kyiv to Lviv, running right though Korets. This would
involve demolishing the wooden bridge over the Korchyk River
and replacing it with a modern one made of concrete. As a civil
engineer who had founded the town's concrete plant, Moshe
was naturally conscripted as a construction engineer. Although
the Soviets generally distrusted the natives of occupied Poland,
Moshe quickly distinguished himself through his organizational
skills and technical knowledge, resulting in an appointment as a
subsection chief within the Directorate of Highways. He got his
son Simcha a job as a driver for the highway directorate.

In April 1940, the People's Commissariat for Internal Affairs,
a predecessor of the KGB that was known by its Russian acro-
nym NKVD, started issuing Soviet identification cards to Jewish
residents and refugees living in Volhynia. The cards of wealthy
Jews and prominent Jewish leaders included an ominous Paragraph 11 that limited where they could live and subjected them
to arrest and exile to the interior of the Soviet Union, where approximately 320,000 people from Western Ukraine and Western Belarus were deported during the period of communist rule.
Moshe's wife, Golda, received a card with a Paragraph 11, but
Moshe did not, presumably because he had made friends with
enough clout to protect him from being expelled.

Not having a Paragraph 11 did not spare one from deporta-
tion. Moshe did not know it at the time, but on June 21, 1941, the
communist authorities drafted a list of wealthy Jews, including
Moshe, who were to be arrested and sent to Siberia. That plan
was interrupted when Nazi Germany invaded the Soviet Union
the very next day.

CHAPTER 2

"Do You Know the People?"

Do you know the people, the pale people,
Of hardship and torment and misery?
How every day looks like a night,
And how each life is a death?
—SHMUEL SHNITMAN, "DO YOU KNOW THE PEOPLE?"
(JOSEPH GLADSTEIN, *FREEDOM'S SONGS*, P. 34)

IN AN 1860 REVIEW OF Charles Darwin's *On the Origin of Species*, German ethnographer Oscar Peschel described human progress as being shaped by geography. Given humans' ability to adapt to their environments, he posited, different habitats can have either favorable or adverse effects on the development of the people who live there. To describe the distinct geographical region in which a specific population evolves, Peschel coined the term Lebensraum, or "living space."

The concept of Lebensraum quickly took hold in German political philosophy. If Germany was to reach its goal of becoming a leading world power, it would need to benefit from a Lebensraum that was more advantageous than the one Germans had historically inhabited. This would necessitate emulating its economic rival, Great Britain, by expanding beyond its borders into new territories with bountiful resources. In the late nineteenth century, Germany began working toward that goal by colonizing territories in Africa and the Pacific, becoming the third largest colonial empire behind Britain and France. There were, however, limitations inherent in depending on faraway lands for natural resources. Those problems were magnified during World War I, when the Allied blockade of Europe severed Germany's access to much-needed supplies from its colonies and caused severe food shortages.

After the war, German nationalists started envisioning not just the restoration of the territories their country had lost in the Treaty of Versailles, but a new, contiguous Lebensraum that would span all the way into the Soviet Union. Adolf Hitler invoked the Lebensraum concept several times throughout *Mein Kampf*, arguing that the National Socialist movement would need to lead the German people "out of the confinement of their [current] Lebensraum to new lands." This, he declared, would solve the problem of the "disproportion between the size of our population and the extent of our territory."

Hitler called for the eastward expansion of Germany's borders to be accompanied by the elimination of the Jews in those lands, as well as in historical Germany. Hitler and other right-wing Germans blamed the Jews for their devastating losses in World War I, as well as for the social and economic turbulence that followed. Jews were falsely accused of having stabbed the country in the back by failing to adequately support the war effort. The right wing maintained that it was this betrayal, rather than weaknesses in the military, that had ultimately led to Germany's defeat. It would be impossible to restore Germany to its former glory, they contended, without also eliminating the Jews who were responsible for its ruin.

When Hitler violated the Molotov–Ribbentrop Pact by invading the Soviet Union on June 22, 1941, it was to achieve two overlapping goals. The first was to expand Germany's Lebensraum, allowing the so-called Aryan race to spread out into a larger geographical region and gain access to richer natural resources. The second was to impose the Nazi worldview on the newly occupied territories by enslaving and ultimately annihilating all of its Jews, along with Poles, Russians, and Romani people, whom they deemed to be not only subhuman, but unworthy of life. Hitler gave the invasion the code name "Operation Barbarossa," after the Holy Roman Emperor and warrior-king Frederick Barbarossa, who, according to German legend, would someday awaken to lead Germany back to greatness.

THE FIRST DAYS of the war were a whirlwind of chaos for Moshe and his neighbors in Korets. On the same day that Germany invaded the Soviet Union, the Soviet authorities convened a town meeting during which they assured the frightened residents that the Soviet Union was too large and powerful for the Germans to ever advance all the way to Korets. But the Germans had caught the Red Army by surprise. With the overwhelming force of 5.5 million soldiers, 4,300 tanks, and 5,000 airplanes, Germany was slicing through Soviet Ukraine at the same speed with which they had conquered western Poland two years earlier.

The Red Army started retreating from Korets that evening. On the second day of the invasion, members of the government packed up and headed eastward as well. One day later, at two in the afternoon, all men between the ages of twenty-three and thirty-six received an order drafting them into the Red Army; twenty-one- and twenty-two-year-olds had already been conscripted. Parents cried, screamed, and begged for their sons to be spared. One family was successful in convincing the Soviet authorities that their two sons were too important to the community to go into the army, only to have those young men become the first casualties when the Germans reached Korets just a few days later.

The Soviet authorities in Korets issued a citywide evacuation order on June 25, initiating even more panic. The Jews who had served in official capacities in the Soviet regime were provided with transportation, and left the city with the remaining members of the Soviet government. Other Jews followed them on foot or in carts they had rented from the Ukrainians at steep prices. Several walked to Novohrad-Volynskyi, only to return to Korets after being unable to secure transport on the overcrowded trains. Many of those who were able to get tickets were killed when the Germans bombed the train station. Of the five thousand Jews who lived in Korets prior to the German invasion, four thousand stayed behind and braced for the worst.

By June 29, the residents of Korets could hear the roar of heavy military equipment as the Soviets withdrew from the west. The Germans had already captured Rivne, and the Red Army was retreating rapidly. By the next day, there was no trace of the Soviets in Korets, other than a few NKVD officers who had remained behind to maintain order. They were gone the next day. Jubilant Ukrainians walked the city streets, excitedly awaiting the arrival of the Germans, whom they saw as liberating them from the Soviet regime.

The Germans occupied Korets on July 2. By dawn, the residents could hear the booming of artillery and the explosions of numerous houses and other buildings being bombed. The streets were soon filled with the roar of engines and triumphant battle cries in German. The first wave of Germans rode into town on motorcycles, followed by the infantry and later by the heavy equipment.

The arrival of the Germans signaled the start of a new murderous chapter in the history of the Korets Jews. After burning down the Great Synagogue and several *beth midrashes*, the Germans roamed the town, beating and killing every Jew they saw.

No Jews dared to go into the streets. They stayed in their homes, anxiously waiting behind closed doors to see what would happen next.

AS HITLER SHARED with some of his most trusted advisors, he envisioned a three-step process for conquering the Soviet Union: occupying it, administering it, and then plundering it. In Korets and throughout Ukraine, the military occupation was followed immediately by the arrival of a police force that established order, conscripted workers for forced labor, and, ultimately, dismantled the existing power structure by murdering community leaders. To assist with the implementation of Nazi laws and regulations, the Germans created local and mobile branches of the Ukrainian auxiliary police—a paramilitary force of Ukrainian nationalists who were eager to assist with the persecution of Poles and Jews. The Ukrainians who joined the auxiliary police in Korets had grown up there and knew exactly which Jewish homes to ransack. They brutalized the occupants and plundered their belongings.

On July 5, there was a loud knock at Moshe's door.

"Open the door, or I'll kick it in," a hostile voice shouted in Ukrainian.

Moshe complied. An auxiliary policeman barged in, accompanied by three Germans.

"All men must come to work for us," the Ukrainian ordered.

As Moshe and Simcha gathered their belongings, the Ukrainian rifled through the cupboards and the food on the table, grabbing whatever he wanted.

Moshe asked how long the work would take, and whether they should bring some food with them.

"You've been eating our meat and drinking our blood for years," the Ukrainian responded. Since the Middle Ages, the Blood Libel myth has maliciously alleged that Jews murder Christian children and use their blood in religious rituals. "Now you can starve a little."

Moshe and Simcha were taken to the local hospital, which had been transformed into a military hospital. Along with several dozen other Jews, they worked without breaks until the late evening, cleaning the rooms and stocking them with pillows and blankets plundered from neighboring Jewish homes. Before they returned to their own homes, their work supervisor gave them certificates documenting that they were official workers. As laborers, they would receive 250 grams of bread each day from designated bakers. Jews without work details would not receive any bread.

Flour mill owner Yehuda Chimenes and his daughter Ita lived across the street from the hospital. They, too, were conscripted into working there on July 5. Yehuda was assigned to sweep the hospital courtyard, while Ita washed laundry. After the first day of work, Yehuda begged his son and two daughters, "Children, don't leave me. They're going to kill me."

Yehuda was beaten at work the next morning. When his eleven-year-old daughter, Shaindel, brought him breakfast, she found him bleeding from a head wound. Next to him stood a German holding a whip. Shaindel walked up to the German and cried, "Why are you hitting my father?"

Yehuda was allowed to return home a few hours later. His wife helped him clean off the blood. Shaindel ran to get the doctor, who bandaged Yehuda's head and ordered him to stay in bed.

Around midnight, the family was jolted awake by loud knocks on the door. Two Germans entered the house and ordered Yehuda to come with them. They refused to explain why, nor did they let him get dressed. He left the house in his underwear.

A few days earlier, a unit of German soldiers had come through Korets on their way to the Eastern Front. They had stopped at Yehuda's house to rest, and had set up a field kitchen in his yard. They had ordered Yehuda to give them two sacks of flour, leaving their empty sacks behind. Yehuda's Ukrainian neighbor had noticed the sacks with swastikas on them and had reported him for theft of military property.

Yehuda was brought to the military hospital and led to the fence that surrounded the hospital yard. The Germans handed him a shovel, forced him to dig his own grave, and shackled him to a tree with iron chains. After bringing Moshe, Simcha, and the other Jewish workers over to witness the spectacle, Yehuda was put on trial and quickly sentenced to death. Yehuda's desperate explanation that the empty sacks had been left there by German soldiers in exchange for two full sacks of flour fell on deaf ears, as did his pleas to let him say goodbye to his wife and children. After the first shot, Yehuda called out, "That's it! This is the end!"

The Germans shot him again, and then bashed in his head with a rifle butt. They threw his body into the grave and ordered two Jews to cover it up with dirt. Everyone else was ordered back to work.

ON JULY 8, the German military administration hung large posters in German and Ukrainian throughout Korets announcing restrictions on Jewish activity:

1. All weapons owned by Jews must be immediately handed over to the German authorities.
2. Jews are forbidden from leaving the city without permission of the authorities.
3. Gentiles are forbidden from crossing the thresholds of Jewish homes.
4. All Jewish homes must be prominently marked with a large blue Star of David.
5. All Jews aged twelve and over must wear two yellow patches: one on the left side of the chest and one on

the back (they should be round and seven centimeters in diameter).

6. Jews are allowed on the street only if they are on their way to or from work.

7. Jews may shop in the market only on Thursday mornings between eight and ten.

At the bottom of the poster an inscription read: *Failure to comply with these orders will result in death.*

The Jews quickly learned that these regulations brought grave repercussions. The Ukrainian peasants who sold vegetables at the market knew that the Jews had limited time to shop. They demanded exorbitant prices for their goods, asking for valuables or nice clothing in exchange for a little grain or beans. Ukrainian auxiliary policemen used the prohibition against weapons to rob and beat any Jew they encountered on the street. Despite the new rules, Germans and Ukrainians barged into Jewish homes, shouting "Jew!" and "Swine!" In addition to stealing food and belongings, they dragged whomever they wanted, regardless of age or gender, down to their headquarters, where they beat them and forced them to pick up trash and broken glass with their bare hands.

Moshe never forgot the first time he wore yellow patches in public. The Germans stared at him with smugness and contempt. Whenever a German walked behind him, Moshe would fear for his life. He imagined that at any moment the German would take out a pistol and aim at the yellow patch that provided a perfect target against the back of his black jacket. Some of the Ukrainians he knew looked at him with compassion, but others pointed and laughed. The stigma of being ostracized was more humiliating than any of the degrading work the Germans would force him to perform. He felt like a leper who had been cast out to avoid infecting the rest of the community.

The Jews of Korets had lived alongside their gentile neighbors in relative peace for several generations. There had always been some antisemitism, including a few merchants who had hung anti-Jewish posters in their store windows, but there had rarely been anything like the murderous pogroms—Russian for "violent riots"—that had occurred throughout the Russian Empire in the late nineteenth and early twentieth centuries. A tragic exception to this coexistence had occurred in 1919, when Ukrainian nationalists had murdered an estimated 150,000 Jews throughout Ukraine during the country's brief period as an independent People's Republic.

The relationship between Jews and Ukrainian nationalists had soured again during the Soviet period. Well aware of the destruction a German occupation would bring to their community, the Jews had welcomed the Soviets as protectors and allies. At the same time, the Ukrainian nationalists had grown to resent the Soviets—and the Jews who collaborated in Soviet political institutions—as occupiers who stood between them and their dream of reclaiming their independence.

Ukrainian independence proved to be out of the question, as it conflicted with Hitler's plans for the former Soviet territories. Nevertheless, Ukrainian nationalists still envisioned an ethnically homogenous state that was cleansed not only of Jews, but also of the Poles who had been transferred from Central Poland a few generations earlier to bring Polish culture and Catholicism to what was then eastern Poland. "The element that settled our cities, whether it is Jews or Poles who were brought here from outside the Ukraine, must disappear completely from our cities," declared the editor of the Ukrainian newspaper *Volhyn* on September 1, 1941. "The Jewish problem is already in the process of being solved, and it will be solved in the framework of a general reorganization of the 'New Europe.'"

In Korets, there was no figure who better represented the radicalization of ethnic Ukrainians than Mitka Zavirukha.

Mitka had been a notorious criminal in his youth. When he had hit rock bottom, he had been taken in by Avraham Bardach, the owner of the largest Jewish bakery in town. Avraham brought Mitka into his home, took him on as an apprentice, taught him Yiddish, and helped him assimilate into the Jewish community. But as soon as the Germans arrived, Mitka turned on the Jews. He got himself appointed as the commandant of the Ukrainian auxiliary police force in Korets and placed himself at the forefront of every murderous action. Wrapping himself in a cloak of piety, Mitka claimed that he had been sent by God to wash his body in a bath of Jewish blood.

Mitka loved to toy with members of his former community by promising that they would be kept alive a little longer. "The Germans are strangers who came here from far off. They intend to kill all of you Jews, but first they'll make sure to take control of all of your property and wealth," he would tell them. "So you have nothing to worry about; the Germans still haven't finished transferring all Jewish property to Germany."

But what Mitka was most interested in was transferring property and wealth to himself. Taking advantage of his rank in the auxiliary police, he would arrest wealthy Jews, holding them in the cellars used by the Ukrainian auxiliary police and the German Gestapo—the Geheime Staatspolizei, or "Secret State Police." He would murder them, even if large bribes had been paid for their release. "Doesn't the Ukrainian police commandant deserve to be rich?" he would cruelly ask his Jewish victims, not in his native tongue of Ukrainian, but in their language of Yiddish.

Two DAYS AFTER posting the restrictions on Jewish activity in Korets, the German military administration created a Jewish Council. The Germans had established Jewish Councils throughout occupied Poland in 1939, and were now extending that practice into their new territories. The Jewish Councils represented their communities in various dealings with the German authorities, and often convinced themselves that their influence with the Germans would allow them to protect their constituents. In reality, the Nazis placed rabbis and other Jewish leaders on the councils to project a false sense of legitimacy, while giving them no autonomous authority. The Jewish Councils were responsible for keeping order in ghettos and other confined communities, implementing and enforcing Nazi regulations. They were also charged with surrendering Jewish homes, clothes, valuables, and other belongings to the Germans on command, as well as providing the Germans with rosters of their Jewish populations that facilitated the conscription of Jews for work details, and, in some areas, the transfer of Jews to ghettos and concentration camps. In Korets, the Germans appointed five community leaders to the Jewish Council, with Moshe Krasnostavski as the chair.

On August 8, the Germans delivered to the Jewish Council a list of 120 names of some of the most prominent and influential members of the Jewish community, including Moshe and Simcha. Those on the list were ordered to report at ten in the morning to the headquarters of the German military police, where, they were told, they would be dispatched to work details. After providing their names, professions, and other information, eight of the prospective laborers were removed from the list because they were providing essential services. Moshe was excused because of his ability to repair watches, as was Simcha, who was an electrician. Both would later be put to work renovating the post office building. The other six essential laborers were a cobbler who made shoes for the local commandant, a tailor who worked for the military, a baker who made bread for the army, a worker from the sugar factory, and two brothers who were carpenters renovating the Ukrainian school. The remaining 112 Jews, among them two members of the Jewish Council, were put on trucks and driven toward Novohrad-Volynskyi, never to be seen again.

It was not until after the war that the few survivors of the Jewish community would learn what had happened. The Jewish leaders were taken to a field near the village of Sukhovolya, seven miles northeast of Korets. They were ordered to dig a mass grave and climb down into the pit, where they were shot.

IN ADDITION TO being threatened with theft and murder at the hands of the Germans, Jews in Ukraine were continually subjected to violence from Ukrainian nationalists, often with the blessings of the Germans. "Locally undertaken attempts to purge communist and Jewish circles in the occupied territories must not be interfered with. On the contrary, they must be supported without reservations," ordered Reinhard Heydrich, who as chief of the Reich Security Main Office oversaw the Gestapo as well as the SD—the Sicherheitsdienst, or "Security Service."

With not just the encouragement, but also the active participation of Germans, Ukrainian nationalists would enter one Jewish home after another, armed with iron bars, axes, and knives. They filled their satchels and carts with clothes, food, and valuables. While the Ukrainians were primarily interested in looting Jewish property, they also eagerly engaged in brutality, rape, and murder.

On August 20, a group of Ukrainian nationalists rampaged through Korets, tormenting and abusing Jews. They were led by Mitka, who excitedly proclaimed that God had sent him to punish the Jews and eliminate them from Ukraine. Mitka plundered Jewish homes, along with his Ukrainian auxiliary policemen, a group of men from the local SS—Schutzstaffel, or "Protection Squadron"—and an SS unit from the city of Zhytomyr. They stole money, bond certificates, silver, and gold—including four gold dental crowns—from seventy-seven Jews and sent the "war booty" to Berlin.

Mitka personally went from house to house, dragging Jews from their homes and killing them. He made a blacksmith and his wife watch as he murdered their six-year-old son and twelve-year-old daughter in front of them. He entered the home of

Shunye Shapira, took an elegant coat from his wardrobe, and put it on.

"Fine. Take it all!" Shunye's mother told him.

"Now give me your son!" Mitka replied, ordering Shunye out of the house. Shunye's family never saw him again.

All of the men who had been dragged out of their homes, including Shunye and yet another member of the Jewish Council, were herded toward the Ukrainian auxiliary police station. When the women and children cried out, a Ukrainian administrator assured them that the men were being sent away for a work detail in Zhytomyr, and would return home soon, safe and sound. Some 350 Jewish men were loaded into covered trucks and were instead taken to the village of Szyntia, just over a mile from Korets. As with the 112 Jews two weeks earlier in Sukhovolya, they were forced to dig their own graves before being shot by men from the SS units.

THE FINAL STEP in establishing control over the occupied territories was the transfer of power from the military administration to a German civil administration. Reich Commissar Erich Koch was put in charge of Reich Commissariat Ukraine, which was headquartered in Rivne. Reich Commissariat Ukraine was divided into six General Commissariats: Volhynia-Podolia, Zhytomyr, Kyiv, Mykolaiv, Dnipropetrovsk, and Crimea-Taurida. Korets was located in General Commissariat Volhynia-Podolia, which was governed by General Commissar Heinrich Schöne. Each General Commissariat was further divided into regions that were named after their capital cities. Korets was in the Region of Rivne, which was governed by Regional Commissar Dr. Werner Beer. Korets itself was designated as a District Center and was placed under the control of District Administrator Oberleutnant Hanzelman.

While the Ukrainians brazenly entered homes to steal valuables, the German civil administration preferred to loot Jewish belongings through pressure and extortion. On August 25, Werner Beer arrived in Korets and took twelve Jews hostage, including Moshe. Beer demanded that the Jewish community provide him with one thousand reichsmarks, several Persian rugs, silverware, and other items. If he did not receive the ransom, he declared, he would shoot the hostages and confine the remaining Jews in a closed ghetto. Although this was a large ransom, the community was able to collect everything Beer had demanded, and he released the hostages.

Moshe and two other prominent members of the Jewish community were appointed to the Jewish Council to replace the three councilmen who had been taken away. As a member of the council, Moshe shared the responsibility of collecting the valuables that were demanded by the German and Ukrainian authorities. The most exacting of those figures was Hanzelman, who had the authority to transfer Jews to other districts and even hand them over to the Gestapo. Hanzelman was constantly requisitioning items that he could send back to Germany or to the Eastern Front. The poorer the Jews became, the more he took from them.

On September 15, Hanzelman sent a note to the Jewish Council ordering them to bring him a fur coat, a sheepskin coat, two women's silver-fox fur coats ("only the best," Hanzelman specified), five plates and cutlery sets, and two quilts by six o'clock the next evening. The Jews were able to round up everything he demanded—except for the women's coats. Even the Ukrainians from whom the council had hoped to purchase the coats were unable to find any. Hanzelman was so angry with the Jewish Council that he locked Krasnostavski and Moshe in the basement, threatening to shoot them if he did not receive the coats by ten o'clock the next morning. After four rounds of negotiations, Hanzelman finally agreed to accept ten other valuable items instead of the two silver-fox fur coats.

Whenever a German officer or anyone else from a military unit spent a night in Korets, the Jews were required to provide pillows, sheets, and blankets, which would subsequently be stolen by Ukrainian auxiliary policemen or Ukrainian peasants. Later, the Germans would issue a decree ordering the Jewish Council to collect and surrender anything that was made of copper or brass: pots, candlesticks, menorahs, and even the handles of doors and windows. "Don't worry," the Ukrainians jeered when they came to collect the copper. "We'll give the copper back to you in a different form." The copper, they cheerfully explained, would be sent to Germany and melted down for bullets.

KNOWING THAT LABORERS received 250 grams of bread daily, every Jew in Korets applied to the Jewish Council for work details that offered steady employment. They also naively believed that their work supervisors would protect them from being murdered by the Nazis or from being sent away to work, as nobody ever returned. At the very least, consistent employment spared them from the random jobs that the Germans and Ukrainians forced on unemployed Jews, which were more likely to be torturous and even deadly.

Even the children and elderly were put to work. Every Ukrainian official or auxiliary policeman had a young Jewish boy or girl as a servant, working in their homes at their beck and call. Men and women who were too old for hard labor were ordered to sweep the streets to earn their bread certificates. All day, every day, they could be seen walking up and down the road, brooms in their hands.

As many as six hundred or seven hundred Jews worked at the sugar factory, which the Germans had repaired after partially destroying it during the invasion. Although the local Poles who had been running the factory for several generations had never hired Jews prior to the German occupation, they now welcomed Jewish workers. The Ukrainians who had previously worked there now refused to do so, nor had any reason to for the paltry wages. During the brief period between the Soviet evacuation and the German occupation, the Ukrainian workers had stolen large quantities of sugar, and they were now selling it to neighboring cities at high prices.

While Poles had historically viewed Jews with suspicion, they became more sympathetic during the Nazi occupation, when they, too, were subjected to discrimination. The Poles who owned the factory even instructed their Ukrainian foreman to pay the Jews not the standard salary of two reichsmarks a day, but in the beet molasses that is the byproduct of extracting sugar from sugar beets. The Jewish workers took the molasses home and either used it as a sugar substitute or sold it to Ukrainian peasants, who distilled it into alcohol.

The work in the factory was dirty, physical labor, carried out in brigades under the supervision of Ukrainians. Jews were still not allowed inside the factory building, so they worked outside, often in heavy rain. Dora Rabinowitz later recalled getting a job sewing and repairing sacks in a large, unfinished warehouse in freezing temperatures. "Our fingers shriveled and contracted. We were frozen like blocks of ice," she wrote. "But the whips of the murderers lashed us and demanded 'production.'" Despite the difficult conditions, the steady work at the sugar factory was one of the most sought-after jobs among the Jews.

Up to a hundred Jews were conscripted into forced labor for Organisation Todt, an engineering and construction corps that was named after its founder, Fritz Todt. As Inspector General of German Roadways, Todt had been responsible for building the Autobahn, largely with German workers from the Reich Labor Service. After the invasion of Poland, Todt had been named the Reich Minister for Armaments and Munitions, and his organization had turned its efforts toward planning construction projects for the military that were built by civilian prisoners, prisoners of war, and Jewish forced laborers. In Korets, the Jewish craftsmen who worked for Organisation Todt were treated well and enjoyed their work.

As an engineer, Moshe would have been well-suited for Organisation Todt. Instead, he was put to work in a job that was much more strenuous: laying underground cable that would allow the front line of the German Army to communicate with Berlin. Moshe and thousands of other Jews were forced to dig deep trenches along the side of the highway. They would then climb down into the ditch. Standing in the narrow, uncomfortable channels, they would pull heavy cables over their shoulders, stretching them as tightly as possible. The German supervisors walked around holding thick clubs, beating anyone who did not appear to be pulling as hard as they could.

Every day, dozens of Jewish workers died of brutality, exhaustion, and starvation. When local farmers started taking beets to the sugar factory, they tried to secretly throw a few to the Jewish laborers. The Jews would scramble to pick them up, and would devour the raw, dirty vegetables. If the guards noticed it, they would beat the offenders ruthlessly, sometimes to death. When it was decided that the sick, injured, and weakened prisoners were not making enough progress, the Germans forced women and children, as young as ten years old, to dig the ditches with them.

One day, Moshe was working behind a Jew from the nearby hamlet of Kylykyiv. The refugee was one of many escapees from Jewish villages that the Nazis were liquidating who had made their way to Korets. The Jews in Korets would hide the refugees in the attics of schools and basements of ruined houses. With the help of the Jewish Council, they would place the refugees on the list of Jewish workers that was maintained by the Labor Office, thus giving the refugees legal status as Korets residents, as well as access to daily bread certificates.

The refugee from Kylykyiv had hidden for several weeks in cornfields, and was so exhausted that he could barely stand. Just as the refugee was about to collapse, Moshe and the worker in front of the refugee propped up the cable so that none of its weight would fall on the refugee's shoulders. All the refugee needed to do was stay in line and pretend to work, while secretly resting and regaining his strength. But the German supervisor saw that the refugee was not pulling his weight. He ran over, whipped out a thick club, and killed the refugee with two angry blows to the head. He looked at his watch and gave the Jewish workers one minute to remove the body from the ditch before getting back to work. For the rest of the day, as German officers and other officials drove or walked by the dead body with a smashed skull and a yellow patch on its chest, most did not even look at it. Those who did notice the body glanced at it with satisfied smiles and kept on going. Late in the evening, when the workday was finally over, Moshe and a few other Jews carried the body to the Jewish cemetery and buried it.

Jews were subjected to harassment and torture on a daily basis. One of the Germans' favorite forms of abuse was to hitch as many as eight elderly Jewish men with long beards to wagons that were usually drawn by pairs of horses. The Germans would climb aboard the wagons and ride them around, whipping the old men with long crops. The old men would cry out in agony, blood flowing from their wounds and collapsing from exhaustion, but they would not be allowed to stop until the end of the workday. Once, Moshe watched as three old men with gray beards were forced to pull a wagon through the entire town, down to the river, and into the water, to the great amusement of German and Ukrainian onlookers. The unbridled sadism served as daily reminders that Jewish life, like Jewish property, held no legal protection and was at the mercy of Nazi whims.

THE WINTER OF 1941 through 1942 was very difficult. There was a severe food shortage in Korets, and the daily ration of bread each laborer received was reduced from 250 to 130 grams. The only way Jews could supplement their allocation was by exchanging their remaining valuables with Ukrainian peasants for flour and potatoes.

It snowed nonstop that winter, with temperatures sometimes dropping to more than twenty degrees below zero Fahrenheit. The Jews battled the harsh Ukrainian winter in light shoes and clothing, as their warm clothes and fur coats had been traded for food or taken by the Germans to be sent to the soldiers on the Eastern Front. Many Jews suffered frostbite on their hands and feet. A few hundred died in the streets. Their bodies were abandoned to the frost and snow.

Starving and shivering from the cold, the Jews were forced to perform grueling physical labor, such as quarrying stones, digging ditches, and excavating underground tunnels. They were also expected to help dig out German vehicles from under the snow and clear snow from the roads.

When the long days came to their ends, the Jews returned home to freezing houses. In previous winters, they had lit fires with wood purchased from peasants, but the Nazis had forbidden the Jews from having fires and had banned the locals from supplying firewood to them. But the fear of freezing to death was greater than the risk of getting caught, so the Jews would bring home dry twigs or branches they had found on the road. Other times, they would burn household items, furniture, and even floor panels. By the end of the winter, things had grown so dire that some Jews moved in with their neighbors and dismantled their old homes for firewood. Sometimes, when Germans and Ukrainian auxiliary policemen would see smoke coming out of a chimney, they would barge into the house, drag the freezing occupants onto the street, and force them to gather snow to extinguish the fire.

By January, Moshe had gotten a job at the sugar factory, building a railway spur from Sukhovolya that would transport wood to the factory. One day, on their way back to Korets from Sukhovolya, Moshe and some other Jewish workers heard a woman screaming and sobbing loudly. As they approached a bridge, they saw two German soldiers laughing. One had balanced the bloody body of a seven- or eight-month-old infant on the tip of his rifle. When the baby's mother ran toward him, he whipped the baby's body to the other guard. When the mother ran to the second guard, he tossed the body back to the first. The mother cried and begged for mercy until she fainted, falling unconscious in the middle of the road. One of the soldiers pulled out his bayonet and nonchalantly stabbed her in the back between her shoulder blades. Wiping the blood from his bayonet on the mother's skirt, he ordered a passing peasant, "Clean this dirt off the street."

CHAPTER 3

"May Song"

Whose voice do I hear ringing?
Let new songs be sung!
All of our troubles have passed,
Along with the long, cold winter...
Rich in colors, rich in sounds,
The First of May arrives.

—M. SORERIVES, "MAY SONG"
(JOSEPH GLADSTEIN, *FREEDOM'S SONGS*, P. 39)

IN EARLY MAY 1942, THE German police administration ordered a group of Soviet prisoners of war and peasants from the villages of Morozivka, Holychivka, and Kozak to dig two pits in a forest near Kozak. They were to be sixty-five feet long, sixty-five feet wide, and ten feet deep. In an effort to keep anyone from finding out about the excavations, the Nazis kept the Soviets and peasants under heavy guard. The Soviet soldiers were not sent back to the prisoner-of-war camp, and the villagers were not allowed to return to their homes.

Despite the secrecy, it did not take long for word of the digging to reach the Jewish community just down the road in Korets. When the Jews asked their forced labor supervisors about the pits, the Germans assured them that the dirt was simply being excavated for road repairs. But Ukrainians told the Jews the truth: The Germans were planning to murder thousands of them and bury their bodies in the newly dug mass graves.

While many Jews grew fearful, others chose to believe that the horrifying gossip about mass slaughters was nothing more than fearmongering. There had been, and would undoubtedly continue to be, murders of individual and small groups of Jews, but they found the idea of a wholesale annihilation to be inconceivable. "It is true that here and there some Jews have been shot," they conceded. "But when in history have Jews *not* been shot and killed?"

"All we need is patience, and everything will blow over," the Jews convinced themselves. "After all, human beings are inherently good."

The pits were completed on May 10. After the next ten days passed uneventfully, the chatter slowed down, and life started to return to normal in Korets. The Jews were preparing for Shavuot, the Jewish holiday that celebrates both the harvest and God's revealing of the Torah to Moses and the Israelites.

At four in the morning, on May 21—the Eve of Shavuot—a German SD squad from Rivne descended on Korets. The SD was joined by Germany's Reserve Police Battalion 33 and units from the German military police, as well as Lithuanian policemen and Ukrainian auxiliary policemen. The Nazi forces went from street to street, barging into Jewish homes like wild animals. They pulled Jews out of their beds, shouting slurs and taunts in German, Lithuanian, Ukrainian, and Russian. "Yids! Kikes! Out! Get out! Death awaits you!"

Jews who were bedridden or housebound were killed on the spot. The rest were forced outside, some barefoot and in their bedclothes, and marched toward a building on Old Monastery Street that had once been owned by Jews, but which had been

commandeered by the Nazis as the district administration building. Anyone who tried to resist was beaten. Anyone who tried
to escape was shot.

Simcha was on his way to his work detail when he learned
what was happening. Earlier that spring, he and several hundred
Jewish laborers had been assigned to construct a barracks building for the German Army. Simcha was heading to the construction site following side streets, as he did every morning to avoid
being harassed on the main roads, when a Polish neighbor called
out to him. "Where are you going? There's an *Aktion,*" the neighbor warned, invoking the term Germans innocuously used to describe their murderous operations. "Run home!"

Simcha hurried home and repeated the news to his parents,
but he was too late. The Nazis broke down the door to the Gildenman house at six that morning. Within seconds, the rooms
were filled with armed Germans and Ukrainian auxiliary policemen. The family was quickly surrounded and dragged outside.

"All Jews must go to a special registration!" one of the Nazis
barked.

Moshe asked one of the Ukrainians, "Should I bring my identity card?"

"The only thing you need to bring is your head," the Ukrainian replied. The others laughed cruelly.

Simcha tried to escape. The Germans shot at him, but
stopped firing when another group of Germans arrived from the
opposite direction. They apprehended Simcha and beat him.

Moshe, Golda, and their daughter, Feigela, were marched
down the narrow cobblestone streets toward the administration
building. They joined a crowd of panicked and confused Jewish
neighbors, many of whom were bleeding from the beatings they
had received. Parents held babies in their arms. Small children
clung to their fathers' shirttails and their mothers' dresses. The
streets and alleys were littered with the bodies of murdered
friends and neighbors. The air was filled with the sounds of gun-

fire, the desperate screams of people being dragged from their homes, and the moans and cries of the wounded. Stretching their arms to heaven, some of the men started to recite *"Shema Yisrael"*—"Hear, O Israel"—the most important prayer in the Jewish faith.

As they made their way through town, Moshe and his family saw Ukrainian peasants looting Jewish homes. The Ukrainians lurked in the streets like hungry jackals, brazen looks on their faces and empty sacks in their hands. As soon as a Jewish home was evacuated, peasants would rush in to plunder whatever clothes and valuables still remained in the house. When their sacks were full, they would rip apart the feather beds, dump out the feathers, and fill the empty quilts with loot. Moshe watched as an elderly woman came out of a Jewish house with a bulging sack on her back. She looked like she might snap in two under its weight.

Moshe and his family reached the square in front of the administration building. There was a large crowd of Jews gathered there, some barefoot and naked. The air was filled with the sound of them sobbing with fear and desperation. The Jewish prisoners were sitting on the ground, overwhelmed with terror, whispering questions to each other about what would happen to them next. They were surrounded by Germans and Ukrainians, who beat and shot at them. The assaults brought more cries from the wounded victims.

Moshe, Golda, and Feigela were led into the building. A German officer sitting beside a table ordered them to empty their pockets, place all of their belongings on the table, and turn their pockets inside out to confirm that nothing remained. The Nazis confiscated whatever clothes and valuables they wanted, down to the last pencil and matchbox. The family was then brought back outside and separated. Golda and Feigela were led to a group of women and children. The adults were trying to put on a brave face for the children, who were bawling loudly, convinced that their tears would evoke pity from their captors.

Moshe was directed to a group of men standing next to the butcher's house. There, he was reunited with Simcha. After being apprehended and beaten, Simcha had been marched to the square. "I'm still young. What have I ever done to you? Why do you want to kill me?" he had pleaded. When they were not far from the castle ruins, Simcha had realized that if he could make his way there, he could find a place to hide. "Give me a chance. Just look away, and I'll disappear."

But the German would not let him go. He had handed Simcha a cigarette, and then had given him the rest of the pack. "Keep it for yourself," the German had said.

At the square, Simcha had continued to beg for his life. "I'm still young," he repeated. "I work at the barracks. I'm an electrician."

AT EIGHT IN the morning, under the watchful eyes of the German military police and the Ukrainian auxiliary police, the Jews were lined up in rows of six for the march to Kozak. The prisoners screamed and wailed as children were torn from their fathers. Women fainted; some even died from heart attacks. A German officer walked between the columns, stopping now and then to ask some of the Jews their age and profession. He instructed a few of the younger and stronger-looking Jews to step to the side and stand with their backs to the columns.

Simcha's supervisor from the construction site arrived. He was a German from Alsace-Lorraine who is remembered only by his first name, Robert. As Robert had explained to his workers, he was an engineer who had been stripped of his rank as a German officer because he was deemed to be insufficiently loyal to the Nazi Party. According to one rumor, Robert was a communist who was working in the Nazi ranks as a spy for Soviet intelligence.

Robert began negotiating with the German commandant to spare some of his Jewish workers. Without tradesmen, he argued, he would be unable to finish the army barracks. Simcha was among the laborers Robert hoped to spare. "He works for me at the barracks as an electrician," Robert explained.

After a lengthy conversation, Robert was allowed to pull Simcha from the ranks, along with nineteen other Jewish men. Just as Moshe's group was about to start marching away, Simcha stepped up to one of the Germans. Pointing at Moshe, he implored, "That's my father. He's still young; he can still work. He's healthy—"

"Shut up," Robert warned him, "or you'll be joining your father right now!" But then, he changed his mind. "Which one's your father?" he asked.

Simcha pointed to Moshe. "That's my father."

"You can get out of line as well," Robert told Moshe. Simcha was able to convince Robert to save his sixteen-year-old cousin, Siomke Geifman, as well.

Around 135 men were allowed to stay, including carpenters, tailors employed by the German Army, and construction workers who had been conscripted into Organisation Todt. There were also fifty-one young women who were spared to provide housekeeping services for the German authorities. Those prisoners were instructed to sit motionlessly on the ground, with their legs tucked underneath them.

The Jews who had not been pulled out of the lines were surrounded by guards and marched toward Kozak. Those who stumbled and fell to the ground were crushed to death under the feet of their neighbors. The sick and elderly who lacked the strength to walk the four miles were loaded into trucks and horse-drawn wagons and driven there. They were joined by children, whom the Nazis grabbed by their hands, legs, heads, and shirts. The children were tossed into the wagons like rag dolls. If one fell off, a Ukrainian auxiliary policeman would scoop them up and throw them back into the wagon.

Around noon, a number of sick and injured Jews who had moved too slowly to be included in the morning caravan were brought to the administration building. Some, like a man whose leg had been broken a few days earlier when he had been hit by a German motorcycle, were carried by auxiliary policemen. The Ukrainians tied the feet of a paralyzed man to their car and dragged him down the street, his head bouncing on the cobblestones. The broken bodies were stacked one on top of the other, like sacks of potatoes.

A red truck arrived. The Germans called the vehicle a *Gaswagen* (gas wagon), but Moshe knew it as a *dushegubka*—Russian for "soul killer." It was a mobile gas chamber, a hermetically sealed box truck that had been customized so that the exhaust from the engine could be piped into the cargo area, suffocating everyone inside. The Nazis started packing the disabled Jews into the back of the truck.

As the last of the sick and injured Jews were being loaded, a delegation of gentile workers from the sugar factory arrived and asked the commandant to release a physician who was inside. They explained that he was the only good doctor in town. He had served as the factory physician for many years, and it would be difficult to replace him. The commandant agreed that the doctor could get out of the truck until the factory manager could arrive to clear things up.

An artist who painted signboards for the German military administration was taken out of the truck a few moments later, after a Nazi official showed up to request his release. But then, the Germans had a change of heart. In an instant, they grabbed the doctor and the painter and forced them back inside the truck. They slammed the doors and locked them shut. The mobile gas chamber sped off, and the doctor and painter were never seen again.

Moshe and the other prisoners looked on in horror. There was nothing they could do but sit there and await their own fate.

Suddenly they heard screaming. It was a local Jewish woman being led down the street by an auxiliary policeman. She had a history of mental illness, but had been stable for a few years. She had even gotten married and started a family. But the day's trauma had triggered an episode. She repeatedly broke free, but the auxiliary policeman caught her each time and savagely beat her for the trouble.

When she reached a telegraph pole in front of the administration building, the woman grabbed it with both hands and started dancing around it. As the auxiliary policeman approached her yet again, she started sarcastically shouting, "Heil, Hitler! Heil, Hitler!" and laughing hysterically. Several Germans gathered around, watching the spectacle with amusement. Seeing the Germans, she stopped laughing and instead started singing "The Internationale." One of the Germans drew his gun and shot her twice, bringing her defiance to an end.

Around two in the afternoon, several peasant carts filled with colorful clothes arrived at the administration building. The Germans who were guarding the transport ordered four of the prisoners, including Moshe's nephew Siomke, to unload the carts. Among the clothing, Siomke discovered the coats that Golda and Feigela had been wearing when they had been taken away that morning. Then the peasants who had brought the cart told them what had happened in Kozak.

AT FOUR THAT morning, just as the Nazis were entering Korets, a Gestapo chief had come to the house of a woodsman who lived near Kozak, accompanied by a large detachment of German soldiers and Ukrainian auxiliary policemen. The chief had ordered the woodsman and his wife to slaughter several chickens and geese and prepare them for dinner, explaining that his men would be working up a hunger all day. The chief stationed some of the Germans to guard the forest surrounding the pits, while others opened crates of brandy and wine, sat on the grass, and started drinking. As the day unfolded, they would get increasingly drunk and increasingly sadistic.

At nine, the first group of Jewish men from Korets arrived, exhausted from the four-mile journey. Many were severely bruised and bloodied from the beatings they had endured along the way. They were ordered to take off their clothes and line up, still in rows of six. The first row was directed to walk down a set of stairs that had been carved into the side of one of the pits. Next to the mass grave, a German officer sat at a little table covered with snacks, bottles of liquor, and a submachine gun. After telling the Jewish men to lie face down at the bottom of the pit, he ordered the German soldiers to shoot them in the backs of their heads with machine guns.

There was a blast of bullets, followed by painful cries as the first six victims were murdered. Then the next row of Jewish men was forced into the pit. They were ordered to straighten the bodies of the first victims before lying on top of the corpses. The officer took a drink, and ordered the soldiers to shoot them. Between each sip of cognac, he gleefully ordered the murders of the Jewish prisoners, six at a time.

The first group of Jewish women and children from Korets were brought an hour later, at around ten that morning. With insults and beatings, they, too, were forced to strip naked. Once again in rows of six, they were ordered into the second pit and shot. Mothers carried small children in their arms into the mass grave and were shot with them. The children who arrived on the trucks and wagons were thrown into the pit and blown up with grenades. From miles away, one could hear the gunfire and explosions, the moaning, crying, and wailing of the women and children, and the loud laughter of the Germans and the Ukrainians.

The pace of the murders could not keep up with the large number of Jews who kept arriving from Korets. By noon, there were a few hundred of them gathered around the pits, horrified by what they were being forced to witness. To keep the prisoners occupied, the Nazis forced them to sort through the clothes of those who had already been sent to their deaths. The

Jews had to carefully create separate piles for pants, jackets, shoes, and underwear, sorted by gender. Some of the prisoners recognized the clothes of their loved ones. The clothes that were not stolen by the Ukrainian auxiliary policemen were sent back to Korets, and then on to Germany.

With the exception of the 186 skilled laborers who had remained behind and a few Jews who had succeeded in hiding, by two in the afternoon, all of the Jews from Korets had been brought to the Kozak Forest. As the numbers of Jews dwindled, the cries and screams grew quieter. Religious Jews sang psalms, while some young women defiantly sang Russian songs. Mothers calmed their children and sobbed quietly. Other prisoners remained silent, resigned to their fate and hoping that the end would come quickly. Before too long, the only sounds that could be heard were the bursts of machine-gun fire and the muffled moans of the wounded.

By three o'clock, the Germans were so drunk that they could barely drag their feet. The auxiliary policemen finished the task of sorting the clothes, searching for any money, gold, and valuables that had not been confiscated earlier, and arguing over who would get to keep the best garments.

At four o'clock, exactly twelve hours after knocking on the woodsman's door, the Gestapo chief declared the mission completed. There were six hundred bodies in the men's pit. The second pit was filled to the brim with the bodies of 1,600 women and children. The local peasants covered the mass graves with a thin layer of soil and walked away.

AT THE EXACT same time that the Gestapo chief in the Kozak Forest officially ended the massacre, the German commandant in Korets addressed the skilled laborers whose lives had been spared.

"The *Aktion* is over!" he announced. "Tomorrow morning the remaining Jews must report to their places of work. Any Jews who managed to hide may return to the ghetto. They are no longer in danger."

Moshe stared in disbelief at the man who stood before him in his elegant German uniform. Other than a few drops of blood on his shiny black boots, Moshe could not detect any hint that the commandant had been impacted in any way by what he had overseen that day. There was a look of satisfaction on his plump face, with a hint of the type of fatigue that comes with completing a strenuous yet rewarding task. The commandant spoke quietly and dispassionately, showing no remorse for having ordered the massacre of 2,200 husbands, wives, sons, and daughters.

For several moments, Moshe and his fellow survivors did not move. They were too shocked by the enormity of the day's tragedy to even begin to process their losses. Then, their knees aching from hours of sitting still, they slowly stood up. Noting that it was the Eve of Shavuot, one of them suggested that they go to a nearby *beth midrash* and commence the Jewish grieving rituals of rending their garments and reciting the prayer of mourning known as the Kaddish. For Moshe, the very idea of the Kaddish was inconceivable. Still overwhelmed by the losses of his beloved wife and daughter, he was not ready to grieve.

When they arrived, the survivors discovered that the *beth midrash* had been vandalized by Ukrainian peasants. The reading table for the Torah had been smashed, and the Torah ark had been yanked open. Two Torah scrolls had been thrown to the ground. Some of the men picked up a scroll that had been pulled from its decorative cloth mantle, laid it on what was left of the reading table, and started carefully rolling it back up. As they performed this ritual slowly and ceremoniously, the others watched intently. To Moshe's dismay, it seemed as if their only concern at the moment was whether the scroll had been damaged.

The Jews started to rend their garments, wailing loudly. When the praying began, Moshe just sat in a corner and watched.

His heart ached, but no tears formed in his eyes. "This is the Eve of Shavuot," he said to himself. "The eve of the feast celebrating the offering of the Torah. The eve of the anniversary of God revealing His presence to the world, along with the commandment 'Thou shalt not kill!'"

Moshe felt anger rising in his heart. He started to hate the whole world, even his Jewish neighbors who were responding to the murders of their loved ones through peaceful ritual and prayer. A voice called out from inside him, "Not this way! We must respond to the innocent blood that was shed today not with prayer, but with revenge!"

When the Kaddish was over, Moshe ran to the dais and banged the pulpit loudly. "Listen to me, you unfortunate, doomed Jews!" he shouted. "An hour ago, I looked at the smug face of the German commandant and thought, 'If this is a human, then I'm ashamed to be human.' Now, as I watch your reactions to the terrible atrocity that the Germans and Ukrainians have committed against us, I think to myself, 'If this is a nation, then I'm ashamed of this nation. If these are the descendants of the heroic Jewish Maccabees, then I'm ashamed to call myself a Jew.' Know that we're all going to die, sooner or later. But I will not go like a sheep to the slaughter!"

"Be quiet!" the congregants urged. They were worried that the Nazis would overhear him, and punish them all for his insubordination.

"I'm not afraid of anyone!" Moshe continued defiantly. "I'm not even afraid of death. But before I die, let me strangle at least one German with my own hands. Let at least one German woman become a widow, and let one German child become an orphan. Only then will I be able to rest in peace!"

Quoting the biblical hero Samson, who died as a martyr while killing thousands of enemy Philistines, Moshe vowed, "Let me die with the Philistines!"

AFTER THE *AKTION,* the Jewish survivors returned to their homes to find them in ruins. The doors and windows had been smashed, any remaining valuables had been plundered, and whatever was left of the furniture had been destroyed. The floors were littered with broken dishes and feathers from the blankets and pillows that the Ukrainians had ripped open to make sacks for their loot. The survivors walked around the empty houses in shock, unable to process the magnitude of their losses. They were grieving not for their lost belongings, but for their devastated families. Every single house was missing at least one person—a father, a mother, or a child—and many houses were empty because nobody from that family had survived.

When Moshe and Simcha arrived back at their house, they went to the courtyard and stood near their well. Their Ukrainian neighbors were surprised to see them. "What? You're still here?" they asked.

Simcha made a decision. "Papa, I'm not coming back home," he said. "We're leaving for the forest."

"Where?" Moshe demanded. "To the forest? Why would you go to the forest?"

It was time for Simcha to share a secret he had been keeping from his father. During the previous winter, Moshe had brought Simcha to work with him on the construction of the railway spur from Sukhovolya to the sugar factory. Moshe would return to Korets every Friday for the Sabbath, but Simcha would stay safely behind. While hiding in the forest near the village of Pishchiv, Simcha had met up with Soviet soldiers who had escaped from prisoner-of-war camps. The men had befriended Simcha and had put him in contact with some partisans—Soviet soldiers who had either gotten cut off behind enemy lines or had escaped captivity. The partisans were starting to organize themselves in nearby forests in the hopes of engaging in guerrilla combat against the Germans.

Simcha had returned to Korets to assemble a group of friends who would join the partisans with him. Most of them had refused, fearful of crossing the Nazis. One friend who had volunteered was Hershel "Zvi" Pe'er, who worked in the slaughterhouse and had survived the *Aktion* by hiding in the slaughterhouse attic with his son, Yaakov. Simcha and his underground operation had established contact with the partisans, secretly providing them with food, clothing, and shoes, at times even sneaking them into the ghetto. As Simcha's contacts with the partisans had deepened, so had his resolve to eventually join them in the forest. It gave him a purpose to know that there was a heroic alternative to life in the ghetto.

Simcha had gotten a job at a stone quarry just outside of Korets where Soviet prisoners were also working. At night, the prisoners of war would return to a detention center that was located in Korets, in the house of a former baker. The Germans had surrounded the building with two rows of barbed wire and placed Germans and defectors from the Red Army on guard, but Simcha had devised a plot to help his new friends escape. With the assistance of Jakob Wulach, a Jewish doctor who had served in the Red Army during World War I and who now attended to the captured soldiers in the detention center, Simcha had passed along a bolt cutter to the prisoners. On January 15, eight prisoners of war had broken through the barbed wire and had made their escape.

Simcha tried to convince Moshe to come with him, but Moshe did not want to abandon his community when it needed him the most—at least, not right away. Before he would leave, the engineer wanted to make sure they had a plan. "We're not going anywhere. We need to figure everything out and assemble a group to escape," he told Simcha. "Introduce me to everyone. I want to see them and talk to them. Let's start organizing ourselves."

CHAPTER 4

"Come to the Forest"

Young and old, come to the forest!
Break out of the ghetto!
Ten may fall, but ten will survive.
Onward, Jews, let's fight!

—MOSHE GILDENMAN, "COME TO THE FOREST"

THE GERMANS CONCENTRATED THE JEWISH survivors in Korets, along with Jews from nearby villages, into a few blocks along Synagogue Street. The Jews assembled new households out of the remnants of old ones. Widowers, widows, and orphans moved in together to form communes they facetiously called kolkhozes, using the Russian word for "collective farms." There were as many as twenty survivors in each kolkhoz. Out of necessity, they were true communes, with neither distinct families nor personal possessions. Everyone helped raise the orphans, and everyone shared whatever food they had. Moshe and Simcha moved into a house that had been owned by a Jewish miller. They lived there with several other survivors, including Moshe Krasnostavski, who had lost his wife and three children in the massacre, and Krasnostavski's one remaining son.

Over the next several days, the ghetto population was further augmented by the return of the Jews who had escaped the massacre by hiding in attics and cellars, in the Jewish cemetery, or in the castle ruins. By the beginning of June, there were 1,100 Jews living in the ghetto. Still processing their unimaginable losses, a number of them sought refuge in alcohol that they obtained from peasants in exchange for their last articles of clothing. Some of the survivors became too depressed to even move, while others returned to their work details out of fear of further persecution.

On June 10, District Administrator Hanzelman summoned Moshe and ordered him to assemble a crew of bricklayers. Moshe and his workers were to leave the ghetto, demolish houses in Korets that had belonged to Jews, and use the reclaimed bricks and wood to build an ox stable in the village of Holovnytsya, three miles west of Korets. Seething with anger at the Ukrainians who had made themselves at home in Jewish houses, Moshe decided to start with those dwellings first. After dismantling a house that had been partially destroyed by a bomb during the German invasion, Moshe and his crew started on the house next door, which a few Ukrainian families had occupied. The Ukrainian peasants complained to the police, but the Ukrainian policemen were powerless to stop an initiative authorized by the Germans. The peasants ran to Hanzelman, who ordered Moshe back to his office.

"Why are you demolishing a house where Ukrainians are living?" Hanzelman demanded. "Didn't I tell you to tear down only Jewish houses?"

"The house that I started to tear down is a Jewish house," Moshe replied innocently. He explained that the Ukrainian peasants were actually residents of the New Town. "I chose to demolish this house because it is built of hard, well-baked bricks that are ideal for constructing solid buildings like the ox stable you told me to oversee."

Satisfied with Moshe's explanation, Hanzelman kicked the peasants out of his office and ordered Moshe to continue working. Within a few days, the house had been razed to its foundation. If the Jews who had originally built the home could no longer live there, then nobody could.

FOR THE FIRST few months after the *Aktion*, there were not many administrative tasks for Moshe, Krasnostavski, and the other members of the Jewish Council. Hanzelman had mostly stopped ordering the Jews to surrender their personal possessions, because he knew there was little left to take. The Jews were now confined to the ghetto, and there were no more requests for laborers to work outside of Korets. With the exception of dealing with minor incidents, such as drunken Germans entering the ghetto to terrorize the Jews who were confined there, the Jewish Council's tasks were limited to making sure there were sufficient Jewish laborers for local work details and preparing questionnaires for new personal identification cards.

In August, Moshe and Krasnostavski were pressed into service by a distressing development at the detention center for captured Soviet soldiers. On August 6, the German supervisor of the detention center, who had become friendly with Krasnostavski because Krasnostavski baked bread for the prisoners, came to Krasnostavski with some alarming news. "Tonight, one of the guards at my camp shot a Jew who was approaching with the intention of incapacitating the guard and freeing the prisoners," he shared. "When they ordered him to halt, he ran away. A guard chased him down and killed him. He's now on the road, about one hundred feet from the camp.

"This is a terrible situation that can have grave repercussions," the German supervisor continued. "I won't take any action unless the Ukrainians get involved, but you need to get him off the road soon. If another German passes by, sees him lying there, and learns why he was shot, there could be retaliation against the Jews in the ghetto."

Moshe and Krasnostavski immediately went to the detention center. They found the body of a pale, emaciated man with a blond beard lying in a pool of blood. The man was barefoot and was wearing a cap, a linen shirt, and linen pants. Moshe and Krasnostavski did not recognize the man, but from his circumcision, they determined that he was indeed Jewish. They did not, however, believe that he was a spy, as the German supervisor had asserted. Instead, they suspected, he was a Jew from a nearby town who had dressed as a peasant to avoid attracting attention on his way into the Korets ghetto.

While some women from the ghetto scrubbed the blood from the cobblestones and covered up any traces of what had happened, Moshe and Krasnostavski rounded up a few Jewish men to load the body onto a stretcher and carry it to the Jewish cemetery. In accordance with Jewish custom, they wrapped the body in a prayer shawl and began to dig a grave.

Suddenly a squad of Ukrainian auxiliary policemen arrived, led by Mitka Zavirukha. Mitka informed Moshe and Krasnostavski that he would witness the burial to make sure the Jews did not bury anything with the alleged spy. The policemen examined the body and confirmed that the man had been circumcised. They searched his clothes and discovered in his pants pockets a sharpened pencil, a blank piece of paper, and three small wooden blocks with Roman numerals. Moshe thought the blocks looked like children's toys, but Mitka suspected otherwise. He spent several minutes scrutinizing them.

"These aren't ordinary blocks," Mitka finally concluded. "This is a secret code that the spy used to communicate with his accomplices, which undoubtedly included Jews in the ghetto who were trying to help him liberate the camp."

Moshe and Krasnostavski immediately realized that Mitka was preparing the justification for a bloody retaliation that would be catastrophic for their community. They begged Mitka not to punish the Jews, but he would not relent. The Jews buried the body, recited the Kaddish, and left the cemetery, dreading Mitka's response.

On the next day, the Jews learned that the retaliation might be even more devastating than they had feared. Mitka had sent the wooden blocks to Regional Commissar Werner Beer in Rivne with an accompanying report and a request for an official inquiry. The Jews started bracing themselves for the very worst.

On the third day, the Jewish Council was visited by an elderly farmer from the village of Dermanka, eleven miles north of Korets. The farmer explained that his thirty-year-old son, who suffered from a mental illness, had disappeared a week earlier. The farmer had heard about a circumcised man who had been shot in Korets, and suspected that he might have been his son. The Jews immediately asked the farmer to share his story with the Nazi authorities. In the presence of a commander from the Ukrainian auxiliary police and a representative from the German military administration, they exhumed the body and removed the prayer shawl. The farmer immediately recognized his son, and tearfully kissed the body. The farmer reclaimed his son's body, the Nazis closed the case, and the Jews breathed a sigh of relief.

As THE SUMMER continued to unfold, the Jews in the ghetto tried to reestablish some sense of normalcy in their daily lives. Now that the Germans and Ukrainians had taken almost everything from the Jews, there was less interest in harassing them. There were even slight improvements to nutrition. In addition to earning 130 grams of bread from their work details every day, some of the Jews started sewing clothes that they exchanged with local farmers for flour and other staples. On occasion, bartered sheep and cows were even brought into the ghetto and slaughtered in accordance with Jewish law. With assurances from the Germans that they were too useful as skilled laborers to be eliminated, many of the survivors started planning for the future. Potatoes and firewood were stored for the upcoming winter. There was even a marriage between a widower and an elderly bachelorette.

The optimism that better days were finally ahead grew stronger when the Germans started the process of issuing new documentation for the Jews. All Jews over the age of fourteen were required to complete the questionnaire that the Jewish Council had prepared, which asked for information such as one's birthplace and year, mother's maiden name, any previous domiciles, education level, the languages they spoke, and whether they had any relatives living abroad. This information, along with a photo, was compiled in new identity cards. Moshe would receive his card on September 11, 1942, the day that marked the beginning of Rosh Hashanah. It was printed on gray paper with a Star of David on its cover to quickly identify its bearer as being Jewish.

Moshe would also receive a registration card from the Employment Office that identified him as an official worker. If he were stopped by the Ukrainian auxiliary police on his way to or from work, the card ensured that the police would not be able to transfer him to another work detail. Workers were instructed to carry the card with them at all times, and present it to their supervisors at the start and end of every work assignment. All workers were required to have registration cards, but naturally Moshe's card included a prominent stamp designating him as not just any laborer, but as a "Jewish Skilled Worker."

Most of the Jews in Korets interpreted the efforts to collect so much information and issue new documents as signs that the German authorities now considered them to be permanent residents of the occupied territory. Their confidence that they were no longer in danger was unwavering, even after an escapee from the Rivne ghetto informed them that the Jews in Rivne had been issued new identity cards just one month before the German SS

and Ukrainian auxiliary police had liquidated their ghetto on
July 13, 1942.

Moshe had seen too much indiscriminate killing to harbor
any hope that the Jewish community in Korets would be spared.
While others were preparing for the winter, he was making
plans to escape to the forest. First they would need to buy some
weapons. Simcha's German supervisor, Robert, who knew that
Simcha was planning on joining the partisans, offered to sell him
a rifle and a pistol, but he did not have any bullets for the pistol.
Robert did, however, have a large dog that had been trained to
hunt down partisans. "Get to know the dog," he instructed Simcha. Robert trained the dog to walk with Simcha and obey Simcha's commands. "If we ever come across a group of partisans
with you in it, he won't attack you," Robert explained.

At a well-attended meeting that had been convened to raise
yet another payoff demanded by the Germans, Moshe called on
the community to set aside a portion of the collected funds to
secretly purchase weapons from the local Poles. They refused
to listen, and admonished him for even suggesting it. When
Moshe confided to his friend Yulik Molir that he was negotiating
with a Polish peasant from Dermanka to buy some guns, Yulik
started shaking with fear. "You'll ruin us all!" he shouted. "If they
find out that you went to the partisans, then, God forbid, they'll
murder all of the Jews in the ghetto. Don't risk it!"

IT WAS DURING his time in the ghetto that Moshe wrote a song
titled "Come to the Forest," in which he urged others to join him
and Simcha in preparing to flee. It became something of a call
to arms to the Jews in Korets and nearby ghettos.

> Days of anguish and suffering
> Are slowly receding into the past,
> And they are replaced, like faraway shadows,
> By nights of uncertainty and fear.

And the heart, full of pain,
Cannot find peace anywhere.
It desperately wants to live, and, above all, to live to
     see
The joyous hour of revenge.

It is neither alive nor dead,
Always in fear and privation.
Is it not better to die as men,
In a heroic death in battle?

Young and old, come to the forest!
Break out of the ghetto!
Ten may fall, but ten will survive.
Onward, Jews, let's fight!

To Moshe's disappointment, very few of his friends and neighbors heeded his call. In addition to the fear of bringing retaliation to the rest of the community, there were doubts as to whether it would even be possible to successfully organize such an escape without getting caught. When the Jews had first learned about the Soviet soldiers hiding in the forest, they had dispatched two young men to sneak out of the ghetto and establish contact. But the Jewish men had been betrayed by a member of their own community, who turned them over to the Ukrainian auxiliary police. The young men were being taken to Rivne for interrogation when they tried to escape. While crossing the bridge on the way out of town, one of them jumped into the river and drowned. The other was unable to get away, and was shot. Their deaths convinced many of the remaining Jews that any attempts to flee the ghetto would be equally futile.

The overwhelming military might that Germany had displayed when it had rolled through Soviet Ukraine during the first weeks of the war had instilled a sense of hopeless resigna-

tion throughout the community. When Moshe asked fellow Jewish Councilman Yukel Marcus to join him in escaping to the forest, Yukel laughed in his face. "Moshe, I thought you were
smarter than that. What's the point of going to the forest now,
when the Germans have already reached Moscow and will soon
take over the whole world?"

Many of the Jews had once again convinced themselves that
they were not in any danger. Yuzik Michelsohn, who worked in
the printshop, was among those in denial. "The head of the printing house, who's a highly respected German, assured me that
Hitler's plan doesn't include killing all of the Jews," Yuzik explained when Moshe tried to recruit him to become a partisan.
"Only Jews who can't provide essential labor are murdered. But,
for example, since you work as an engineer and I work as a type-
setter, we won't be killed.

"If Hitler killed us all, he'd have to fill our positions with
workers from Germany, and he needs them for the war," Yuzik
rationalized. "Hitler's not that foolish. He wouldn't do that."

Others agreed with Moshe's assessment that the ghetto
would be liquidated at some point, but still did not plan to escape. Krasnostavski confessed that he had simply lost the will
to fight after the murders of his wife and three children. He
would remain in the ghetto and wait for the end. Moshe urged
Krasnostavski to reconsider, arguing that he could avenge the
murders of his loved ones. At the very least, Moshe contended,
somebody had to survive to bear witness about what had happened in Korets.

"Can you imagine how happy you'll make Mitka if you allow
him to lead you into the pit and shoot you?" Moshe pleaded.

"Relax," Krasnostavski replied. "I'd never give him that pleasure. Moreover, he won't steal a single penny from me. Nothing
in our house that belongs to you or me will fall into his hands."

"What are you going to do?"

"I've prepared a few bottles of gasoline. At the last minute, I'll lock the door, set the gasoline on fire, and burn down the house with myself inside."

"That will take quite a bit of courage and resolve. It's heroic," Moshe acknowledged. "But it won't help the Jewish people."

Moshe remained convinced that he would die by German hands, sooner or later, but he hoped to be able to take at least one German with him. "I don't want to die as a religious martyr. I want to follow in the footsteps of our great Jewish heroes Mattathias and Judah Maccabee," he told Krasnostavski. Mattathias and Judah were the father-and-son Jewish priests who led the victorious Maccabean Revolt that is central to the story of Hanukkah.

Evoking the sacred Hebrew prayer that observant Jews traditionally recite on their deathbeds, Moshe resolved, "I want to die with 'Shema Yisrael' on my lips and a gun in my hand."

ON AUGUST 31, 1942, Reich Commissar Erich Koch issued an order for the liquidation of all Jews in General Commissariat Volhynia-Podolia. After fifteen thousand Jews had been killed in executions and pogroms during the first few weeks of the occupation, the Germans had launched a new wave of *Aktions* throughout Volhynia-Podolia that had resulted in the murders of thirty thousand Jews between September and November 1941. The killings had largely ceased in December, at least partially because the Germans had realized that they still needed large numbers of Jews, especially skilled craftsmen, for the labor force.

The recommencement of large-scale exterminations marked a new phase in the efforts to eliminate Jews from the occupied territories. Once again, Jews were rounded up, marched to pits that had been prepared nearby, and murdered by the thousands, with the full knowledge and sometimes the cooperation of the local population. It has been estimated that 28,800 Jews from Volhynia-Podolia were executed in May, June, and July 1942, with another 150,000 Jews massacred between August 10 and October 15; a final group of 3,500 survivors and skilled laborers would be murdered by the middle of 1943.

On September 11, the Jews of the Korets ghetto observed the beginning of Rosh Hashanah by praying in the former synagogue of the Shoemakers Guild. The synagogue had been one of the smallest houses of worship in Korets, but now it was the only one left. After burning down the Great Synagogue, the Nazis had converted the other synagogues into grain warehouses. Even those who had not been observant before the Nazi occupation prayed intensely, as everyone now realized that any help they received would only come from God. The most emotional moments came during the Kaddish, when all the congregants recited the prayer as one. Everyone had deaths to mourn.

On the second day of Rosh Hashanah, the Jews began to hear rumors that the Germans were planning to liquidate the remaining Jews, not only in Korets, but throughout Volhynia-Podolia. When they asked the Ukrainians whether the reports were true, the peasants simply shrugged their shoulders and asked, "Do you think the Germans tell us their plans?"

The work supervisors once again tried to assuage the growing fears, but this time the Jews were not fooled. They had heard this story before, right before the Shavuot massacre. Sympathetic Ukrainians started coming into the ghetto to warn their Jewish acquaintances of the impending danger. Less compassionate Ukrainians persuaded Jews to hand over their last remaining valuables for safekeeping, knowing they would never be reclaimed.

On September 24, the Jewish Council learned that more pits were being dug near Kozak. When Dr. Wulach had reported to the prisoner-of-war detention center that morning, he had discovered that the Soviet soldiers, with the exception of a few sick prisoners, were gone. One of the patients who had been left behind had informed Dr. Wulach that the prisoners had been dispatched to the Kozak Forest to dig more mass graves for the remaining Jews in Korets.

The Jewish leaders were finally convinced that the ghetto was going to be liquidated, but it was too late. A German SD unit from Rivne was surrounding the ghetto, along with German military policemen and Ukrainian auxiliary policemen.

Everyone ran around in a panic, trying to figure out how to escape. But every street was blocked and guarded by Ukrainian auxiliary policemen. The Jews who tried to run were shot. Those who fought back were overwhelmed by the combined German and Ukrainian forces. Two brothers managed to hide in their attic. When they were discovered, they attacked the murderers with pitchforks, killing a few before being killed themselves.

The Jews were rounded up, tortured, and murdered. A group of young women were locked in a basement of a house that was set on fire. A group of men were led to the highway and beaten mercilessly. Some Jews managed to escape the encirclement and made it to the small wooden bridge over the Korchyk River, only to be gunned down as they tried to run across.

Two sisters who managed to escape were recaptured, brought back to Korets, and murdered in the Christian cemetery. When their father learned of their deaths, he hanged himself in the sugar factory.

Among those who took their own lives rather than being killed by the Nazis were some of the Jews who had ignored Moshe's pleas to run away with him. Having learned that his two sisters had been killed trying to flee, Yuzik Michelsohn hanged himself, as did another Jewish worker in the printshop, just as the Germans were surrounding them. Yukel Marcus, who had laughed at the idea of escaping to the forest, also committed suicide. When his sister-in-law found his body hanging in her attic, she hanged herself as well.

Krasnostavski fulfilled his vow to burn himself alive, along with the home he and Moshe had shared in the ghetto. The fire

quickly consumed the entire house and spread to nearby buildings. Soon there was a wall of fire separating one side of Synagogue Street from the other. Within a half hour, the entire
ghetto was engulfed in flames, forcing the Germans and Ukrainians to retreat.

Taking advantage of the pandemonium, several of the men
who had been rounded up ran back into the ghetto, preferring
to die in the flames rather than at the hands of Nazi murderers.
Others ran away, hoping to find refuge in the cemetery or the
castle ruins. They were quickly recaptured.

On September 25, 1942, the remaining Jews from the Korets
ghetto were marshaled to the market square and taken to the
Kozak Forest. Just like their neighbors, friends, and family
members four months earlier, they were ordered to strip naked,
line up in rows of six, and lie face down in the pit, where they
were murdered.

BY THE TIME the Nazis had entered the Korets ghetto for its
final liquidation, Moshe and Simcha had escaped to the forest.
On September 24, after hearing the news that more pits were
being dug near Kozak, Moshe dispatched two Jewish teenagers
to spy on the Jewish home that the Ukrainian auxiliary police
had commandeered as its headquarters. The lookouts warned
Moshe that several trucks carrying additional auxiliary policemen had arrived. An hour later, the surveillants reported
that four large units of heavily armed auxiliary policemen had
left the station headed in different directions.

Moshe immediately understood that the Ukrainian auxiliary
policemen were going to reinforce the German military policemen who had established a surveillance perimeter around the
ghetto. He apparently did not know about the German SD unit
that had also arrived from Rivne to provide even more fortification. But he did know that once the Nazis fully encircled the
ghetto, nobody would be able to escape.

Moshe initially decided to leave that night, sneaking out under the cover of darkness. In the meantime, he sent Zvi's son Yaakov to confirm the rumors about the new pits near Kozak. Before Yaakov returned, the streets started filling with Ukrainian auxiliary policemen. Moshe realized there was no time to wait. Anybody who hoped to survive would have to leave that afternoon.

Everyone in the ghetto had known that Moshe and Simcha were making preparations to join the partisans, but only the few who had expressed interest had been given any details. Moshe decided that they would sneak out of the ghetto in small groups, following different routes in case any of them were caught. They would rendezvous just outside of town, at the home of Vasil Kovalets, a Ukrainian thief and drunkard with connections to the criminal underworld who was nevertheless known for his big heart.

"Whoever can come, should come!" Moshe urged.

At four in the afternoon, Moshe snuck out of town with Simcha and Siomke. They passed through the densely wooded park that surrounded the old castle and headed toward a section of the Korchyk River that they knew would be shallow enough to cross. To minimize the risk of being seen, Simcha went first, followed by Siomke twenty-five steps behind him. Moshe brought up the rear.

Moshe took with him his copy of *Freedom's Songs*, along with the only weapon he had managed to get from his Polish source: a revolver that he had been quickly shown how to fire, along with five bullets. Moshe, Simcha, and Siomke agreed that if they were discovered, they would not allow themselves to be taken alive. Moshe would shoot his son and nephew, and then himself. They knew that an even worse fate would await them if they were captured.

After crossing the Korchyk River, they tore the circular yellow patches from the fronts and backs of their coats. They spent a moment wondering what they should do with the patches. They considered tossing them aside, but instinctively stuffed them in their pockets. "If they kill us, it won't make any difference whether they find the patches on us," Moshe and Simcha both realized. "But if we survive, we'll keep them as a reminder of the days of suffering, pain, and humiliation."

An hour later, at around five o'clock, Moshe, Simcha, and Siomke reached Vasil's house, near the stone quarry where Simcha had worked the previous winter. Zvi Pe'er had already arrived, along with Avigdor Zayka and sisters Dvora and Faige Kaftan. Lazar Gershfeld, who had the only other gun besides Moshe's, was also there. A little bit later, they were joined by four other Jews from Korets.

At the age of forty-four, Moshe was the oldest of his group and its leader. Zvi was the only one who had served in the army, but he had not received any weapons training. Lacking arms and training, Moshe and his group hoped to meet up with Soviet partisans who would provide them with both.

WHEN THE DARKNESS of night arrived, it was time to leave. Moshe and his group had waited as long as they could for Yaakov to join them, but he had not shown up.

"Do you have bread? Do you have food?" Vasil asked before they headed out. He gave them two loaves of bread. In exchange for hiding them, feeding them, and promising to shelter them again if they ever returned to Korets, the group gave Vasil all of their remaining money. It would be of no use to them in the forest.

Moshe and his group set out in search of partisans. They headed northward and disappeared into the safe seclusion of the dense woods. They walked all night, without the benefit of maps or guides. It was frightening to be wandering in the woods at night as untrained, barely armed fugitives. Every branch sticking out of a shrub looked like the muzzle of a rifle. Every birdcall sounded like a signal from a hidden enemy. They crossed the Sluch River just as the sun was rising.

Over the course of the night, Simcha had developed pneumonia with a high fever. He could barely walk. The group risked entering a village in search of schnapps that they could use as a homeopathic cure. There was no schnapps or vodka, but the villagers did give them some denatured alcohol. After returning back to the forest, the group massaged Simcha with the alcohol and wrapped him in every scrap of clothing they could spare. While Simcha fell into a deep sleep, the rest of them also settled in for the day. They were so close to the Germans and Ukrainians that they could see the Nazis through the trees. It was only by luck that the Nazis did not see them. "We were no master strategists," Simcha later quipped.

The group continued to travel only at night to avoid being discovered. They spent the next day near Mishikova, a village that is a little under twenty miles north of Korets, where Lazar Gershfeld had a close friend. By this time, Moshe's group had been augmented by a few other Jewish refugees they had met in the forest, including a woman named Rachel Weinstein and a man from the village of Mezhyrichi, thirteen miles west of Korets.

As the sun was rising, Moshe and his group heard the clattering of wagon wheels and snorting of horses. They were sure that the Germans or Ukrainians had followed their tracks. Instead, they saw villagers with carts filled with large milk cans. They jumped up and ordered the villagers to get off the carts so they could inspect them. Instead of the explosives that were often hidden in milk cans, the Jews found milk, which the villagers explained had been requisitioned by the Germans. Moshe and his group dumped the milk onto the ground. When the villagers complained that the Germans would kill them for not delivering the milk, Moshe's group provided them with a note claiming that the milk had been seized by partisans. They signed the note with a stamp carved from a large potato.

Moshe and his group were in constant fear of the very real possibility of being captured by the Nazis. One day, when Rachel and the man from Mezhyrichi went looking for bread, they were apprehended by Ukrainian auxiliary policemen. The Ukrainians looped a rope around Rachel's neck and choked her to death. They tied a rope around the man from Mezhyrichi's neck as well, but he played dead and they left him alone. He still had the rope around his neck when he returned to the group to tell them about Rachel's murder. Three other Jews who had joined the group were captured during a roundup. They were killed slowly, to prolong their agony.

Frustrated by the group's inability to find partisans, Lazar and Avigdor decided to go back to Korets, taking with them not only Lazar's pistol, but also one of the two loaves of bread that Vasil Kovalets had given the group.

While they were in Mishikova, Moshe's group received confirmation from the locals that the Korets ghetto had been liquidated. They lit a candle, hiding its flame from view by placing it in a box. Gathering around the candle, they recited the Kaddish for all who had been lost.

CHAPTER 5

"In Struggle"

Unfurl the large banners,
Wake those who slumber, being weak.
Bring the scattered together one by one.
Tell them: today the sacred cause is calling us
Against the bloody enemy!

—MORRIS WINCHEVSKY, "IN STRUGGLE"
(JOSEPH GLADSTEIN, *FREEDOM'S SONGS*, P. 23)

O**N SEPTEMBER 27, MOSHE AND** his group arrived near the village of Voronovka, twenty-seven miles north of Korets. At one o'clock, an hour after midnight, they heard footsteps. "Halt! Halt! Who goes there?" someone called out in Russian. The Jewish refugees had stumbled upon a reconnaissance unit from a Soviet partisan detachment commanded by Dmitry Medvedev.

In a radio message that was broadcast on July 3, 1941, less than two weeks after Germany invaded the Soviet Union, Joseph Stalin had announced a plan to create partisan units that would disrupt the German rear by blowing up roads and bridges, destroying communication lines, burning down forests, stores,

and warehouses, and terrorizing the Germans and their collaborators. This type of guerrilla warfare had been part of the Soviet
arsenal for decades. Vladimir Lenin had called for similar tactics
against the tsarist authorities in 1906, and the Bolsheviks had deployed a number of partisan units during the Russian Civil War
of 1918 through 1922. Soviet partisans had also spearheaded guerrilla activities during the Spanish Civil War of 1936 through 1939.

Medvedev had volunteered for the Red Army in 1917, during
the October Revolution. After the Russian Civil War, he had
joined the cheka—the secret police organization that was formed
to protect the new government from reactionary forces. As a che-
kist, Medvedev had mastered the techniques of guerrilla warfare
while fighting anti-Bolshevik partisans in the Bryansk Forest,
near Russia's border with Ukraine, as well as in Ukraine itself.

In August 1941, Medvedev snuck behind enemy lines with
thirty-three volunteers. While there were many Soviet soldiers
who were living in the forests, stranded behind enemy lines after
escaping German imprisonment, Medvedev's unit was the first
group of partisans to travel from the Soviet Union into German-
occupied territory. They spent the next six months in the
Bryansk Forest, successfully organizing partisan units throughout the region. They lost many men in combat, and Medvedev
himself was wounded on two occasions. But by the time they returned to the Soviet Union in February 1942, the detachment
had swelled in size to three hundred partisans.

In spring 1942, Medvedev was assigned to venture much
deeper into German-occupied Ukraine, all the way to the forest
around the Volhynian city of Sarny. His new partisan detachment, named "The Victors," would be composed of around
ninety men and women—Soviets, Ukrainians, and Poles, some
of whom were Jewish, and fifteen Republicans from the Spanish
Civil War. Well-equipped with radio transmitters and radio operators, the detachment would inform Moscow of the strength
and movements of the German Army, as well as of the locations

of factories and military depots. Their proximity to Rivne, fifty miles south of Sarny, would allow them to spy on the capital of Reich Commissariat Ukraine and tap into the underground resistance movement there.

To avoid detection, Medvedev's detachment was flown over German-occupied Ukraine at night. The distance to Sarny was too great for a plane to make it there and back before sunrise, so the plan was to fly the detachment to the forest near Mukhoedy, a village twenty miles south of Naroulia that is now known as Kirov. They would proceed the rest of the way to Sarny—some 120 miles west of Mukhoedy—on foot. In late May 1942, the first group of fourteen men was dropped by parachute, missing the landing spot by almost two hundred miles to the south. They were attacked by an SS unit, and only two men survived.

The second unit parachuted into a swamp near Tovstyi Lis— Ukrainian for "Thick Forest"—a village fifteen miles southeast of Mukhoedy. Once there, they set up signal fires to help the remaining groups identify their location from the air. But the third group, which included Medvedev's chief of staff, Fyodor Pashun, mistook fires lit by railway workers for the signals and bailed out over one hundred miles away. The next three groups, including Medvedev's, were more successful, and met up with the second unit in Tovstyi Lis. On June 23, they set off for Sarny, reuniting with Pashun's group and adding escaped prisoners of war to their ranks along the way. They fought and won several battles with Germans and Ukrainian auxiliary policemen as they worked their way westward.

Medvedev's partisan detachment reached the Sarny Forest at the end of July. Their orders were to lay low by keeping their numbers small and avoiding combat, but repeated skirmishes with Germans and Ukrainian nationalists forced them to defend themselves and even go on the offensive on several occasions. Accordingly, Medvedev started fortifying his detachment with even more members. Most of the new recruits were Red Army soldiers who had escaped captivity, but Medvedev was also known to welcome Jewish refugees into his ranks.

When Moshe and his group met up with Medvedev's reconnaissance unit in late September, they introduced themselves as fellow partisans and asked if they could join the detachment. The Soviets agreed to introduce the Jews to their commanding officer, and set up a time and place for a rendezvous.

The next day, Moshe met with Pashun, who asked how many fighters and what kind of weapons they had.

"My group consists of ten men and two women," Moshe replied. "We have one revolver with five bullets and one butcher's knife that's half a yard long." Zvi Pe'er, who had worked in the slaughterhouse, had taken the knife during their escape from the Korets ghetto.

Pashun smirked. "First of all, you don't have enough weapons," he explained. "Second, our unit is about to go on a special mission. We don't need any new fighters in our ranks right now."

Refusing to accept defeat, Moshe asked where he could find other partisan units.

"Head east, toward the Bryansk Forest," Pashun replied. "You'll find tens of thousands of partisans there."

Pashun told Moshe about a caravan of Jewish refugees whom the Soviet partisans had sent in that direction a few days earlier. He explained that the group was rather disorganized, and recommended that Moshe track them down and provide them with much-needed leadership.

ONE OF THE Jews whom Medvedev had sent eastward was Aleksander "Sasha" Kuc, a partisan from the Jewish town of Berezne, some thirty miles northwest of Korets. Sasha had joined Medvedev's partisan detachment shortly after the partisans had arrived in the Sarny Forest, and had used his knowledge of the area to infiltrate German and Ukrainian institutions. Sasha was specifically tasked with establishing contact with members of the underground resistance movement.

The Soviets gave Sasha and other young Jewish men uniforms and *pilotka* side caps with red stars. They taught them how to fire weapons, as well as how to use explosives and other tools of sabotage. They would even let Jews guard the rear of squads as they went out on patrol. But they never included Jewish refugees in combat missions. There was widespread antisemitism among the Soviet partisans, many of whom believed that Jews were genetically predisposed to cowardice and were therefore unfit for combat.

When the commander who oversaw the Jewish refugees indicated that he agreed with the notion that all Jews should be barred from combat, Sasha took offense. "I'm the only one left from my family," he argued. "I don't see why my life should be sheltered." When the commander explained that he was simply trying to save the Jews from being killed, Sasha retorted that anyone who wants to go on combat missions should be allowed to, and that it was unfair to force Jews to work only in service roles. As punishment for his insubordination, Sasha was removed from intelligence operations and assigned to an agricultural unit.

As the summer progressed, Sasha started hearing from his contacts that the ghettos in nearby cities and towns were being liquidated. On the night of July 13, five thousand Jews in Rivne had been forced out of the ghetto, herded into freight cars, and taken to a quarry, where they had all been shot. Other large-scale *Aktions* took place in Sasha's hometown of Berezne on August 25 and in Sarny on August 27, 1942. When the Nazis arrived in Tuchyn on September 23 to kill the three thousand Jews living there, the Jews fought back, setting fire to the ghetto and to nearby German warehouses, shooting at the Germans and Ukrainians, and running away. An estimated two thousand of them were able to escape, only to find it impossible to survive

in the forest. Around one thousand of the escapees were captured and killed within three days, while three hundred women
with children returned to Tuchyn.

When Sasha and his friends Yosef and Yechiel asked Medvedev if anything could be done to help the Jews who were wandering in the forest after escaping the ghetto liquidations,
Medvedev gave them permission to find the refugees and bring
them back to the base camp. The Soviet partisans welcomed the
Jewish refugees, providing them with warm food and medical
care. By the end of August, Medvedev found himself sheltering
150 Jews, including women, children, and the elderly. Living in
the camp, the refugees slowly started to feel human again after
spending months in ghettos and several days in the woods.

AT FIRST, THE Jewish refugees were simply absorbed into the
camp population. The men assisted the Soviet partisans on noncombat missions, the elderly cleaned, and the women cooked
and cared for the children. One of the women taught school,
while another woman and her husband sewed shirts out of para-
chutes for the children.

Medvedev knew that he could not safeguard so many refugees indefinitely. He suggested arming the able-bodied men and
assigning them to a fighting unit—just not his. "All around we
are encountering groups of Jews, around ten to twenty people
each, who escaped execution," he radioed Moscow in early September. "Their wives and children were shot. They thirst for revenge. A partisan detachment can be formed. Weapons and
ammunition are needed." The new Jewish unit Medvedev proposed never came to fruition.

But many of the refugees were unfit for combat. They were
too young or too old, or too weakened by sickness, starvation,
and exhaustion. Medvedev knew that he would not be able to
protect them in the Sarny Forest, especially with the Soviet partisans regularly leaving the camp to go on missions. Moreover,

if the camp was ever attacked, it would be impossible to evacuate them all in time.

Medvedev made a plan to send one hundred of the Jewish women, children, and elderly to Moscow on planes that were bringing ammunition and other supplies to the partisans. Medvedev's men located a large meadow near their camp where a plane could land, and lit signal fires to guide the way. When the first plane neared, Sasha and the other partisans gathered a group they wanted to send to safety, including an old man from Berezne who, Sasha hoped, would bear witness to what was happening to the Jews in Ukraine. But the pilot misread the signals and overshot the makeshift runway. The plane crash-landed and was damaged beyond repair. After unloading the ammunition and medicine, the Soviets burned the plane to the ground.

Medvedev abandoned his plan to fly the women, children, and elderly to Moscow and instead decided to send them on foot to the Bryansk Forest, an area controlled by the Soviet partisans. The Jewish refugees would be safe there, while still being able to contribute to noncombat operations. Medvedev did not know enough about the partisans who were operating in that forest at the time to point the refugees in a specific direction, but he did provide them with two horse-drawn wagons loaded with enough flour, meat, and other supplies to last for several days. Medvedev also gave them paratrooper jumpsuits and weapons, including eighteen rifles with ammunition. He dispatched three Soviet scouts to accompany the caravan as far as the railway line that ran from Ukraine's western border all the way to Kyiv, and assigned Sasha, Yosef, and Yechiel to escort the refugees the rest of the way. Other young Jewish men went along voluntarily, unwilling to be separated from their parents and younger siblings.

Early into the journey, the caravan was attacked by a gang of Ukrainian nationalists. Unwilling to protect so many women, children, and old people, the Soviet scouts abandoned the Jewish refugees and returned to Medvedev's base. One antisemitic

scout later blamed the Jews for being too greedy and lazy to war-
rant protection. He claimed, falsely, that the Jews had not
wanted to leave Volhynia because they had hidden gold there,
and that they had refused to dig latrines when the caravan had
stopped to rest.

When they deserted the Jewish refugees, the Soviet scouts
took with them the two horses, a cart with a machine gun, two
submachine guns, all of the money, and all of the food. Nothing
remained except a few hand grenades and no more than ten rifles, which only Sasha, Yosef, and Yechiel knew how to fire.

While a few refugees returned to Medvedev's camp for new
instructions, the rest remained behind in a dangerous area.
There were Germans nearby, and the Jews would be apprehended and no doubt murdered unless they maintained absolute
silence. The caravan included a doctor from Berezne, his wife,
and their two children, one of whom kept crying from hunger,
cold, and bugbites. The refugees urged the doctor to silence the
boy, but the child was inconsolable. Fearful that the Germans
would hear the crying, the doctor allowed the other refugees to
kill his young son. "Take the child. I cannot keep him quiet. Do
with him as you wish," he told them. "Let us not all be lost!"

When the refugees who had returned to Medvedev's camp
came back, they reported that the caravan would not receive
any further assistance from the Soviets. Most of the Jews, including Yosef and Yechiel, decided to leave the caravan. They were
not interested in walking all the way to the Bryansk Forest, only
to be assigned roles that did not involve combat. "If I'm just
going to ride out the war, then I'd rather do it in an area I know
and where people know me," they rationalized.

Sasha and around forty other Jewish refugees continued on.
Moshe and his group caught up with them a few days later, close
to the railroad line between the towns of Klesiv and Rokytne.
Moshe took one of the rifles Medvedev had given to Sasha's
group and handed two other rifles, along with some of the gre-

nades, to Simcha and Siomke. The newly combined unit elected Moshe as their leader. Since Sasha had the most military experience, particularly the training in reconnaissance that he had gained during his time with Medvedev, he became Moshe's chief of staff.

MOSHE AND HIS newly augmented group continued their journey, still walking at night and spending their days eating and resting. Sasha, Simcha, and three other refugees quickly organized themselves into a reconnaissance unit. They would set out early in the day, in search of the best routes. Whenever they encountered roads, they would look for places where the caravan could emerge from the forest just long enough to cross the roads without being detected, before disappearing back into the woods on the other side. It took two days of surveillance before they figured out how to safely cross a railway bridge near the village of Osnytsk, four miles west of Rokytne. Each night, the reconnaissance unit would lead the larger group through the route they had planned that day.

After crossing the bridge near Osnytsk and continuing northward, the caravan walked for another three miles before stopping at the end of another long night. Early in the morning, the refugees saw a peasant gathering fodder. They discussed killing the peasant to make sure he could not tell the Germans where they were, but decided just to swear him to secrecy and allow him to continue on his way.

But the peasant informed on them. A half hour later, the refugees heard shouts of "Halt! Halt!" followed by a hail of gunfire. A large group of heavily armed Germans encircled the refugees and launched a massive offensive. Simcha lobbed a grenade, killing two Germans and wounding another, but the Jews were clearly outgunned. Many of them died in the battle, including Noah Reisenberg, who had been among the eleven Jews who had left Korets with Moshe.

While a few refugees stayed behind to provide cover fire, the others ran away as fast as they could. Moshe and Simcha escaped with nine women and hid in a swamp. They stood silently in the water, where they could avoid detection by the search dogs the Germans had brought to track them down. By the time night finally fell, they had been standing all day and had not eaten or slept for twenty-four hours. Simcha had caught dysentery from eating contaminated food, and had not slept in seventy-two hours.

Moshe and Simcha led the nine women to Staryky, a village three miles south of Osnytsk. They had stayed there the day before they had crossed the bridge, and Moshe had designated Staryky as where the group would rendezvous if they got separated. Simcha was exhausted. He was able to keep his feet moving, but was otherwise asleep. Moshe kept having to rouse him back to consciousness so that Simcha could show him how to get back to Staryky.

When they arrived back in Staryky, Moshe and Simcha reunited with Sasha and Siomke. The only ones left from the forty-member caravan were the four of them and six other men, including Zvi and a Polish Jew from Łódź named Maryan. There were also eleven women, most of whom would not survive partisan combat.

"Ladies, we can't continue like this," Moshe told them. "What kind of army would we be?"

They decided to stay with the women for a few days before leaving nine of them behind in the forest with food and money. The women would be able to provide for themselves; they knew the area and the local villagers. The refugees retained two women in their ranks, including Faige Kaftan from Korets.

Moshe's newly restructured group set off in the direction of Klesiv, crossing the railway bridge for the third time. They were in Polesia, a region on Ukraine's border with Belarus that is known for its dense forests and large swamps. Because the villages in Polesia were few and far between, Moshe and his group would be able to travel throughout the region undetected. Whenever they needed to lie low, they could hide in the thick forest, where it would be next to impossible for the Germans and Ukrainians to find them. The impenetrable terrain would be the perfect place for them to resume their search for partisans.

ON OCTOBER 5, Moshe and his group were resting in a pine forest. But Moshe could not sleep. Neither could Simcha nor Zvi. They had been searching everywhere for experienced partisans, hoping to be accepted into their ranks, but had so far been unsuccessful.

"It's not going to be easy to find partisans," Moshe conceded. "We need to get our hands on some weapons at any cost, and become partisans on our own."

"But how are we going to get weapons?" Zvi asked.

Moshe had been in contact with a sympathetic Pole who had provided him with intelligence on the German military police and the Ukrainian auxiliary police in the area, as well as where one could find weapons. "I heard that there is a Russian rifle and a double-barreled shotgun in a woodsman's lodge about twelve-and-a-half miles away from here, in the village of Ozera," Moshe told Zvi and the others. "We have to get them."

Moshe started thinking about how to commandeer the woodsman's weapons. "This will be our first guerrilla mission. If we want it to be a success, we'll need to plan everything carefully," he concluded.

Moshe decided that the best strategy would be to convince the woodsman to lay down his weapons without engaging in a firefight. He formulated a plan to trick the woodsman into believing that there were over a hundred heavily armed guerrillas in their group rather than a dozen aspiring partisans with limited weaponry. To make the woodsman believe that the few partisans he would see were all armed, Moshe had Zvi fashion fake pistols out of birch bark, which they stitched together and colored black with a chemical pencil.

At midnight the next night, Moshe and his group approached the woodsman's lodge near Ozera, a village seventeen miles north of Klesiv. The lodge was a large house at the outskirts of the village, facing the road from the nearby village of Shakhy into Ozera. Moshe stood on the front porch and barked orders that he knew could be overheard from inside the house. "I need six of you to stay with me, and ten of you to go with Siomke to guard the back door."

"Yes, sir!" Siomke shouted.

Ten members of the group marched loudly to the back of the house. After making some noise, they quietly tiptoed back to Moshe.

"I need twenty men to surround the woodsman's house! Micka, you lead them. Be vigilant! If you see anything suspicious, shoot immediately."

The group stomped away, again returning silently a few minutes later.

"Sasha, run to the horsemen and make sure they're not blocking the road. They should stay on the roadside and watch the road to Shakhy. No one is to enter or leave the village," Moshe commanded. "Everyone else, stay with me. Ready your weapons!"

Moshe banged on the woodsman's door. "Open up!" he shouted. He banged again.

The door opened slowly. A woman stood before them, wearing only her nightclothes. "Who are you looking for?" she asked, her entire body trembling with fear.

Moshe gave the door a little push, forcing the woodsman's wife to step backward. He entered the house with Simcha and Zvi. Simcha turned on a light, and the men followed the woman into a large kitchen.

"What do you want?" she whispered, pleading with her hands.

"Where's the woodsman?" Moshe asked.

"He isn't here. He went to the Vysotsk region."

"Where are his guns?"

"He took them to give to the German commandant. Rumors are circulating that there are partisans in our forest who could steal the weapons, and he would be executed if he allowed that to happen."

"That's a lie!" Moshe snapped. "The Germans don't shoot people like your husband." He ordered her to grab a shovel that was propped in the corner and follow him outside.

"Where are you taking me?" she asked fearfully.

"You're going to dig your own grave. And your husband will be hanged."

The woman's knees buckled. She called out her husband's name, fainted, and fell to the floor.

The kitchen door flung open. A tall man stood in the door-way, wearing only his underwear. The woodsman approached Moshe and fell to his knees.

"Good men, I'll give you my weapons. I'll give you anything you want," he pleaded in a broken voice. "But, please, spare my wife. She has a weak heart."

Moshe pointed his revolver at the woodsman and shouted, "Show us where your guns are, and your wife won't be harmed." Turning to Zvi, he commanded, "Wake her up and tend to her."

While Zvi grabbed a bucket of water to splash on the woman, Moshe and Simcha followed the woodsman through several rooms to a large office. The woodsman pushed aside a heavy desk and removed a plank from the wooden floor. He pulled out a Russian rifle, a shotgun, and some ammunition.

Zvi entered the office with the woodsman's wife, who ran to the woodsman and embraced him. "Whatever you do to my hus-band, do the same to me," she whispered weakly.

"I won't hurt you. We're just going to lock you in this room. Don't leave until dawn. There are two guerrillas armed with automatic rifles who are guarding both windows. If either of

you gets close to a window, they'll shoot you on the spot,"
Moshe lied.

"Aren't you hungry?" the woman asked, a little calmer. "We
have fresh bread and butter."

"We'll take a few loaves of bread," Moshe acquiesced. "Our
bread has gone quite stale."

Moshe and his group were about to lock the couple in the office when the woodsman asked him to leave some proof that the
weapons had been taken at gunpoint. If the Germans came asking, the woodsman wanted some evidence that he had surrendered them only under duress.

"No problem," Moshe agreed. "I'll give you a receipt."

He wrote: *On October 6, 1942, rifle number 60240 with 40 bullets
and a double-barreled shotgun with 12 shells were taken from the
hands of this German servant. The weapons are now in the hands of
those who will avenge the blood that has been shed by innocents.*

Moshe started his signature—*Head of the Partisan Detachment*—and then hesitated, unsure of how he should sign his
name.

Siomke appeared at the window. "Uncle Misha!" he called
out, using the affectionate diminutive of the name Moshe. "A
farmer's cart is approaching the village. Should we stop it?"

"Just a moment," Moshe replied. He had reached a decision.
He signed the note with the name under which he would terrorize Nazis and Nazi sympathizers for the next two-and-a-half
years: *Uncle Misha.*

CHAPTER 6

≡≡≡≡≡

"Death to the German Robbers!"

And now we have come to you,
In partisan detachments,
To poison the lives of Germans,
To destroy all of their depots, bases, and warehouses.

    —MOSHE GILDENMAN, "DEATH TO THE GERMAN
    ROBBERS!"

F OR THE NEXT TWO WEEKS, Uncle Misha and his partisans traveled around Polesia, taking advantage of weather that was unusually warm and dry. Without a long-term plan, they wandered from place to place, spending one or two nights at each location before moving on to avoid being caught. Just as they had convinced the woodsman in Ozera that they were a much bigger group than they actually were, they told anyone they met in the forest that they were just a reconnaissance squad from a large partisan detachment that was operating nearby. They wore the jumpsuits that Sasha's group of Jewish refugees had gotten from Medvedev to convince the local peasants that they were Soviet paratroopers.

Upon entering a village, Uncle Misha would go to the local government building and make a telephone call to the district office. He would report that the village had been overrun by Uncle Misha's partisan detachment and was in desperate need of assistance. When the official on the other end would ask who was speaking, he would reply, "Uncle Misha!" He would destroy the telephone, burn all of the documents in the building, and quickly escape to the next village, cutting the telephone and telegraph lines along the way.

While ethnic Ukrainians had been in the majority in Volhynia, most of the locals in Polesia were indigenous Poleshuks, who did not support Ukrainian nationalism. In order to earn the Poleshuks' sympathies, Uncle Misha and his partisans shared with them the spoils of the stores and depots they ransacked. The Poleshuks were especially happy to receive salt, which was a rare commodity during the war. The partisans looted several tons of salt from German depots and distributed it among the impoverished Poleshuks.

Uncle Misha also engaged in anti-German propaganda. From the earliest days of the war, the Soviets had been dropping leaflets onto occupied territories. The flyers contained brief declarations and calls to action: *The Red Army Is Fighting for the Freedom of the People, Rally for the Patriotic War!* and *Death to the German Robbers!* In efforts to arouse a sense of patriotism and inspire local populations to take up the fight, the notices reported that the Germans wanted to colonize Ukraine and enslave the people living there. The leaflets often referenced the German commandeering and looting of property that was rampant in Polesia.

Uncle Misha wrote a number of similar leaflets and pamphlets that he and his partisans distributed to the villagers. One flyer included a new song that he wrote in Russian. Taking inspiration from the Soviet flyers, he titled the song "Death to the German Robbers!"

Hello, people of Polesia!!!!
Uncle Misha has come to you.
And he has brought reliable and honest men
With him by the hundreds.

Uncle Misha knows everything:
How the Germans rule here
As your children perish
And are taken to Germany.

How the Germans took your last cattle,
Your chickens, and your grain.
And how they demand about five yards of cloth
From every woman.

The Germans are obsessed with fat.
They devour all the butter and honey they want,
And the people are dying here
Without medicine and without salt.

And now we have come to you,
In partisan detachments,
To poison the lives of Germans,
To destroy all of their depots, bases, and warehouses.

And give away all of the goods
To all aggrieved peasants.
They burn bridges, and give you no peace,
These Germans and German overlords.

To the Germans, partisans mean
A blow to the rear.
And our friend, Comrade Stalin,
Will deal a blow to the Germans on the front.

And then we will throw this garbage
Out of our homeland.
But only if you help us
In that combat mission.

Here is the mission of the partisan:
To beat the Germans hard in the back.
And with this, people of Polesia,
Uncle Misha sends his greetings!!!

The leaflet is signed, *Uncle Misha's Partisan Detachment.* It concludes with a note urging the local youth to form their own partisan units, obtain some weapons, and join the war to drive out the occupying Germans.

As they became acclimated to life as fugitives, Uncle Misha and his partisans became more confident in their ability to survive in the forest. They also grew more resolved in their mission to avenge the murders of their loved ones.

"We should imagine ourselves lying in the mass grave in the Kozak Forest, along with our mothers, brothers, and sisters. We already have nothing to lose," Simcha would remind them. Invoking the Jewish dynasty that had once created an independent Jewish kingdom in the Land of Israel, he urged his fellow partisans, "Don't forget that we're the descendants of the Hasmoneans. We have to be willing to sacrifice our lives in the forests of Polesia, just as they did by the walls of Jerusalem."

Like Uncle Misha, several of the partisans adapted noms de guerre. Simcha became "Lionka Semyonov," and Zvi fought under the name "Grisha Khapkes."

The band of partisans also continued to grow in size, accepting into their ranks Jews they found wandering, hungry and scared, in the woods. Some of the refugees had fled ghettos, while others had been duped by Ukrainian peasants into handing over everything they had in exchange for hiding places, only to be chased away. Uncle Misha welcomed the refugees into his detachment, including a sixteen-year-old boy from Davyd-Haradok named Sashka and two young women from Berezne named Anya and Dusia. With these additions, there were sixteen men and four women among Uncle Misha's partisans.

ON OCTOBER 20, Uncle Misha and his partisans stopped to rest in a forest near the town of Hlynne. Uncle Misha assigned two partisans to stand guard, while everyone else settled in for a short rest. They planned to sleep until midnight and then continue on through the night. Uncle Misha fell asleep immediately, but was awakened by Faige, who had been standing guard.

"Uncle Misha," she whispered. "I hear some voices."

Uncle Misha listened carefully. He heard two men speaking in Ukrainian. They were coming closer.

A peasant cart stopped about fifty yards from them. Uncle Misha heard barrels being rolled out of the cart. A few moments later, he saw a small flame flickering from between the dense shrubs. When the wind carried a familiar musty odor in his direction, he realized that the men were distilling alcohol. He crawled closer for a better look.

He saw two peasants standing next to a still. One was around forty-five years old, and the other was slightly younger. Both wore ragged clothes and shoes woven from tree bark. They were working quickly, while constantly looking around nervously. These men were no threats to the partisans. They were bootleggers, making their contraband in the forest.

Uncle Misha grabbed his revolver, crawled closer, and rose to his feet. The sudden presence of an armed man frightened the peasants, and they started to run away.

"Don't run," Uncle Misha implored. "I'm not your enemy. I'm a partisan."

When they stepped closer, Uncle Misha put his revolver away and greeted them. They shook hands.

"Carry on. I won't disturb you," he said. "What village are you from?"

"We're from Hlynne. We're making schnapps, but not for our own enjoyment," the older peasant explained. "The Germans have taken all of our bread. We have a large family, and we have to eat. We take the schnapps to the steppe, where we exchange it for bread. Sometimes we sell the schnapps in Klesiv, to the stonecutters, to earn enough money to pay our taxes. Ah, may we live to see better times."

"There's no shame in this, my friends," Uncle Misha comforted them. "The Germans aren't going to be here forever. Have patience and everything will go back to what it was like before."

The peasants invited Uncle Misha closer to the cauldron. Tossing a couple of dry branches into the fire, the older peasant started to open up.

"Ah, how we used to live," he reminisced. "We were never wealthy. You know our land: either forests or swamps, nothing more. But each of us had ten cows. There was milk and butter. We would sell one cow in the fall, buy some corn with the money, and be set for the entire year. And when the Soviets came, they wanted to drain the swamps. We could have never done that on our own, but a government can do anything. Ah, how good that would have been! We would have had such good land that even the peasants of the steppe would have envied us. Then the devil brought the Germans to our land and misfortune to our homes. We all wanted to leave, like the birds do in the fall. Those damned Germans take everything: horses, cows, whatever they come across." The old peasant then lamented that the Council Chair and the District Administrator from Yelne, a village thirteen miles southwest of Hlynne, would be coming the next day to recruit child laborers to send to Germany. "And if they don't go voluntarily, they'll be taken by force," he added. "Oh, this is such a disaster. A disaster!"

Something clicked for Uncle Misha. "Are they coming by themselves?" he asked casually.

"Two or three policemen are coming with them. Those policemen, our own henchmen, are even worse than the Germans. They rummage through every home, plundering and tormenting their own kind."

Uncle Misha returned to his partisans, woke them up, and shared the plan he had just formulated. "Tomorrow the Council Chair, the District Administrator, and two or three policemen are coming from Yelne to Hlynne. I've decided to mount an attack on them. If we succeed, we're going to get some more rifles, and perhaps some more revolvers," he explained. "This is a serious matter, and has to be approached as such. As soon as day breaks, we'll head to the road and look for a suitable position to lie in wait."

"Very good!" everyone agreed in unison.

AT DAWN, WITH a light fog still covering the ground, the partisans walked over to the road. When they emerged from the woods, the land sloped downward, opening up a beautiful vista. It was a welcome sight for partisans who had been living in the forest for a month.

"Papa, just look at how big the sky is!" Lionka exclaimed, his voice a mixture of joy and frustration.

"Yes, son, a lot of sky and a lot of land," Uncle Misha replied. "But little room for us Jews!"

While the others stood at the edge of the forest, Uncle Misha, Lionka, Siomke, and Grisha went in search of the perfect spot for an ambush. About two hundred yards down the road, there was a small bridge over a muddy riverbed.

"As an engineer, couldn't you rebuild this bridge so that it would collapse under the policemen? Wouldn't that be pretty easy for you to do?" Lionka asked half-jokingly.

"I'll try!"

They examined the bridge. It was sixteen feet long and five feet high, and was of simple construction. Its wooden planks were supported by three birch beams that spanned the riverbed.

The beams rested on logs that had been sunk into the banks as footings. Uncle Misha realized that if they removed one of the footings, the bridge would lose its structural integrity without appearing to be damaged. But to get to the footing, they would have to tear out the beams.

"That's no big deal!" Grisha proclaimed.

He crawled under the bridge and pushed against a beam with his broad shoulders. He grabbed a plank with both hands and started to wiggle it back and forth with all his strength. He worked it free and emerged victoriously from the mud holding the plank. Using the plank as a lever, the partisans lifted the beams and slid the log footing into the riverbed. After raking the dirt, they rested the beams on the loose soil.

Uncle Misha called the other partisans over and told them the plan. They would hide in thick shrubs on the other side of the road. As soon as the wagon carrying the Nazi officials fell into the riverbed, they would open fire, jump from behind the shrubs, and overrun the enemy before they even knew what hit them. Uncle Misha distributed the few weapons they had. He held on to his revolver and gave Lionka the rifle. Siomke got the shotgun, but only after Grisha had turned it down, preferring to stick with his butcher's knife. The others were armed only with sticks and extra planks from the bridge.

Then they waited. By ten o'clock, there was still no sign of anyone. The partisans watched the road, growing more impatient with each passing hour. The still silence was interrupted only by the knocking of woodpeckers on nearby trees, the gentle breeze, and the distant echo of creaking gates from the nearby village. At least it was a fine autumn day, with the rising sun providing a nice warmth.

Uncle Misha was starting to doubt whether the peasants had given him reliable information, but soon he heard the Ukrainian folk song "Unhitch the Horses, Boys" being sung far away.

"They're coming!" he whispered.

The singing grew louder and louder until the partisans could see two small Polesian horses coming down the road, pulling a peasant cart. In the front sat the driver and a man in a black coat and green hat. On one side of the cart, a man in a police uniform and a man in civilian clothing reclined in a haystack, singing. Across from them, two policemen sat in black overcoats, talking loudly and laughing.

The horses sprang onto the bridge without difficulty. But as soon as the front wheel of the cart touched the bridge, it collapsed under the additional weight. There was a loud crash as the horses and cart fell into the riverbed. The cart toppled over, trapping the policeman who had been singing.

Uncle Misha gave the signal, and the partisans started shooting. The smoke from the opening salvos had not yet cleared when they leaped from their hideout, rushed to where the bridge had been just seconds earlier and started pummeling the men with sticks and the butts of their guns. Uncle Misha was delighted to see how efficiently the partisans were working together.

Grisha pounced on the policeman who had freed himself from under the cart. He plunged the long blade of his butcher's knife into the man's side, all the way to the hilt, shouting, "This is for my murdered wife and child!"

The District Administrator lay under the horses' hooves, sobbing. The left side of his face was riddled with shotgun pellets and soaked in blood. The partisans left him there to die alongside his comrades.

The partisans took the men's shoes to replace their own boots, which had worn down to holes during the long treks through the forests. They grabbed everything they could find from the cart: pencils, notebooks, pocketknives, sausage, and a few loaves of bread. Most importantly, they gained more weaponry: two revolvers, three rifles, and six grenades. All without any injuries to their side.

———

KNOWING THAT THE Nazis would be looking for payback after the ambush on the officials near Hlynne, Uncle Misha moved his partisans back to Ozera. Eleven miles north of Ozera is the town of Perebrody, where there was a well-known fishery called Rybałki—"Fisherman" in Polish. Surrounded on all sides by hundred-year-old pines and oaks, the large lake, which the locals called the "warehouse," was fed by a network of canals and streams that ran through nearby forests and meadows. On the shore, there was a large house built on pine pilings. At the start of the war, the attendant who had lived in the house had been conscripted into the Red Army, leaving behind his wife and two children. Since then, his wife had managed the fishery, taking orders over the telephone.

Every Saturday, the dam on the lake was opened, draining into canals that carried the water to the Horyn River. When the water lowered, the golden carp that were bred in the lake were trapped in specially designed tanks. The best-looking carps were hauled in barrels to the Regional Commissar and the District Administrators of nearby towns. Quite a few of the fish would be poached in transit by Ukrainian policemen who assisted with the harvesting and transporting of the fish.

Uncle Misha took great offense to the thought that the Germans and Ukrainians, the slaughterers of thousands of Jews, were gorging themselves on a dish that was such an important staple of Jewish cuisine. Although he had planned to lay low after the ambush near Hlynne, he decided to destroy the fishery and release the carp into the river.

On the morning of Friday, October 30, 1942, Uncle Misha set off for Rybałki with Lionka, Sasha, Siomke, and Grisha, along with Anya, Dusia, and a Jewish partisan named Suliko. The warm weather they had enjoyed just a few days earlier had passed, so they marched quickly to stay warm in the frosty air. A chilly eastern wind blew, biting at the tips of their ears and their flushed cheeks. With each gust, yellow leaves blew from the trees and rustled to the ground. The partisans broke two large branches off trees and made a footbridge to cross one of the canals that led to the river.

As they approached the attendant's house, Uncle Misha saw a woman's head flash in a window before quickly disappearing.

Uncle Misha knocked on the door. Nobody answered, but he thought he heard voices inside. As he grabbed the door handle and started to rattle the door violently, he heard a telephone ringing. Finally a young woman opened the door and invited the partisans inside with exaggerated politeness.

"Oh, I'm so happy to see real Russian partisans," she gushed, noting their Soviet paratrooper jumpsuits. "My husband is also Russian, from the city of Gorky. Please sit down, my dear guests, you must be hungry. I'll make tea and fry some fish." She spoke very quickly and anxiously, in a dialect of mixed Belarusian and Russian. It was clear that her hospitality was forced and insincere.

"Show us how to access the fish tanks," Uncle Misha demanded.

"Of course, my darlings. I'll show you everything," she promised. "But first, eat something. Such dear guests!"

Sasha looked through an open door and saw a telephone in the other room. "She must have notified the police station in Perebrody of our arrival," he whispered.

Remembering the telephone ringing as they waited at the door, Uncle Misha grabbed the woman's hand and led her to the telephone. He pointed his revolver at her and sternly commanded, "You must say whatever I tell you to say over the telephone. If you add one word or change anything, you'll get a bullet in the head."

When the line connected, he held the handset in such a way that she could speak into the receiver while he could hear the speaker. "Ask them, 'Have you left yet?'"

She repeated his words in a trembling voice.

"The entire police force is on its way to Rybałki," came the response.

"'Uncle Misha was at my house with more than fifty men. I
heard them saying that they're going to attack the police station.
Get ready!'"

She repeated Uncle Misha's words, but exclaimed at the end,
"They're going to shoot me!"

Uncle Misha covered her mouth with his hand and hissed, "If
you betray us with one more word, you'll be shot immediately!
Speak faster!"

"'Which road are you using?' Repeat it," he instructed, moving the receiver back to her mouth.

"Uncle Misha is here! Hurry! Help me! I—"

Before she could finish the sentence, Uncle Misha shot her
twice in the head.

THE PARTISANS RAN out of the house. They jumped over the
canal and darted across the damp meadow, sprinting to the forest that loomed on the other side like a dark green wall. When
they were fifty yards away from the forest, they heard shouting.

"There they are!" someone yelled in Ukrainian from the forest. "Fire!" Gunshots rang through the air.

Uncle Misha, Lionka, Sasha, and Suliko reached some bushes
at the edge of the forest and threw their bodies to the ground.
Siomke, Grisha, Anya, and Dusia hid behind a large haystack in
the meadow.

Uncle Misha took notice of how inexperienced the Ukrainian shooters were. In addition to making the tactical error of not
shooting the partisans when they were in the open meadow,
they were firing their weapons indiscriminately. Their bullets
were flying everywhere, but were not hitting anybody. The bullets whistled over the partisans' heads and landed several yards
behind them, kicking up tiny fountains of mud. Although the partisans were outgunned, Uncle Misha realized that they could
win the shoot-out if they were more disciplined.

He told his partisans to remain calm and only fire on his command. There were three Ukrainian auxiliary policemen to their left, about forty yards away. One of them had a submachine gun, and was continually firing short bursts at the partisans. "Left, all together, two bullets each. Fire!" he ordered.

A short burst of gunfire erupted from the partisans. They heard a cry, and then cursing. The machine gunner had been neutralized.

Meanwhile, Siomke crawled on his hands and knees from behind the haystack and started working his way toward the bushes. The policemen saw him and started shooting in his direction. The bullets continued to miss their target, and within a few seconds, Siomke was lying next to Uncle Misha, carefully wiping the mud from his rifle with his cap.

Anya tried to follow Siomke's lead, but as soon as she appeared from behind the haystack, the policemen started firing at her. She quickly ducked back behind the haystack.

Suddenly the gunfire stopped. Through the silence, Uncle Misha could hear the policemen arguing. One voice stood out, saying, "There are only eight of them and forty of us. Attack them! Follow me!"

The policemen jumped up and started rushing toward the partisans.

"Aim carefully," Uncle Misha commanded. "Fire!" They shot and killed a handful of the policemen. The others stopped their advance.

"Forward, Ukrainian swine, or you'll be shot!" their commanding officer shouted in German.

A policeman in a black jacket jumped out first. "Follow me, brothers," he yelled. He ran forward, and the others started to join him.

The partisans responded with a hail of gunfire, killing a few more policemen. The other policemen quickly hid behind the trees. They started advancing again, darting from one tree to the next, firing on the run.

When the policemen were twenty yards away, Uncle Misha ordered the partisans to stop firing and take out their grenades.

The police commander had the same idea. "Ready the grenades!" he shouted.

But the partisans were a few seconds ahead of them. Before the policemen were even able to touch their grenades, Uncle Misha gave the order, "Lionka, Sasha, are you ready? Throw!"

Two grenades flew into a group of policemen, followed by loud explosions that reverberated throughout the forest.

Lionka heard a hissing sound nearby. One of the partisans had pulled the pin from a grenade, initiating the fuse. Lacking any training, he had set the grenade on the ground between himself and Lionka. "There were some real 'experts' among us," Lionka later recalled sarcastically.

"What do we do now?" the partisan asked.

Lionka quickly snatched up the grenade and threw it as hard as he could. It exploded just a second later.

The policemen were just as inexperienced. A few seconds later, there were explosions from grenades that three policemen had failed to throw before they detonated.

The forest quickly filled with the sounds of badly injured policemen thrashing on the ground screaming, some missing arms or legs. As the smoke cleared, the partisans saw four dead policemen and six who were seriously injured, not counting those who had been blown to bits. Any survivors ran off.

ANYA LIMPED OVER to Uncle Misha after emerging from behind the haystack. "Uncle Misha, I'm wounded," she said sheepishly, holding her hand in her pants pocket. She had been shot when she had tried to crawl toward the bushes. Luckily, the bullet had hit the aluminum mug that she carried on the right side of her belt. The bullet had slowed when it passed through the mug, and had burrowed into her upper thigh.

"Can you walk?" he asked.

"I'll try."

"Be brave, Anya. We have to get as far away from here as possible. When we're in a safe place, we'll dress your wound," Uncle Misha promised. "For now, cover the wound with a handkerchief, and let's get out of here."

"Are we just going to let the Germans eat the fish?" Suliko asked. "Let me and Sasha release them. It's not far from here. We'll catch up with you."

Uncle Misha agreed, and Sasha and Suliko went to the lake. The rest of the partisans took off for the village of Karasyn, eighteen miles south of Perebrody and eleven miles north of Klesiv. Anya had no problem walking for the first three miles, but the farther they traveled, the weaker she became. Eventually they had to carry her.

After an hour, Sasha and Suliko caught up with them and reported that they had broken the dam in three places and had released all the fish into the canals.

When the partisans arrived in Karasyn late that evening, Uncle Misha cleaned Anya's wound. The injury was in a delicate place, but did not appear at first to be life-threatening. But when the wound started to swell the next day, he started worrying about lead poisoning.

Uncle Misha learned from a local villager that there was a Jewish doctor hiding nearby with his wife and son, and immediately sent some peasants to summon him. They returned at dawn.

"I'm leaving this partisan girl with you, along with the doctor and his family. The doctor will be treating her until she makes a full recovery. You must protect them so that nothing bad happens to them. If anyone betrays them, or fails to protect them from an attack by Ukrainian auxiliary policemen or Germans, I'm going to hold the entire village responsible. I'll round you all up in one barn and burn you alive!" he warned. "But if she recovers, you'll be amply rewarded."

Uncle Misha and his partisans spent the next three weeks on the run to avoid the Germans who were hunting them in the forest. While moving quickly from place to place, they also started carrying out missions with greater frequency. They destroyed flour mills, set fire to granaries, and plundered the farms of German collaborators. The attacks were relatively small in scale, but quickly became vexing to the German authorities because they never knew who their attackers were, nor where they were located. The local peasants would add to the legend of Uncle Misha and his partisans by telling the Germans that it had been a large detachment that had attacked the sites.

In one particularly successful mission, Uncle Misha and his partisans attacked the police station in Vezhytsya, a village twelve miles northeast of Karasyn. They threw two grenades through the window and then gunned down the policemen who ran out of the station in panic. Making off with twelve rifles and two submachine guns, they once again escaped back into the forest.

When the partisans returned to Karasyn, they found Anya in good health. Although the doctor did not have proper medical equipment, he had used a knife, a pair of scissors, and some tweezers to remove the bullet that had lodged in her upper thigh. In the absence of medicine, he had treated the wound with a topical ointment concocted out of rendered lard mixed with the powder of pulverized flowers that he and his son had picked in the fields. "I formulated a salve that could surely not be found in any pharmacy," the doctor later recalled. There were also no bandages, so he dressed the wound with strips of coarse cloth that the peasants wove. Anya was young and otherwise healthy, and had been back on her feet in no time.

As he had promised, Uncle Misha rewarded the peasants with a large supply of salt from a depot he had ransacked on his way back to Karasyn.

CHAPTER 7

"Awake!"

Preach freedom from the barricades of battle,
Declare war on the tyrants!
Courage and determination, brave comrades,
Will lead you to victory!

—DAVID EDELSTADT, "AWAKE!"
(JOSEPH GLADSTEIN, *FREEDOM'S SONGS*, P. 50)

ONE MORNING, UNCLE MISHA AND his partisans were hiding at a farm near Karasyn when one of their sentries spied a group of armed men approaching. Uncle Misha dispatched a squad of five partisans, who observed three men wearing Ukrainian auxiliary police uniforms, ten wearing German uniforms, and one in civilian clothes. With two rounds of gunfire, the partisans killed twelve men, capturing eleven rifles and two submachine guns. They allowed two wounded Ukrainians to escape to tell everyone that it was the Jewish partisans who had attacked them.

A boy emerged from the bushes. "Friends, don't shoot!" he shouted in Polish.

It was Tadeusz Weinberg, the fourteen-year-old son of the doctor who had treated Anya. The Weinbergs had escaped from Poland during the German invasion, and had ended up in Karasyn, where Dr. Weinberg had found work as a physician. In late August 1942, when Jews in the Sarny area were being rounded up for a final liquidation, the Weinbergs and a few other Jews had found refuge on a small, dry island amidst the wetlands of the Pripyat Marshes, ten miles from Karasyn. While they were there, Dr. Weinberg had discovered that the villagers were willing to give him food in exchange for medical treatment. Sometimes, as he had done with Anya, Dr. Weinberg would assist Jewish partisans who had been wounded in combat.

When Tadeusz told Uncle Misha that there were twenty Jewish refugees living on the marsh island, Uncle Misha invited them to join his partisans. Half of them were assigned to specific units and given some of the weapons that the partisans had just confiscated. The other half were old men, women, and children who were unfit for combat. A few of them had been wounded, but others were able to help. Some of the women prepared food and washed clothes, while Tadeusz and his parents formed a field hospital, known as the "Sanitary Battalion."

In addition to having learned first aid from his father, Tadeusz knew every path in the area. He also had an instinctive sense for how to navigate through the woods without being detected; this later earned him the nickname "Forest Eyes." Accordingly, he took part in every combat mission as both a paramedic and a guide.

The largest mission in which Tadeusz participated was the destruction of a retreat for German soldiers in Klesiv. It was a rather dangerous operation that involved traveling a long distance and infiltrating an occupied city.

Tadeusz and seven other partisans left the partisan camp on horseback. About halfway to Klesiv, as the forest started to thin, they left the horses with one of the partisans and traveled the last several miles by foot.

When they arrived in Klesiv, the partisans rendezvoused with a communist engineer named Kirill, whom Uncle Misha had known before the war. Kirill took ten sticks of dynamite that the partisans had brought, and hid them in a milk can. He gave the can to the peasant who delivered milk and cheese to the retreat's canteen. When the peasant brought the milk to the canteen's cellar, he placed a grenade underneath the can in such a way that its weight held down the safety lever. He pulled out the pin and left.

That evening, when one of the canteen workers moved the milk can, the grenade discharged, detonating the dynamite. The massive explosion tore the building into pieces and ignited a large fire that spread to neighboring buildings that were inhabited by Germans and the Ukrainian auxiliary policemen who guarded the retreat.

The partisans had already escaped when the dynamite exploded, but they could hear the howl of fire sirens and see the red sky over Klesiv. They found their horses and returned to the dense forest.

WHEN THE SNOW started to fall, it became more difficult for the partisans to travel through the forest without leaving tracks. Uncle Misha started thinking about where they would spend the winter. He decided to go deeper into Polesia, into the Pripyat Marshes, which were impassable in the winter.

By this time, Uncle Misha's group had grown to include fifty vulnerable refugees—old men, women, and children. They had escaped the *Aktions* in their hometowns and were desperately in need of sanctuary from the bands of Ukrainian nationalists rampaging through the forests. Knowing that he would not be able to protect so many defenseless refugees, Uncle Misha decided to leave them behind when he went to the Pripyat Marshes.

Ozera proved to be an ideal place to shelter them, as there were several partisan detachments encamped in the nearby forests. There were so many partisan detachments operating there that the Germans and Ukrainians had started avoiding the area out of fear of confronting enigmatic enemies.

The Jewish refugees were disappointed to learn that Uncle Misha and his partisans would be leaving. "What will become of us?" they wondered. "What will we do?"

Uncle Misha decided to leave the refugees with enough food to last through the winter. They commandeered as many as thirty wagons and went to a nearby village to steal enough food to fill the carts. The noise of the wagons, combined with shouting and gunfire as the Jewish partisans approached the village, was so loud that the villagers assumed that a much larger force was descending on them. The partisans raided a store where villagers would receive salt in exchange for mushrooms, blueberries, and gooseberries. They plundered milk, jam, and everything else in the shop, including ten cartloads of salt.

While distributing their spoils to the Jewish refugees, the partisans learned that the Germans had been informed of the raid and were searching for them. The partisans fled to the forest with their carts, but the Germans found one of the Jewish refugees and killed him in the swamps.

Uncle Misha had hoped that Tadeusz and his parents would come with him to the Pripyat Marshes, but they decided to stay behind to tend to the Jewish refugees who needed further medical care. The Weinbergs did, however, agree to set up a Sanitary Battalion to which Uncle Misha could send sick and injured partisans from his group, but there is no evidence that he ever did so.

UNCLE MISHA AND his partisans ventured deep into the Pripyat Marshes, around twenty-five miles north of Hlynne, to an area known as Merlinskie Farms. When they went into a peasant's house for breakfast, Lionka noticed a violin under a bed and opened its case. The label said it was a Stradivarius, but it was almost certainly a fake. Upon learning that the instrument had been left there by Jews who had passed through while fleeing the German invasion of Poland, the partisans confiscated the violin. For the next two or three years, until the instrument broke, Uncle Misha and Lionka took the violin with them wherever they went.

Finding Merlinskie Farms to be an ideal location for a winter base, Uncle Misha and his partisans started constructing shelters. These *kiboshes*, as they called them, were conical tents fashioned out of thin branches of pine or birch that the partisans would strip and bind together at the top with switches, leaving an opening as a chimney. The partisans would cover each *kibosh* with a thick layer of hay to protect it from the rain. If there was no hay, they would use dried leaves from the ground, or even moss. The partisans would leave an opening on one side for the entrance, with an old sack serving as a curtain. In the middle of the *kibosh*, they would place four thick logs as benches for the fire that would be built inside the square. They would throw a thick layer of hay on the ground surrounding the benches, to give themselves soft beds for sitting and sleeping. Although each *kibosh* was large enough to accommodate ten to twelve people, the partisans could build one in just a few minutes.

There were always two partisans on watch for every *kibosh*. One partisan would stand guard outside, while the other stayed inside, maintaining the fire, boiling water for tea, and, at night, making sure sleeping partisans did not accidentally set themselves on fire. The partisans usually slept fully clothed, with their boots facing the fire. When one of them would stretch his leg out, the monitor would smack the leg with a long stick, and the leg would reflexively withdraw before coming too close to the fire.

During the winter, the darkness of night fell early in the dense forest, as early as four in the afternoon. After dinner, the partisans would chat with each other. Sometimes one of them would play a balalaika—a Russian folk guitar with three strings and a triangular body. Other times, they would sing together. At around five in the evening, they would retire to their *kiboshes*, lie down on the soft hay, and fall asleep. Before long, each *kibosh* would be filled with the loud snoring of sleeping partisans.

It was not uncommon for one of the partisans to be woken up in the middle of the night by the intense itching of lice bites. To delouse their clothes, the partisans would take them off and dangle them over the fire to "fry" the lice. The lice carcasses would fall into the fire with a dry, crackling sound, and the partisan would experience the immense satisfaction of putting back on clothes that were both hot and lice-free. In the meantime, a second or third partisan would wake up, and soon the entire *kibosh* would be stirring. Someone would suggest that they have some tea, and they would toss a handful of dried blueberries into the pail of water boiling over the fire. After a few minutes, they would all be sitting around the fire, telling jokes as they sipped tea with honeycomb. For a short while, they could forget about the fighting from the previous day or the next day, forget about being hundreds of miles behind enemy lines, and forget that there were many more days of hunger and coldness ahead of them. The warmth of the fire, the hot tea, and the loyal camaraderie of their fellow partisans would make them feel like they were at home. They could then lie back down on the hay and sleep until dawn.

After setting up the base camp in Merlinskie Farms, the partisans started preparing for the winter. They hunted for meat, gathered fruits, and collected other food. It took many trips to stockpile all the food they would need to survive.

During one such expedition, Lionka met up with some of the Red Army soldiers whom he had helped in Korets. The soldiers had since formed a reconnaissance team for a detachment of Soviet partisans led by Sydir Kovpak.

The son of Ukrainian peasants, Kovpak was awarded two Saint George's Crosses for heroism in World War I. During the

Russian Civil War, he commanded a Soviet partisan detachment that battled the German occupation of Ukraine. After serving in various governmental positions in the interwar period, Kovpak returned to partisan warfare to once again drive the Germans out of Ukraine. On October 25, 1942, 832 men from Kovpak's Sumy Partisan Federation left Soviet territory, along with 1,408 partisans in the United Partisan Federation commanded by Alexander Saburov.

Over the next month, the two partisan federations fought their way through northern Ukraine, adding 1,580 escaped prisoners of war to their ranks along the way. Among the many successes of Kovpak's federation was an attack on November 26 on the administrative city of Lyelchytsy, forty miles southwest of Mazyr, during which they killed members of the German administration and burned all of the buildings occupied by Germans and their collaborators to the ground. The victorious campaigns exposed weaknesses in the German rear and earned Kovpak a reputation among the Soviets as the "father of the partisan movement in Ukraine."

After the attack on Lyelchytsy, Kovpak's Sumy Partisan Federation had established its headquarters in Glushkovichi, a village fifteen miles east of Hlynne and around thirty miles southeast of Merlinskie Farms. They were actively recruiting more partisans, almost doubling their membership from two thousand to 3,500 fighters during that period.

"Come with us!" Kovpak's reconnaissance team invited Lionka.

"What are you thinking?" Lionka responded. "I have a father and many things to take care of." He explained that he was committed to helping Uncle Misha and the other partisans make preparations for the winter.

"No problem. Kovpak will arrive in two days, and we'll introduce you to him," the Soviet partisans assured him. "Everything will be fine."

Back at the base camp, Uncle Misha had heard that there was a German unit searching for them. According to the intelligence, the Germans were disguised as Soviet partisans. He dispatched two partisans to warn Lionka that the men who had promised to introduce him to Kovpak were impostors.

"Idiots! I know these men from the forests. I know this area; I know the people," Lionka scolded them. "This is Kovpak, I'm sure of it."

Nevertheless, Lionka did not show up for his meeting with Kovpak. When he and his fellow Jewish partisans arrived back at their base, they found a note: *I was here. I would very much like for you to contact me.* The note was signed by Sydir Kovpak.

The realization that anyone had found their base camp made the partisans feel vulnerable and convinced them to abandon the camp. They left behind the meat of five or six cows they had slaughtered, along with flour and other food. They would later return to the camp, only to find that the entire stockpile had been completely raided. All that was left was a note reading in Russian: *Thanks so much for leaving us the food, but why did you run away?*

As UNCLE MISHA and his partisans continued to move through Merlinskie Farms, they learned that there were several other bands of partisans in the area. One group was led by a Soviet soldier named Dmitrii Ivanovich Popov, but Uncle Misha was more impressed by a band of ten Red Army soldiers, including two Jews, who had escaped from German prisoner-of-war camps and were being led by a Major Sasha.

Major Sasha's group accepted Uncle Misha and his partisans into their ranks, but the alliance did not last long. The former prisoners of war were not interested in actually carrying out operations. They were too engrossed with drinking vodka and abducting local girls. They plundered villages and murdered the residents, not for self-protection, or even as part of military offensives, but simply for sport. The unit was one of many bands of Soviet soldiers who were living in the forest without engaging in warfare. "All these familial partisan detachments are not battle-worthy; they engage in drunkenness, [and] the confiscation of property from the population," Soviet partisan commander Vasilii Ushakov complained in an encrypted message to Soviet command. "Disorder reigns in detachments."

Major Sasha's partisans also displayed a callous disregard for Jewish lives. One day, Sashka—the Jewish teenager from Davyd-Haradok—went out to gather food. He sat down to rest, then fell asleep. When Sashka returned to the base camp, Major Sasha quickly convened a court-martial, sentenced Sashka to death, and had him executed. This deeply offended the Jewish partisans, who knew that the harshness of the sentence was the result of antisemitism. Sashka had indeed fallen asleep on duty, but any danger he had put the rest of them in was minimal. He had been killed simply for being Jewish. Uncle Misha and the other Jewish partisans began making plans to leave Major Sasha's partisan group as soon as possible.

In the meantime, Lionka, Sasha Kuc, and another Jewish partisan set out for a nearby village. When they were about twelve-and-a-half miles away from the village, they smelled charred meat. They assumed that they were near another partisan camp and went to investigate. They found an empty campsite, but that was not the source of the scent. They continued on until they were close to a village that they had visited before. There had been ten families in the village with sons who were working with the German police, so Uncle Misha's partisans had ransacked their granaries and stolen their cattle.

Usually, when the partisans approached a village, dogs would sense them and start barking. But this time, there were no signs of life. The village was dark and eerily quiet.

Sasha decided that they would not go straight into the village. Instead, they visited one of the small clusters of houses that were scattered on its outskirts. When they arrived, they found the outpost crowded with people. The villagers started cursing at them. "Why have you come here?" they demanded. "You're the reason for this disaster."

Someone had falsely told the Germans that the villagers were collaborating with the partisans. Two days earlier, a large German unit had arrived, encircled the village, and rounded up all of the villagers. "Since you're giving food to the partisans, we're going to destroy your village," the Germans said. "Collect your things, each according to his own ability, and we'll transfer you to the town of Vysotsk."

As the villagers started to pack food and other belongings, another German unit arrived and started going from house to house, shooting everyone inside. Some villagers were able to escape, but everyone else was killed, including the village priest. Then the houses were set on fire, with the bodies of the victims still inside. That was the smell that had gotten the partisans' attention.

When the partisans returned to their camp, they learned that a second Jewish fighter had been executed. Chanan Gruszko—a Jewish partisan from Sasha Kuc's hometown of Berezne—had been very sick, and had been covered with sores. He had been left behind to guard the camp, but he had passed out. When Chanan had regained consciousness, he had realized that he was in serious trouble and had tried to run away. One of the Soviet soldiers had chased him down and had shot him. This time, there had been no court-martial. The Soviets justified Chanan's execution by saying that they were worried that he would be caught by the Germans and tortured for information.

The Jews decided that they could not wait any longer to leave Major Sasha's group. They walked away, with Uncle Misha reassuming command. The Soviets chased after them, threatening to shoot the Jewish partisans if they did not return, but Uncle

Misha's group would not relent. "Enough! We're done!" Uncle Misha told them. "We can't take it anymore!"

ONE DAY IN early January 1943, as Lionka, Sasha, and Grisha were entering a village looking for food, they learned that a large military unit was approaching. They ran back into the forest to see who it was. Riding horses and wearing Soviet uniforms, with red ribbons in their caps, the partisan detachment made quite an impression as they paraded into town, bringing with them carts of wounded combatants and several sleighs filled with equipment. As Lionka, Sasha, and Grisha snuck back into the village, they heard the partisans speaking to each other in Russian.

The three Jewish partisans walked up to two of the Soviets, introduced themselves as being from Uncle Misha's partisan detachment, and asked to speak to the Soviets' commander.

"Which commander?" the Soviets asked, explaining that they had a platoon commander, a company commander, and a detachment commander.

"We'd like to talk to the commander in chief of your entire camp."

The Soviet partisans agreed to take the Jews to Alexander Saburov, the commander of the United Partisan Federation.

The son of Russian peasants, Saburov joined the Communist Party when he was twenty-four, while serving in the Red Army. Six years later, he joined the NKVD, for which he is thought to have been the director of political instruction. In the fall of 1941, just a few months after Nazi Germany invaded the Soviet Union, Saburov was put in charge of a partisan detachment in the Bryansk Forest. Operating behind enemy lines, he convinced other Soviet partisans in the area that he was the NKVD Deputy People's Commissar for the Ukrainian Soviet Socialist Republic. As Saburov was the only one with a two-way radio, he persuaded the other partisan commanders to dispatch updates on their combat activities to him, so he could report their successes to Moscow. Instead, by taking credit for their victories, Saburov established a reputation as a tactical genius, earning a promotion and the distinguished title Hero of the Soviet Union.

In March 1942, eight partisan detachments operating in the Bryansk region were combined into one large federation of 1,408 men under Saburov's command. It was this United Partisan Federation that fought its way through Ukraine, along with Kovpak's Sumy Partisan Federation in late 1942. Saburov was a more aggressive fighter than Kovpak, and developed a particular reputation for killing policemen. "Wherever Saburov has passed through, there are no police," reported a correspondent for *Pravda*. Saburov was especially adept at creating independent partisan detachments and units, earning the nickname "the incubator of the partisan movement" from fellow partisan commander Mikhail Naumov.

By December 1942, Saburov's United Partisan Federation reached northern Zhytomyr, where they created a stronghold. One of the first things they did was clear an airfield that allowed Soviet planes to bring them ample supplies. "General Saburov is sitting north of Ovruch, armed to the teeth," complained Naumov. "He is always supplied by Moscow right down to the highest quality of cigarettes. This 'talented' military commander, who sits on his butt, never lacks for anything, including medals."

Although he was based in northern Zhytomyr, Saburov had men operating throughout northwest Ukraine, from the Kyiv region through Volhynia. During the night of January 15 and 16, 1943, one of Saburov's units would attack the town of Stolin, twelve miles north of Perebrody, where they would destroy the telephone station and capture one hundred guards. They would also loot and set fire to the Regional Commissar's residence, the guard barracks, and the local distillery.

When Uncle Misha, Lionka, and Sasha were brought to Saburov, he told them that he had heard a great deal about their group, but that he had thought that they were a much larger partisan detachment.

"The entire unit under Uncle Misha's command numbers ten people, but apparently everyone thinks that a division of partisans operates here," Sasha explained. "We have ties to the locals, who help us. We distribute proclamations, leaflets, and the like. We make a lot of noise. What we're able to do, we do. That's all we can do."

While Saburov was disappointed by the small size of Uncle Misha's partisan group, he was impressed by everything they had accomplished. "You've done well!" he congratulated them. "You'll stay with us."

Uncle Misha and his partisans had finally been admitted into a real partisan detachment. There was just one catch: The group would have to split up. The Ukrainian Staff of the Partisan Movement, which oversaw the activities of the Soviet partisans in Ukraine, was opposed to the idea of having distinctly Jewish detachments. They worried that such units would bolster propaganda from the Nazis and Ukrainian nationalists that the partisan movement was a tool of Judeo-Bolshevism. Saburov was in agreement with this policy. "I'll redistribute you between all of the units in the camp," he told the partisans in Uncle Misha's group. "I don't want a separate Jewish partisan unit here."

As Uncle Misha, Lionka, and Sasha got to know Saburov, he earned their trust. They had initially been worried about joining his federation, because they had seen how Major Sasha had treated the Jews under his command. They had also heard stories of Medvedev's men killing Jews under the weakest of pretexts. A Jewish man whom the Nazis had forced to serve as a police chief in the Lutsk ghetto was executed as a collaborator. When Jews who had escaped German captivity found their way to Medvedev's unit, they were accused of having been dispatched to spy on the partisans, and were sentenced to death.

"Yes, I've heard about this," Saburov admitted when Sasha brought up the murders. "That's why I don't want a separate Jewish partisan unit. There are different people among us, including antisemites. We are, in fact, not far removed from the socialist revolution, and we haven't yet managed to rid Soviet society of every negative thing, including the antisemitism we inherited from tsarist Russia. Within the short time since the revolution, we haven't succeeded in getting rid of all the issues we have in our country. This isn't so easy."

The Jewish partisans would indeed cross paths with a number of antisemites while fighting alongside the Soviet partisans, including a Red Army commander who once remarked, "Whatever the future holds, the Jews will never hold the same bloated status they used to have." That commander later died during one of the partisan operations. It is not clear whether the bullet that killed him was fired by a German soldier or a Jewish partisan. Lionka believed that it was one of the Jews who shot the commander, in defense of Jewish pride.

Uncle Misha and Lionka were assigned to the 1st Stalin Partisan Detachment, while the other Jewish fighters were distributed among other detachments within Saburov's partisan federation. Although Uncle Misha was no doubt sad to see his group of Jewish partisans disbanded, he had learned that it was simply too difficult to succeed with a small group. Joining forces with the Soviet partisans would provide him with the access to weapons and military intelligence he needed to participate in missions that were much larger than what he could have ever accomplished on his own.

CHAPTER 8

"Forward into the Ranks of Combat!"

Brothers, swear on the blood-soaked earth
To free the people from tyrants!
Shoulder to shoulder, with armor and sword,
Forward into the ranks of combat!

—DAVID EDELSTADT, "THE JEWISH PROLETARIAN"
(JOSEPH GLADSTEIN, *FREEDOM'S SONGS*, P. 79)

UNCLE MISHA AND LIONKA JOINED the 1st Stalin Partisan
Detachment on January 11, 1943. The detachment had arrived in Rubryn, a village not far from Merlinskie Farms, two
days earlier, and was gathering intelligence in the area. On January 12, the detachment executed four villagers from Rubryn who,
in addition to having informed on the partisans, had captured
and handed over three partisans to the Germans.

That same day, the detachment headed eastward, into the
region of Zhytomyr. On January 21, they established a new
camp near the village of Khilchikha, fourteen miles south of Naroulia. Immediately upon arriving, the partisans started conducting reconnaissance that resulted in the execution of the

starosta of the nearby town of Mukhoedy for being a traitor and a Gestapo agent.

Starostas were administrators whom the Germans had appointed to govern their villages. The *starostas* were in charge of maintaining order, sometimes with the assistance of local policemen. They ensured compliance with all German proclamations and supplied whatever food and laborers the Germans demanded. The *starostas* also reported any signs of anti-German activities and handed over villagers who collaborated with the partisans. They were a constant thorn in the partisans' side, and the partisans hated the traitorous *starostas* even more than they hated the Germans.

On January 22, the day after they executed the *starosta* from Mukhoedy, the partisans confiscated his property, along with that of a local Gestapo agent who had managed to escape. On the next day, they executed a policeman from Mukhoedy who had come to Khilchikha to spy on the partisans on behalf of the German commandant in Naroulia.

That night, the new *starosta* from Mukhoedy led two companies of SS men to the partisans' camp. Luckily, the sentries saw the Germans coming. They alerted the partisans, who were able to flee into the forest without being captured.

During the escape, Uncle Misha stumbled over a fallen tree branch. He careened to the ground, banging his knees so hard that they started bleeding. The big toe of his left foot started burning like it was on fire. When he stood back up, he realized that the sole of his left boot was partially torn off. He quickly tied a rope around his boot to secure the sole and continued scurrying away.

After running for twenty-five miles, the partisans found a safe place to stop and rest. Uncle Misha took off his damaged boot and discovered an enormous blister on his big toe. As he inspected his torn boot, he grew angrier and angrier. He was annoyed by the snow, which fell in large flakes from the gray skies and kept getting under his collar. He was furious at the *starosta* for having informed on the partisans. But, at that moment, he was most of all irate at his damaged boot, which made walking very difficult. Enraged, he ripped off the sole and hurled the boot at the nearest tree, followed by the other boot. The tantrum allowed him to blow off some steam, but left him barefoot in the Ukrainian winter.

He lanced the blister with a needle and squeezed out the discolored pus. Then he stood up, inspected his submachine gun and the grenades hanging from his belt, and called over six partisans.

"We're going on a mission, to the road leading to Aleksandrovka," he told them, referring to a village six miles south of Mukhoedy where the partisans had conducted reconnaissance the day before. "The truck delivering the mail from Ovruch to the nearby garrisons will be coming through today." While large military support units defended German headquarters in major cities, the towns and villages were guarded by smaller security forces stationed in garrisons. "I need to get a pair of thick German boots with studded soles and a wide shaft," he continued. "Let's go, comrades!"

Within ten minutes, the seven partisans were on their way. They walked ten miles, along wolf trails and through thick shrubs, taking precautions to avoid being tracked. For the first few minutes, Uncle Misha's bare feet were so cold that he could barely stand. But soon he was so warmed up from walking that when the partisans stopped to rest for a couple of minutes, the snow melted beneath his feet.

The squad reached the road to Aleksandrovka in two-and-a-half hours. They stuffed an old jacket and a pair of pants with straw and left them in the middle of the road. A hundred yards away, they burrowed a hiding spot deep into the snow. They covered the foxhole with pine branches as camouflage and waited.

Within a half hour, they heard the sound of an engine and then saw a truck coming down the road. As the driver approached, he noticed what appeared to be a man lying in the road, and started slowing down. By the time he passed the foxhole, he was going less than ten miles an hour. The partisans could clearly see the driver and his assistant sitting in the cabin.

On Uncle Misha's signal, two partisans threw grenades at the engine. There was a loud explosion as the grenades detonated, blasting shrapnel that killed the two men in the cabin instantly. The truck veered to the right, rolled about ten yards, and slid into the ditch. The gas tank exploded, engulfing the truck in flames and smoke.

When the partisans reached the truck, a German with a submachine gun leaped out of the back and started running away. Uncle Misha ran up to the German and, using the butt of his own submachine gun, knocked him to the ground with a blow to the shoulder. The German rolled to his side, rose to his knees, and fired in Uncle Misha's direction. Uncle Misha twisted away, but a bullet pierced his wool jacket and grazed his shoulder. He fired two shots, killing the German.

Uncle Misha looked at the dead German's feet. Just as he had hoped, they were clad in thick German boots made of black and yellow leather with studded soles, a wide shaft, and side stitching. He quickly pulled off the German's boots and warm woolen socks. He sat down in the snow and put them on. Before hurrying back to the partisans, Uncle Misha searched the German's pockets and took a wallet, a pocketknife, a notebook, and a cigarette case with several cigarettes.

A few days later, sitting by the fire, Uncle Misha looked through the dead German's wallet. He found several photographs of a young German woman. There were pictures of the blonde by herself and some of her with a two-year-old child. Other pictures included the man Uncle Misha had shot. There were letters in the wallet, in which the woman had written to her husband that she had moved in with his mother, that her love for him had not diminished, and that she was waiting impa-

Iорецъ - Korzec

Moshe Gildenman's hometown of Korets, Ukraine, 1912.
From the collection of Maria Markowska (Muszyńska) in the Cyfrowe Archiwum Dzierżoniowa,
which is managed by the Fundacja Forum Dialogu Między Kulturami.

The Korchyk River, with Korets in the background. After occupying Korets in September 1939,
the Soviets would demolish the wooden bridge and replace it with one made of concrete,
with Gildenman's assistance.
Courtesy of Yousef (Seffi) Hanegbi.

Kościuszko Street, the main thoroughfare in Korets, in 1927.
From the collection of Maria Markowska (Muszyńska) in the Cyfrowe Archiwum Dzierżoniowo which is managed by the Fundacja Forum Dialogu Między Kulturami.

Moshe Gildenman (center, wearing a tie) at his cement plant with his employees and children, early 1930s.
Courtesy of Yousef (Seffi) Hanegbi.

The Gildenman family (Simcha, Golda, Moshe, Feigela), mid-1930s.
Courtesy of Yousef (Seffi) Hanegbi.

A music ensemble in Korets in the late 1930s.
Moshe Gildenman is the second gentleman from the left in the third row.
Family Archive—Polish Roots in Israel Project/POLIN Museum of the History of Polish Jews.

A page from Moshe Gildenman's copy of Joseph Gladstein's *Freedom's*
Several annotations suggest that Gildenman led performances from this Yiddish son₪
Yad Vashem Artifacts Collection, courtesy of Yousef (Seffi) Hanegbi, and Zahava Shanni,

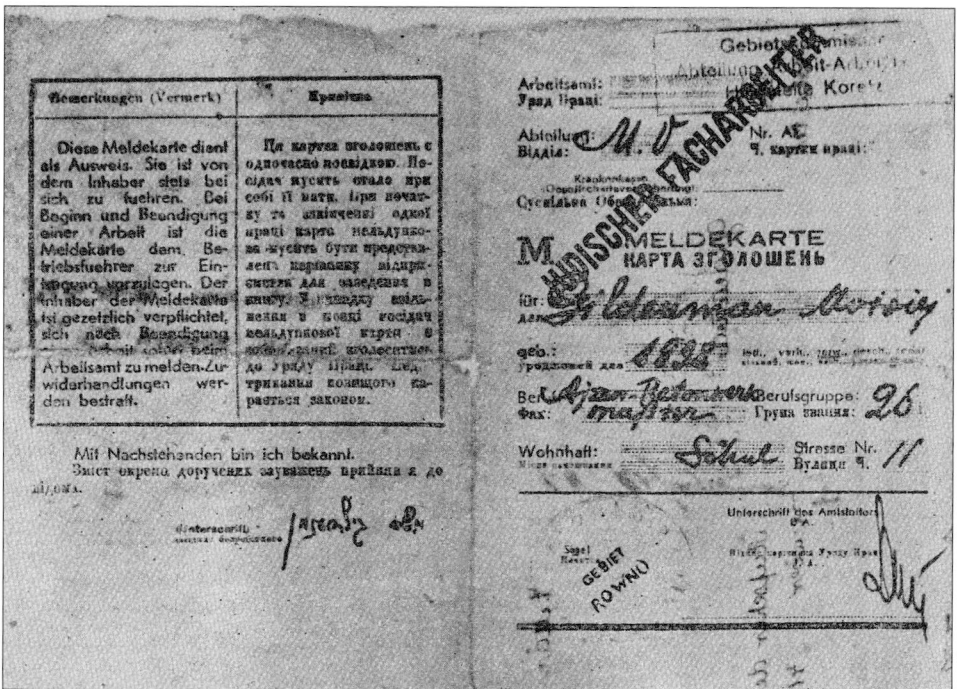

Moshe Gildenman's registration card from the Korets ghetto, identifying him as a "Jewish Skilled Worker."

Handwritten copy of the lyrics to Moshe Gildenman's "Come to the Forest." Gildenman wrote the song in the Korets ghetto, to encourage his fellow Jews to join him in escaping to the forest to take up arms against the Nazis.

From Simcha Gildenman's songbook, Yad Vashem Artifacts Collection, courtesy of Yousef (Seffi) Hanegbi, and Zahava Shanni, Israel.

Hershel "Zvi" Pe'er, who left Korets with
Moshe and Simcha Gildenman on September 24, 1942.
Zvi fought alongside Moshe and Simcha until January 1943,
when partisan commander Alexander Saburov assigned
the fighters in Gildenman's group to different detachments
within the United Partisan Federation.
Ghetto Fighters' House Museum, Israel/Photo Archive.

Aleksander "Sasha" K
who joined up with M
Gildenman after leavi
Dmitry Medvedev's
partisan detachment in
late September 1942.
Sasha served as
Gildenman's chief of
until January 1943. H
wearing the Order of
Red Banner and the "
Partisan of the Patriot
War," 1st Class meda
that he later received
from the Soviet Union
*Ghetto Fighters'
House Museum, Israe
Photo Archive.*

Issachar Trosman, who left
Dmitry Medvedev's partisan
detachment with Sasha Kuc
in late September 1942.
Trosman split from Moshe
Gildenman's group in early
October 1942, after they came
under attack near Rokytne.
*Ghetto Fighters' House Museum,
Israel/Photo Archive.*

Tadeusz Weinberg
(later Gad Karmon),
who served as a
paramedic and
guide for Moshe
Gildenman's group in
the autumn of 1942.
*Ghetto Fighters'
House Museum,
Israel/Photo Archive.*

Moshe Gildenman as a partisan, early 1943.
Ghetto Fighters' House Museum, Israel/Photo Archive.

A group of Soviet partisans in a forest.
Photographed by Yakov Davidson. Ghetto Fighters' House Museum, Israel/Photo Archive.

A group of Soviet partisans setting up an ambush.
Photographed by Yakov Davidson. Ghetto Fighters' House Museum, Israel/Photo Archive.

An attack by a detachment
of Soviet partisans.
*Photographed by
Yakov Davidson.
Ghetto Fighters'
House Museum,
Israel/Photo Archive.*

Soviet partisans sabotaging
a railroad track.
*Ghetto Fighters' House Museum,
Israel/Photo Archive.*

A Soviet partisan unit fording a river.
Photographed by Yakov Davidson. Ghetto Fighters' House Museum, Israel/Photo Archive.

A group of Soviet partisans singing during a lull in the fighting.
Photographed by Yakov Davidson. Ghetto Fighters' House Museum, Israel/Photo Archive.

A group of Soviet partisans dancing during a lull in the fighting.
Photographed by Yakov Davidson. Ghetto Fighters' House Museum, Israel/Photo Archive.

The violin of Motele Schlein, a young partisan who was practically a son to Moshe Gildenman.
Yad Vashem Artifacts Collection, courtesy of Yousef (Seffi) Hanegbi, and Zahava Shanni, Israel.

A German map of partisan
activity in western Ukraine
where Gildenman was
operating, June 21–30, 1943.
*National Archives and
Records Administration,
courtesy of the United States
Holocaust Memorial Museum.*

German troops on the move during an antipartisan operation.
*Belarusian State Archive of Documentary Film and Photography,
courtesy of the United States Holocaust Memorial Museum.*

Moshe Gildenman with his revolver and rifle, October 1943.
He is wearing his "To a Partisan of the Patriotic War," 2nd Class medal.
Yad Vashem Photo Archive, Jerusalem, 122EO6.

Moshe Gildenman (fourth from left) with Soviet officers, ca. 1944–45.
Courtesy of Yousef (Seffi) Hanegbi.

Moshe Gildenman (standing, fourth from right) with Soviet officers,
Chomutov, Czechoslovakia, May 8, 1945 (Victory in Europe Day).
Courtesy of Yousef (Seffi) Hanegbi.

Moshe Gildenman in uniform, wearing his Order of the Red Star
and Order of the Patriotic War, 2nd Class medals, ca. 1945.
Courtesy of Yousef (Seffi) Hanegbi.

Moshe and Simcha Gildenman after the w
1945–46. Simcha is wearing his "For Cou
and "For the Victory over Germany in the
Great Patriotic War 1941–1945" medals.
Yad Vashem Testimonies, Diaries, and Me
Collection, Jerusalem, O.33-524.

Moshe Gildenman, wear
Partisan Cross, Order of the
of Grunwald, and Medal of V
and Freedom 1945 ribbons, ca.
Ghetto Fighters' House Mu
Israel/Photo A

Members of the Akiva youth movement
in Jelenia Góra, Poland, 1947. Moshe Gildenman
is standing, third from the right.
Ghetto Fighters' House Museum,
Israel/Photo Archive.

tiently for Germany's victory, when he would return home and they could be together again. At the end of her letters, she urged him to try to earn a cross by any means, explaining that the wives of decorated soldiers received better ration cards.

"Well," Uncle Misha said to himself, "I made sure he gets a cross." Not one of the Iron Crosses that German soldiers were awarded for valor, but one of the bronze crosses that he had seen marking German graves throughout Ukraine.

The discovery that the German had lived in Breslau reminded Uncle Misha of how as a boy he had perused his grandfather's bookshelves and noticed how many of the Jewish texts had been printed in Breslau. "Once, there were Jews living there," he contemplated. "They had normal lives, businesses, *beth midrashes*, and even their own printing press. And now those Jews have surely been murdered, and their *beth midrashes* have been turned into horse stables, just like in Korets." Once again, Uncle Misha's heart grew heavy with sorrow.

LIKE MOST PARTISAN detachments, the 1st Stalin detachment was a confederation of companies that were subdivided into platoons. At the top was a commander, with a commissar from the NKVD and a chief of staff from the Red Army reporting directly to him; in this case, Evgenii Mirkovsky, Vasilii Volkov, and Vasilii Ushakov, respectively. Underneath the command staff were the leaders of the companies and platoons. Depending on the nature of a mission, the entire detachment, an individual company, or even a single platoon might be deployed.

With the arrival of Uncle Misha and Lionka, Mirkovsky had transferred the other Jews in his detachment into a new unit composed mostly of Jewish fighters. Mirkovsky's decision to ignore the policy against creating special units of Jewish partisans may have been motivated by the success of Uncle Misha's partisan group in Volhynia, but it is also possible that Mirkovsky was simply happy for an excuse to segregate the Jews under his command. He appointed Uncle Misha as the leader of the new unit, which grew to call itself the "Separate Jewish Combat Unit" and "Uncle Misha's Jewish Combat Unit," or "Uncle Misha's Jewish Group" for short. These titles were not official designations. After the Soviet partisans began to sarcastically refer to the unit as the "Jewish Group," its members embraced that designation as their own. The unit grew with the addition of newly arrived partisans of all nationalities, but its leadership was always Jewish.

A few days after the entire detachment abandoned the camp near Khilchikha, Uncle Misha's Jewish Group was distributed between the 1st Stalin Partisan Detachment's 2nd and 3rd Companies. Their assignment was to roam the region hunting for *starostas* and their collaborators. Their order: "Hang the *starostas* and their informants on the gates of their houses, and bomb the families of the policemen." In partisan jargon, "bombing" meant attacking a farm, confiscating its cattle, pigs, and chickens, and burning it to the ground. The campaign would take revenge on the *starostas* and their policemen, punish the Nazi sympathizers who enabled them, and send a warning to anyone who was considering betraying the partisans. For the Jewish partisans, the missions would serve an additional purpose: exacting retribution for the horrors that Jews had suffered at the hands of Ukrainians in the ghettos. They were fighting, as one Ukrainian Jew wrote: *for their homeland* and *their Jewish people.*

The partisans split into four units and left the camp heading in four different directions. Uncle Misha led one unit of thirty partisans, while Lionka commanded a group of twenty-five men armed with submachine guns and a large machine gun. Two units of twenty fighters each were led by Soviet partisans named Dmitrienko and Sobolov.

All four units snuck stealthily through the forest to avoid detection. They left as few tracks as possible by walking in single file, with each partisan carefully stepping in the footprints of the man in front of him. To misdirect any pursuers, the last in line would sweep away the footsteps with a large broom. This would create a narrow path that resembled those created by the wild boars that roamed the area. To complete the deception, the partisan at the end of the line would stamp severed boars' legs into the snow. When he tired of making boar footprints, he would roll around in the snow to emulate the frolicking of a boar. The partisans would walk normally on roads and paths, but when they reentered the forest they would sometimes walk backward, to leave the impression that whoever had left the footprints had been walking out of the forest rather than into it. They continued the subterfuge until they reached a major road or had gotten more than ten miles away from the camp.

The partisans had agreed that they would reunite five days later, at the Iakovets Farm on the border between the regions of Zhytomyr and Kyiv. The farm was an ideal spot for a rendezvous, because it was located in the middle of a large forest. There were no villages or frequently traveled roads nearby, so the Germans rarely patrolled the area. Iakovets was farmed by poor peasant families who had always welcomed the partisans, and the partisans reciprocated by bringing them food and clothing.

Uncle Misha and his unit arrived at the Iakovets Farm at dawn on February 3, and reunited with the groups led by Dmitrienko and Sobolov. Lionka's unit had not yet arrived.

The partisans from the three units shared reports from their adventures. Over the previous five days, they had hanged several dozen *starostas* and policemen, burned down more than thirty farms owned by policemen and their informants, and spread panic among Germans and their collaborators throughout the area. Among the *starostas* whom Uncle Misha had hanged was the one from the village of Pavlovichi. While searching the Pavlovichi *starosta*'s house, Uncle Misha had found a petition to the General Commissar requesting authorization to punish thirty-seven peasants who had gathered dry twigs to heat their homes without permission. Since the *starosta* was illiterate, his wife had signed the petition for him. Uncle Misha had hanged her, along with her husband.

At around noon, the partisans posted sentries around the farm, made themselves comfortable in an empty farmhouse, and went to sleep. But Uncle Misha was restless. He was worried about Lionka, who had still not reported in. Every few minutes, he looked out the window at the narrow path that led to Iakovets, hoping to see Lionka.

Suddenly Uncle Misha saw shadowy figures darting about in the woods, hiding behind the thick trees. He looked more carefully and watched the figures run toward the frozen stream. He quickly woke up a few partisans, but before they could get to the window to see for themselves, they heard a volley of rifle fire, followed by a scream and then groaning from the nearby woodshed. Uncle Misha realized that they were under attack, and that one of the partisan sentries had been killed.

"Ready your weapons!" he shouted, waking everyone up.

Another hail of gunfire erupted, shattering all of the windows. Uncle Misha ordered the partisans to stand against the walls between the windows, and instructed a lookout to climb into the attic for a better vantage point. During a lull in the shooting, the lookout came back down and reported that there was a unit of German military policemen in the riverbed in front of the farmhouse, and that another unit was in the forest preparing to attack them from behind.

Uncle Misha dispatched Dmitrienko and his unit to cover the rear of the farmhouse. As soon as the partisans ran outside, three shots from the forest killed three men. Dmitrienko ordered everyone to crawl back inside. What was left of Dmitrienko's unit returned to Uncle Misha, while the Germans took a comfortable position under the cover of thick bushes more than fifty yards away from the back of the farmhouse.

The lookout returned from the attic again, this time informing Uncle Misha that there were barrels of rifles and submachine guns sticking out of the gaps between the boards of the woodshed. Since the woodshed door faced the farmhouse, the German unit must have torn out the woodshed's rear wall to establish their position inside the structure.

There were no side doors to the farmhouse. With the Germans covering the front and rear entrances, the partisans were surrounded. They had two options: launch an attack on one of the German units—a move to which the Germans would no doubt respond with a hail of bullets from their hiding places—or wait until nightfall, four hours away, and try to escape to the forest under the cover of darkness. The first option would almost certainly result in the loss of many partisan lives, while the second risked giving the Germans time to bring in reinforcements. Uncle Misha decided to wait.

NOT A SINGLE shot was fired over the next two hours. Trapped in the farmhouse, the partisans grew increasingly nervous. One of them suggested that he sneak out the front door and set fire to the woodshed, but Uncle Misha rejected the idea.

At around two in the afternoon, the partisans heard gunshots from the front of the farmhouse, followed by a commotion in the woodshed. They were still trying to figure out what was happening when the lookout from the attic jumped down and shouted, "Lionka is coming! We're saved!"

When the Germans in the woodshed turned around to return fire at Lionka's unit through the missing rear wall, Uncle Misha leaped out the front door of the farmhouse, closely followed by his partisans. They ran into the woodshed and attacked the Germans from behind with their bayonets and rifle butts.

The German unit in the rear of the farmhouse heard the gunfire coming from the front. They assumed that it was the other German unit attacking the partisans, and started running toward the house. Uncle Misha left some of the partisans in the woodshed to finish off the Germans there and to chase after those who were running away. He led the other partisans back into the farm-house, where they started firing from the windows at the Germans who were advancing toward the rear. Within a matter of seconds, the snow-covered clearing was littered with the bodies of killed or wounded German military policemen, but the other Germans kept returning fire. Whenever a partisan peeked out a window to try to aim their weapon, they were met with an immediate hail of German bullets. Uncle Misha darted back to the woodshed and dispatched a unit to sneak across the river and outflank the Germans in the clearing from behind. Some of the Germans surrendered, while others ran back into the forest.

In the meantime, Lionka rode up to Uncle Misha on his horse. Before Uncle Misha could even greet him, Lionka surveyed the fleeing Germans and shouted, "There's an officer! Bondarenko, follow me!"

Lionka jumped off his horse and started running after the German officer. Vladimir Danilovich Bondarenko, a tall partisan from Belarus, could barely keep up. They disappeared into the forest, chasing the officer who was desperately firing two revolvers at them as he ran away.

After a while, the German officer reemerged from the forest, walking with his head bent down, with Lionka and Bondarenko behind him. Lionka was wearing the officer's uniform coat, a belt with a yellow holster, and the officer's cap, which he had comically pulled down over his eyes. The partisans burst out in laughter when they saw the trio coming out of the forest.

In addition to the officer, the partisans had apprehended five German military policemen, along with a submachine gun, two pistols, and six hundred bullets. They had killed six Germans and wounded another ten during the shoot-out. While interrogating the captured military policemen, the partisans learned that most of them were descendants of the German colonists who had settled in Novohrad-Volynskyi in the nineteenth century. Uncle Misha demanded that they give a precise description of the murders of the Jews in Novohrad-Volynskyi, a town less than twenty miles from Korets that had been home to many of his friends. The partisans could tell from the Germans' faces that they had participated in the *Aktions*. At Uncle Misha's command, all of the military policemen were shot.

The officer initially refused to talk, but he ultimately relented after being tortured. He was Oberleutnant Knopp, from Stuttgart. After being wounded in the Battle of Moscow, he had been reassigned as the commandant of the SS unit responsible for hunting down and eliminating partisans in the regions of Zhytomyr and Kyiv. When the local Ukrainians had informed Knopp that it had been Uncle Misha's group that had hanged the Pavlovichi *starosta*, Knopp had resolved to find the partisans and punish them for killing his most loyal *starosta*. Knopp had even hoped to capture a partisan to earn a hefty reward and a promotion. Despite the partisans' efforts to disguise their footprints, the determined officer had tracked them all night. He had followed them to Iakovets, but had not expected to encounter a force more than three times the size of the unit that had attacked Pavlovichi.

Lionka liked wearing Knopp's uniform coat, and decided that it would replace the tattered jacket he had been wearing since leaving Korets. As he emptied out his pockets to transfer everything to the new coat, he found the circular yellow patches that he had torn off his old jacket on his way out of the ghetto. Smoothing out the patches, he walked over and showed them to Knopp.

"Do you know what these are?"

"No," Knopp replied.

"Then let me explain. Your Führer ordered us Jews to wear these patches to humiliate us. We were forced to wear them on our chests and backs."

Knopp mumbled something unintelligible and stared gloomily ahead.

"Take off your shirt!" Lionka yelled. Without waiting, he ripped Knopp's shirt off his body. Lionka took two pins and tacked the yellow patches onto Knopp's bare chest and bare back. "Now strip naked, just as my mother and my thirteen-year-old sister were ordered to before they were murdered."

The partisans reached over and tore off Knopp's boots, pants, and underwear. Knopp remained standing, stark naked in the Ukrainian winter. It was five degrees Fahrenheit, and there was a strong wind.

"Now march forward!" Lionka commanded, gesturing with his pistol toward the pile of dead Germans. When Knopp reached his fallen comrades, Lionka ordered him to return to the original spot. Knopp looked around, terrified.

"What you're feeling now is what we felt all the time when we lived in the ghetto," Lionka explained. "Now lie on the ground, facing down."

Knopp obeyed.

Lionka leaned over and placed his gun on Knopp's head. He held it for a few long minutes.

The German shifted restlessly.

"What you're experiencing now," Lionka said, "is what the 2,200 Jews of Korets, among them my dear mother and beloved little sister, experienced on May 21, 1942, when they were thrown, naked, into a mass grave, ordered to straighten out the corpses that were already lying there, and lie face down on top of them. Then a German shot them all."

Lionka pulled the trigger twice, firing both shots into Knopp's skull.

The partisans returned to their camp with three injured comrades and the bodies of six partisans who had died in the battle.

A peasant from Iakovets later told the partisans that the day after they had left the farm, a large unit of Germans had arrived. The Germans had surrounded the houses, dragged the peasants outside, and interrogated them, demanding to be told where

Uncle Misha and his partisans were hiding. When the peasants had replied that they knew nothing about the partisans, the Germans had tortured them for two hours, beating many of them unconscious.

Afterward, the Germans had ordered the peasants to load the dead military policemen onto wagons. The commander had walked over to the naked body with the yellow patch pinned to its back and had turned it over. The face had been unrecognizable, but the commander had noticed that the chest had a yellow patch as well. He had nudged the corpse with the tip of his boot. "This is a Jew," the commander had sneered. "He can remain here."

The Germans had set fire to the farm and left. Before fleeing to neighboring villages, the peasants had dragged Knopp's body into the woods so the wolves could devour it.

WHEN THEY WERE not fighting with an entire detachment, company, or platoon, individual partisans were often assigned to smaller squads that would conduct reconnaissance, engage in sabotage missions, or participate in special assignments designed to harass the locals who were giving food to the Nazis and to disrupt economic and industrial enterprises that provided aid to the Germans.

The greatest honor was to be assigned to one of the squads that were dispatched to various locations, either designated by the Soviets or selected by the partisans themselves, to blow up German trains. The trains carrying soldiers and ammunition across Ukraine were crucial to the German war effort. "The Army by itself (i.e., not including the Air Force) had a requirement for 120 trainloads of supplies every twenty-four hours," the Chief of the German Armed Forces High Command recorded in his memoirs. "Besides, there were violent fluctuations which could be attributed to the endless railway stoppages caused by the partisans; often there were more than a hundred stretches of railway blown up in one night."

According to one German estimate, partisans damaged or destroyed approximately five thousand locomotives and 17,500 railcars throughout the Soviet Union in 1943.

Carrying twenty-five-pound mines on their shoulders, the saboteurs would traverse dense forests and swamps in squads of eight. After making their way to the railway line, a squad would select a good location, lay the mine, and wait from a hiding spot somewhere close by. When a train rolled over the mine, it would detonate, derailing the engine and destroying some of the railcars. As soon as the partisans heard the explosion, they would run in separate directions to minimize the risk of German manhunts capturing the entire squad. They would rendezvous the following evening at a predetermined location before returning to camp.

On February 7, Lionka led a team of eight saboteurs that included Lieutenant Piotr Tsukanov, a former policeman who had joined the 1st Stalin Partisan Detachment the previous November. The squad headed south, to the train line that ran from Korosten to Kyiv. They arrived near the city of Malyn on February 10. At midnight, with the rest of the squad standing guard, Lionka and Tsukanov climbed up a hill and laid the mine. When the train arrived half an hour later, it was derailed by the explosion. The squad excitedly scattered.

The saboteurs spent the next day hiding in safe locations near Rubezhivka, a village twenty miles north of Malyn. When darkness fell, they went to an abandoned forester's lodge, where they had agreed to meet. Lionka arrived to find three partisans waiting. Another three showed up later, but Tsukanov never came. After waiting a few more hours, the partisans began to worry that Tsukanov had been captured by the Germans. They left the forester's lodge and moved to a different location, where they waited all day before returning to the lodge. Tsukanov was still not there.

Lionka and his squad cautiously visited a few of the nearby villages to ask the peasants whether they had heard anything about the Germans apprehending or killing a partisan. It was rare for the Germans to capture a partisan alive. When they did, they would publicize it widely for miles and miles. Regardless of whom they had captured, they would claim that he was a prominent leader. They would take photos of him and spread leaflets announcing his arrest throughout the villages in the area. The fact that the villagers had not heard about a partisan being captured dead or alive could only mean one thing: Tsukanov had deserted the partisans, taking with him a submachine gun, a map of the area, and a compass.

When Uncle Misha learned about Tsukanov's departure, he quickly grasped that Tsukanov was not just a deserter, but a double agent. Looking back, Uncle Misha realized that the flirtatious behavior in which Tsukanov had often engaged with several of the women partisans had been not only distasteful, but also deceitful.

Shortly after being assigned to Uncle Misha's Jewish Group, Tsukanov had set his sights on Manya, a beautiful and intelligent radio woman from Moscow who had parachuted into the detachment. Manya was one of three thousand Soviets—86 percent of whom were women—who had graduated from a two-and-a-half-month training course that the Central Staff of the Partisan Movement had established for radio operators, where she had been instructed how to operate behind enemy lines. Manya had told Tsukanov that she was not interested in flirting with him, and had asked him to leave her alone. When he had continued to profess his love for her, she had thrown him out of her *kibosh* and had forbidden him from ever returning.

Tsukanov had then moved on to a scout named Khanke, who had turned him away because she did not trust his assertions that he was unmarried. When it came to romance, a professional decorum prevailed in Uncle Misha's Jewish Group. There were some amorous relationships, as one would expect within a unit in which men and women lived in such close proximity to each other, but both parties would exercise discretion. Everyone remained monogamous, and there were no attempts by one partisan to steal another's partner.

Despite these partisan social mores, after being rejected by Khanke, Tsukanov had started pursuing the wife of Semyon Krasnov, the Soviet commander of a squad of machine gunners. Whenever Krasnov had gone on a mission, Tsukanov had paid his wife a visit. She had initially humored him, but after he entered her *kibosh* one evening and started making overtures, she had slapped him twice in the face and had thrown him out. When Krasnov had returned and learned that Tsukanov had been harassing his wife, he drew his pistol on Tsukanov. He might have killed Tsukanov, had Uncle Misha not intervened.

Ultimately, Tsukanov had settled on Khristye, a staff cook. Khristye was a chubby village girl, neither particularly pretty nor particularly smart. She had not seemed like a suitable match for Tsukanov, but she had taken good care of him, even washing his clothes for him.

It was not until Tsukanov's desertion that Uncle Misha understood that Tsukanov's interest in Manya had not been romantic, but an attempt to gain access to the ciphers that were crucial to German efforts to decrypt Soviet radio communications. Tsukanov's relationship with Khristye also finally made sense. As a staff cook, Khristye was always in the large *kibosh* the partisans had erected in the center of their camp as their staff headquarters, and the unit leaders had never given a second thought to discussing strategy in her presence. The partisans were furious at themselves for having allowed Tsukanov to dupe them.

WHILE LIONKA WAS on his sabotage mission, Uncle Misha was participating in a raid with the 1st Company, 3rd Company, and a joint squad of machine gunners. They attacked two village police departments along the way, but their main target was Rozvazhiv, a town located twenty miles northeast of Malyn, in the forested area between the regions of Zhytomyr and Kyiv. According to the partisans' intelligence, there were German warehouses in Rozvazhiv that were filled with food, medicine, fur coats, and blankets. Such supplies would be crucial to surviving the winter in Ukraine, where temperatures are consistently below freezing.

In the weeks leading up to the raid, the partisans would sit around the campfire during the long winter nights, considering every detail of the dangerous operation. Two fighters from Rozvazhiv who had only recently joined the partisans drew a detailed map of the town. They pointed out the houses where the German officers were billeted and the school building where the German soldiers were stationed. They showed their fellow partisans the location of the local police station, as well as the church complex where the German military police force was based. They noted the safest entrances into town and best routes for making a quick escape back to the forest.

The partisans knew that a successful attack on a town as heavily fortified as Rozvazhiv would depend on the element of surprise. They divided themselves into six squads that would launch a coordinated assault, ambushing six strategic targets at the exact same time. To catch the enemy off guard, the partisans slated the incursion for the wee hours of the morning.

That night turned out to provide ideal conditions for a sneak attack. A heavy snow fell from low clouds that cast everything in a gray veil, limiting visibility. Any sounds the partisans made as they hiked the twelve miles through the snow-covered forest paths were concealed by a sharp easterly wind that whistled wildly, at times sounding like wolves howling or children crying.

The partisans arrived at the outskirts of town just before midnight and stopped to rest. At exactly one o'clock, Uncle Misha gave the signal and the attack began.

The team that the partisans had designated as the "Communications Squad" went straight to the post office. They smashed all of the communications equipment and severed the telephone and telegraph connections. The Germans and Ukrainians were cut off from each other and from the rest of the world.

Another squad was dispatched to the police station. The partisans tossed several grenades into a dimly lit hall where policemen were sitting around covered tables, eating and drinking. Policemen ran out of the building in a panic, only to be met by a hail of gunfire. They retreated back inside and surrendered within a matter of minutes. After disarming the policemen, the partisans tied up their commander and took him with them.

A third squad surrounded the school building where two hundred German soldiers were quartered. The partisans successfully blockaded the building, preventing the soldiers from launching a counteroffensive.

Yet another partisan squad attacked the German military police. Garrisoned in a brick church building that was surrounded by a massive stone wall, the military policemen repelled every partisan effort to breach the courtyard by firing machine guns from the bell tower and from rooftops.

After more than a half hour of heavy fighting, the leader of the partisan squad used two mines to blow up part of the stone wall. The partisans swarmed in, shooting everyone in sight. A handful of military policemen survived by hiding in the cellar or running away into the darkness. The rest were killed by the partisans.

While the soldiers and policemen were being pinned down, the "Supply Squad" raided the military pharmacy and ransacked the warehouses. They made off with a large stockpile of coats, blankets, medical supplies, flour, butter, sugar, meat, carrots, French wine, and tobacco.

As soon as he had signaled the other five squads to initiate the attack, Uncle Misha and ten other partisans, including one of the men from Rozvazhiv, had entered the town. They had advanced swiftly but stealthily, pressing their bodies against the walls of houses to avoid being seen. The sounds of the gunfire and explosions elsewhere in town were completely drowned out by the howling wind.

The partisans stopped for a moment when they reached the private residence of the German commandant, on a side street not far from the post office. An armed soldier stood guard at the front door. He wore a thick fur coat with an upturned collar, as well as the lumpy, plaited straw overboots that Germany had issued to soldiers on the Eastern Front to stave off frostbite. Uncle Misha thought the guard looked like an overstuffed doll.

Suddenly a partisan appeared from out of nowhere. With a precise blow to the skull with the butt of his rifle, he killed the guard quickly and silently.

Uncle Misha peered through frosty windowpanes into the house. He could see a German commandant and eight officers sitting around a table, which was covered with food and drinks. Their uniforms were unbuttoned, their faces were flushed from alcohol, and the air was thick with cigar smoke. Their eyes were riveted on a young woman who was standing in the middle of the room, accompanying herself on a guitar while sweetly singing a Russian love song.

The partisans burst through the door and stormed into the room, shooting at all of the German officers at once. The barrage was so swift and unexpected that only one of the officers managed to draw his pistol. He fired one shot, wounding one of the partisans. In the next instant, the German collapsed to the floor with a bullet in his head. Within a matter of seconds, all of the officers were dead. Their bodies slumped forward onto the table or slid to the floor.

Throughout the attack, the woman had stood frozen, her large blue eyes showing more astonishment than fear. One of the partisans grabbed her by the hand and started shaking her. Snapping out of her shock, she remarked calmly in Russian, "It's about time you got here."

"You're Russian?" the partisan who had grabbed the woman bellowed. "Oh, you daughter of a bitch. You're carousing with the enemies of our fatherland, you tramp! Stand against the wall; you're going to be shot."

She dropped the guitar and placed her hands over her heart. "Shoot me," she whispered, starting to cry. "I deserve to die."

Confused, the partisan lowered his pistol.

At that moment, the partisan Sasha Yakimchuk came into the house. The Supply Squad had discovered a large trove of leather, and needed to know whether Uncle Misha wanted them to destroy it or take it with them. When he saw the woman, he ran over to her, grabbed her hand, and called out in surprise, "Sonya, what are you doing here?"

"Don't touch me, Sasha. I've sinned. I deserve to be shot," she replied, pulling her hand away. Turning back to the partisan who had first grabbed her hand, she asked, "So, why haven't you shot me?"

"Do you know this whore?" Uncle Misha asked Sasha.

"She's not a whore; she's a decent woman. I can vouch for her," Sasha replied. "Uncle Misha, I've known her for several years. She's the wife of my best friend, Vasya Zorin, an officer in the Red Army."

"We don't have time to deal with her," Uncle Misha determined. "Tie her up, and we'll deal with her in the camp. We can clear up this matter there."

THE HORSES EXHALED puffs of condensation from their flared nostrils as they pulled the sleds down the forest paths. The partisans were joking and laughing, sharing a celebratory mood inspired by the success of their mission. They had destroyed the commandant's headquarters, the mayor's office, the police station, a butter factory, and four shops. They had also neutralized a large enemy force, plundered and destroyed two warehouses, and captured fifteen rifles, a revolver, and as many as four hundred bullets. Only two partisans had lost their lives in the assault. The one partisan who had been wounded was being pulled on a sled, nestled underneath newly captured fur coats.

The partisans traveled through the rest of the night and for the entirety of the following day. They used misdirection to trick the Germans who were pursuing them into thinking that the partisans were from four detachments, operating in four different districts. As a result, the Germans concentrated their forces into setting up a number of ambushes in the wrong areas. There was an ambush of thirty German military policemen on the route the partisans actually took, but the partisans found out about it and instead passed through the village that the military policemen had abandoned to stage the ambush. As the partisans rode on, a heavy snow continued to fall, covering their tracks.

When they made it back to camp on the evening of February 17, Uncle Misha ordered Sonya to be brought to the staff *kibosh*. He invited Vasilii Ushakov, who was Mirkovsky's chief of staff, Sonya's friend Sasha Yakimchuk, and a few other partisans, including one who had been guarding Sonya, and some women. The partisans sat down on the logs that surrounded the fire and waited for the interrogation to begin.

When Sonya arrived in the *kibosh*, Uncle Misha invited her to sit. He spent several minutes studying her. Her appearance had changed dramatically during the trip from Rozvazhiv. She seemed much older, and even shorter. Her shoulders were slumped, as if they were bowing under the pressure of a heavy burden. She was staring into the fire with an expression of endless gloom. Her lower lip was quivering, as if she were fighting back tears. Uncle Misha found it hard to believe that this broken and resigned woman could have betrayed her people and her country so shamefully.

"Tell us, how were you connected to the German murderers?" he finally asked.

Sonya winced, as if waking from a dream. "I know that I've committed a grave crime, but before you mete out my punishment, let me tell you my story," she responded quietly. "You'll learn how a decent woman, who loved her husband and who was a devoted mother of her child, became a prostitute for the Germans. Allow me, good people, to open my heart to you and describe the terrible tragedy that led to my horrible sin. After that, I'll calmly accept whatever punishment you deem necessary."

As Sonya explained to the partisans, she was a Jewish woman from Korostyshiv, a village less than twenty miles east of the city of Zhytomyr. She had moved to Kyiv with her husband, Vasya Zorin, a gentile officer in the Red Army with whom she lost contact early in the war. She and their young son, Kostik, had moved in with Vasya's aunt Melania in Rozvazhiv, where Sonya had found a job as a dishwasher in the local soldiers' home. When Kostik had become deathly ill with pneumonia, the local commandant had offered to arrange for the boy to receive lifesaving medicine, but only in exchange for a night with Sonya. Sonya had been disgusted by the proposition, but had ultimately relented as Kostik had neared death, convincing herself that allowing her son to die when she had the means to save him would have been an even graver sin than infidelity and prostitution. Sonya knew that she would never be able to look Vasya in the face again, and had resolved to commit suicide once he returned. She had continued to work in the soldiers' home, and had no choice but to comply when the commandant had ordered her to return to his residence to entertain him and his officers.

When she was done sharing her heartbreaking tale, Sonya paused and then looked up with an expression of determination. "Good people, death is the lightest punishment I deserve. I accept that I'll have to pay with my life for the crime I've committed, but I do have one request: grant the wish of a desperate mother and take in my Kostik," she asked. "Aunt Melania isn't going to live much longer, and after her death, my Kostik will be completely alone. Once I'm assured that Kostik is going to be in good hands, I'll be able to die in peace."

A partisan sitting next to Sonya put his arms around her and hugged her to his chest. "It's the Nazi murderers who deserve to be put to death, not you," he proclaimed with tears in his eyes. "You aren't a criminal—just an unfortunate victim of the German beast!"

It was settled. "Who wants to go to Rozvazhiv to get Kostik?" Uncle Misha asked.

"Me," everyone answered in unison.

That night, Lionka and a woman partisan returned to Rozvazhiv on a sled. The woman, dressed as a peasant, went to Aunt Melania and passed on Sonya's wish. The elder woman led Kostik out of town to an agreed-upon location, where Lionka was waiting. They wrapped Kostik in a fur coat and brought him to the partisan camp, where he ran to the arms of his joyful mother.

The partisans also welcomed Kostik with open arms. Some of them had left their children behind, but most had lost their children to Nazi murderers. They adopted Kostik and treasured the opportunity to reawaken their parental instincts. It became an unwritten rule that every partisan who went out on a mission was obligated to bring back a present to the young boy to whom everyone referred as "our Kostik."

Uncle Misha offered Sonya an assignment as a nurse in the Sanitary Battalion, which would have spared her from combat, as well as from being separated from Kostik. Sonya categorically refused. "I want to be a regular fighter," she explained. "I want to kill as many Germans as I can with my own hands. I want to take revenge for my parents and for my humiliation."

Sonya quickly proved to be one of the fiercest women combatants in Uncle Misha's Jewish Group. She eagerly participated in the most dangerous battles, often earning cautions from her fellow partisans not to take so many risks that could leave young Kostik without either of his parents. In her free time between missions, she trained herself in new skills, the harder the better, finding each task to be a welcome distraction from her sorrow.

Although she was always cordial to the other partisans, Sonya never allowed anyone to get too close, and never joined in their camaraderie. She never smiled, and always seemed to be deep in her own thoughts. The only partisans with whom she ever spent time were Sasha Yakimchuk, Uncle Misha, and Lionka. When Sonya became particularly sad, she would visit the *kibosh* that Uncle Misha and Lionka shared. "I miss our Volhynian Jews," she would say. "Let's talk about them for a little while, Uncle Misha."

Uncle Misha was happy to listen to the stories about her childhood in Korostyshiv and her blissful years in Kyiv with Vasya and Kostik. He could see that reliving her happiest memories helped Sonya drive away her sadness.

CHAPTER 9

"The Oath"

We vow to fight for freedom and right,
Against all tyrants and their knaves.
We vow to defeat the darkest night,
Or fall heroically in battle!

—S. ANSKY, "THE OATH"
(JOSEPH GLADSTEIN, *FREEDOM'S SONGS*, P. 14)

B Y FEBRUARY 1943, UNCLE MISHA'S Jewish Group had grown to include thirty-one men and women, most of whom had no prior military experience. They were tailors, shoe-makers, and barbers who had worked in the partisan camps, pro-viding essential services to the Soviets. They had joined the Jewish Group without any weapons, nor any idea how to defend themselves if they were attacked.

These were Jews who had not been forced into ghettos and had not experienced *Aktions*. Some of them had been working for the Soviets before the German invasion, and had gotten trapped behind enemy lines along with the Red Army. Others had been hiding with Belarusian peasants who had presented their "little Jews" to the Soviet partisans as proof that they had not collaborated with the Germans. Since they had not witnessed the horrors of the German invasion, the Jewish workers initially saw their new assignment to Uncle Misha's Jewish Group simply as another place of refuge, where they could ride out the rest of the war.

While some of the Jewish workers were too old to fight, Uncle Misha was committed to converting the rest into Jewish combatants. He spent many hours in front of the campfire telling them about the ghettos, the *Aktions*, and other German atrocities. He inspired them with the story of how he and a few other Jews, armed with only a single revolver and five bullets, had left Korets. He proudly told them how much he and his squad had achieved and how many Germans they had killed in the five months since. Uncle Misha pointed to the very creation of the new Jewish Group as proof that his unit had brought honor and distinction to the Jewish nation.

Uncle Misha and his fellow Jewish fighters convinced their new comrades that it was their duty as Jewish survivors to fight the Nazis. Uncle Misha trained them how to maintain their rifles and taught them that they should never be satisfied with merely staying alive. They had a sacred obligation to use the weapons they now held in their hands to avenge the murders of thousands of innocent brothers and sisters.

Life was very difficult in the forest. In addition to waging war against the Germans, the partisans had to combat starvation, dehydration, disease, and exposure. But even in the worst of times, the Jewish partisans felt proud and optimistic. Knowing that they were taking up arms against Judaism's greatest enemy fortified their spirits and convinced them that they would be victorious. When they would capture a German alive, Uncle Misha would introduce himself by saying, in German, "I am a Jew," and they would forget about their hardships. It was worth all of the suffering to witness every moment of revenge.

ONE EXPERIENCED COMBATANT who joined Uncle Misha's Jewish Group that winter was a soldier from Hungary. Uncle Misha met the young man after a battle with Hungarian forces in Mukhoedy. The Hungarians had the benefit of an abundance of reserves, as well as barricades they had built out of headstones from the Christian cemetery, but their front line was in complete disarray. They fired desperately at the partisans for two hours before giving up. They scurried away like mice, abandoning their camp, along with food, supplies, and several dead and severely injured soldiers.

After the victory, Uncle Misha dispatched a squad to "bomb" the families of the policemen in Mukhoedy. The rest of the partisans gathered in a large school courtyard, surveying with curiosity the newly appropriated field kitchen in which "Timke the Cook" was making soup.

The partisans had informants in nearly every city and town. Uncle Misha's informant in Mukhoedy was a woman named Zoya, who was the administrator and only teacher in the local school. When Uncle Misha paid Zoya a visit after the gunfight with the Hungarians, she opened her office door and whispered, "Uncle Misha, there's a Hungarian, a Jew, in my room. I've gotten to know him over the past few weeks, and he wants to join your partisan detachment. I will happily vouch for him."

Uncle Misha peered into the room and saw a thin young man of about twenty-two or twenty-three years old, wearing the uniform of a Hungarian junior officer. Uncle Misha quickly disarmed him and searched him for additional weapons. When he was satisfied that the Hungarian was unarmed, he sat him at a table.

"I am from Munkács," the Hungarian told Uncle Misha in crisp Yiddish. Munkács, which is known today as Mukachevo, Ukraine, was an important Jewish community. At the end of the nineteenth century, the Hungarian city had been home to the

Grand Rabbi Shlomo Spira, who had formed the Munkács Hasidic dynasty.

As the Hungarian explained to Uncle Misha, he had been raised in the Hasidic community and had studied at a yeshiva until he was sixteen. He had left the small Hasidic circle of Munkács behind to study philosophy at the University of Budapest. When Hungary had started drafting Jews into forced labor, he had been sent to a farm in the village of Uzhhorod, on the Slovakian border, and then to the underground salt mines near Salzburg. After escaping back to Budapest, he had come to the conclusion that he would be safest in the army. Using the Aryan identification card of an old girlfriend's dead brother, he had joined the Royal Hungarian Army.

Unfortunately, the division he joined was sent to the Eastern Front, where the Hungarian had watched in horror as his fellow soldiers committed atrocities against Jews. When he had heard about the partisans, he had started thinking about deserting the army and running away to the forest. At the end of December, he had volunteered for a punitive expedition that had been formed to hunt down the partisans. After meeting and befriending Zoya in Mukhoedy, he had entrusted her with his secret, and she had agreed to introduce him to Uncle Misha.

"I'm particularly glad to meet up with a Jewish partisan detachment. I hope you'll accept me into your ranks, and that I'll be able to fight and avenge the innocent victims," he said. "My name is Ephraim, but my mother used to call me Fridek."

"Good," Uncle Misha simply said. He accepted the Hungarian into his group, bestowing upon him the nickname "Fridek the Magyar."

ALL OF THE partisans quickly grew to like Fridek. He was bold, but not temperamental. "The lightest head is a hothead. The wind could easily blow it away," he would say. "You have to use your brains—assuming, of course, you have any." Fridek was admired for his pragmatic spirit, which he was able to maintain even in the worst of moments, as well as for his talent for rhetoric. He was especially adept at telling stories about the Hasidic Grand Rabbis, introducing the spellbound partisans to the world of Hasidic mysticism.

During long winter nights by the campfire, the partisans would engage in endless discussions, always led by Uncle Misha. Given how early night fell in the forest, it was not unusual for the darkness to last as long as eighteen hours, and he needed to find constructive ways for his partisans to fill the time. He also wanted to give them something to think about other than the sorrowful past. To accomplish both goals, he organized "debates," as they called them, in such a way that everyone present could participate. He wanted to make sure that every partisan, regardless of their background, experienced new perspectives and developed the ability to think both critically and independently.

As the partisans discussed various topics, Fridek usually took the opposite side of everyone else. With his quick mind and broad education, not only in the Talmud and philosophy, but also in general subjects, he delighted everyone with his clever and innovative thinking. Since most of the partisans had little formal education, he was practically unbeatable in any debate.

On more than one occasion, the discussion topic was music. One night, the partisans talked about the musics of different countries, with Uncle Misha demonstrating various musical styles on his violin. The subject captured the partisans' interest, and a lively discussion ensued. This conversation led to another musical topic, which was debated for several evenings in a row: whether major events can permanently change the way a particular culture makes music. Most of the partisans agreed with a Soviet partisan named Nikita Kolosov, who posited that historical developments could reshape the characteristics of a country's music. He used Russian popular music as his example. At the turn of the twentieth century, Russian music was dominated by melancholy songs and sentimental waltzes. But after the Russian Revolution, Nikita argued, the country's music became more upbeat, reflecting the new cadence of a liberated nation and the confident march toward a better and brighter future.

As always, Fridek played the role of the contrarian. His stance was that the passions stirred up by certain events could bring temporary changes to a country's music, but once those moments passed, the music would revert to its original style. He pointed to French music, which has historically prioritized grace and elegance. When "La Marseillaise" appeared in a new militaristic style in 1792, it captured the optimistic spirit of the French Revolution. But the song that three years later became the French national anthem made no lasting impression on the French style. The songs that followed it returned to the lightness that had preceded the revolution.

In this particular matter, Fridek had to concede defeat when Nikita pointed out that the difference between the developments in Russian music and the stability of French music was that the French Revolution did not have as far-reaching and long-lasting consequences on French culture as the Bolshevik Revolution had in Russia.

In addition to loving a good debate, Fridek was a devout Jew who prayed and recited ten psalms every day. When the other partisans would ask how he reconciled maintaining this devotion with disregarding other Jewish precepts, like the restriction on eating pork, he would smile and say, "I've been praying every day for as long as I can remember. It's become a habit, and a habit becomes second nature. I'm also convinced that through my prayers I honor the memory of my devout parents, who rejoice in their graves knowing that their beloved son has not forgotten his faith."

Fridek also rationalized that weapons could be used to serve God. In Fridek's thinking, humans throughout history could be divided into two camps. One believed in the Judeo-Christian

God and followed either the commandments of the Torah or the teachings of Jesus Christ. They believed that if everyone followed their example, peace, stability, and happiness would prevail, and the messiah would come. On the other side of the spectrum were those who defied Judeo-Christian ethics and morality. The Hitlers and Mussolinis of the world had provoked hatred among the nations. Instead of ushering in the messiah, their behavior had fomented injustice, darkness, and brutal authoritarianism. There were also "agents of God" who believed they could triumph over evil with prayers and good deeds, but who were ultimately unsuccessful.

"Then came our generation, which understands that we can only resist the dark forces with weapons in our hands, and which stepped into the decisive battle. We partisans are therefore not just ordinary people. We are emissaries who are fighting in God's name to bring the messiah sooner," Fridek asserted. "By destroying the armies of evil, we're bringing the redemption closer, and are thereby serving God. Killing a Nazi is exactly the same as performing a prayer service."

The partisans in Uncle Misha's Jewish Group took this lesson to heart. Whenever a squad would come back from a mission, instead of being asked, "How did the mission go?" they would be asked, "How did the prayer service go?"

"Very well. We had six weekday prayers and one festive prayer," the returning partisans would answer, indicating that they had killed six German soldiers and one officer.

IN EARLY MARCH 1943, Uncle Misha's Jewish Group was encamped with the rest of the 1st Stalin Partisan Detachment a few miles north of Khilchikha. In May 1942, Medvedev's partisan detachment had selected Mukhoedy, a few miles south of Khilchikha, as the site where they would parachute into Ukraine, based on its location as the farthest point west that a plane could fly from the Soviet Union and back overnight. Now, ten months later, the 1st Stalin Partisan Detachment had established an airstrip in the same area, where Soviet planes could land to deliver supplies.

By that time, the detachment included forty Soviet partisans who had gotten injured or very sick since the partisans had left Soviet territory the previous October. The next plane would transport those partisans back to Moscow. While they were awaiting the arrival of the plane, the partisans were unable to launch more large-scale attacks. At least one unit always had to remain in the camp to defend the Sanitary Battalion, which the partisans shortened to "SanBat."

In the meantime, squads of six to eight men would carry out smaller missions. They patrolled the area to gather information about which German troops were nearby and where they were garrisoned. The partisans wanted to know which garrisons could be attacked with the least amount of risk, and needed to be able to anticipate where they themselves were the most vulnerable. They also surveilled the railway lines and the highway that ran from Shepetivka, through Ovruch and Mazyr, and on to Chernihiv, reporting intelligence back to Moscow via radio regarding the types and numbers of soldiers, as well as the quantities of ammunition being transported to the front.

The partisans remained involved in sabotage. Sometimes they would sneak off to railroad tracks with mines on their shoulders, which they would use to blow up trains carrying ammunition and soldiers on their way to the front. Other times, they would march to villages farther away to assassinate German collaborators: informants, heads of cooperatives, and *soltysi*—village elders who had been elected to town councils.

The Germans may not have been aware of the surveillance, but they quickly felt the presence of partisans in the area when *soltysi* were murdered and newly nominated elders fled to the forest rather than taking their place. Villagers no longer allowed their children to be taken to Germany for labor, out of fear of reprisal from the partisans. They stopped providing bread, butter, chicken, and eggs to the Germans. It did not take long for the Germans to start retaliating.

In early March, German forces started to assemble in Antonovka, a village ten miles southwest of Naroulia and three miles from the 1st Stalin Partisan Detachment's camp. On March 4, two German units from Antonovka were out on patrol when they mistook each other for partisan detachments and engaged in a firefight. On the next day, eight hundred German soldiers arrived in Antonovka as reinforcements, bringing the entire complement to as many as 1,200 men.

Mirkovsky dispatched small squads in shifts to monitor the road leading from the village to the camp. At nine-thirty in the morning on March 6, a squad from the 3rd Company, led by Mikhail Dmitrienko, observed Germans approaching the camp. When the Germans came closer, the partisans opened fire with machine guns, submachine guns, and rifles. The Germans retreated, but the partisans knew that they would return with a much larger force. According to the partisan intelligence operatives who had infiltrated Antonovka, the Germans split into three detachments and entered the forest with the intention of encircling the partisan camp.

At noon, Mirkovsky dispatched the entire 3rd Company under the command of Lieutenant Petr Sergeevich Podiachev to take up defensive positions close to two miles outside of the camp. The Germans reached that position at around one o'clock. The 3rd Company allowed the Germans to get within fifty yards before opening fire. Intensive shooting could be heard from every direction.

Uncle Misha's Jewish Group was ordered to stay in the camp to defend the staff headquarters and the Sanitary Battalion. The emergency escape plan called for the wounded partisans in the SanBat to be dressed in warm clothes, laid on sleighs, and evacuated through the thick forest that stretched westward from the camp for several miles. But the lookouts who maintained contact between the 3rd Company and the camp informed them that the Germans were rapidly encircling the camp and that it would be impossible to get the sick and wounded partisans out in time.

The fighting continued, with only short lulls. The partisans sustained several injuries and deaths. Mirkovsky knew that the Germans would probably return to the village when darkness fell, but doubted whether the partisans could hold out that long. The situation was growing dire.

The sick and wounded lying helplessly on the sleighs gave up hope. They started begging their fellow partisans for grenades, so they could blow themselves up before the Germans could take them alive. Boris Goldfarb, a Jewish fighter from the village of Andrusiiv—seventeen miles west of Korets—was in the Sanitary Battalion with a foot injury. He kept calling Uncle Misha over, asking for updates. With every visit, he would make Uncle Misha promise to shoot him if the Germans captured the camp.

MIRKOVSKY WAS SITTING on a tree stump, surrounded by his chief of staff, Vasilii Ushakov; his aide-de-camp, Gavriil Negrobov; and Uncle Misha. The partisan commander appeared to be calm, but his advisors could not help but notice that he was smoking one cigarette after another and kept readjusting his hat from the back of his head to his forehead and back.

"If we could divert the attention of all three German detachments, if only for an hour, we'd be able to slip through to the other side of the line with the SanBat, and they'd be saved," Mirkovsky said, almost to himself.

Uncle Misha had a plan. "If Antonovka came under attack," he said, "the detachment closest to the road would immediately rush to defend it. Then all of our platoons could launch a joint attack on the middle detachment. The detachment farthest from the road would then be forced to join the middle one to ward off our attack. That would clear the entire western flank, and we could lead the SanBat out."

"That's a good idea, Uncle Misha, but it won't work," Mirkovsky responded. "We can't afford to withdraw even one partisan from the defensive line."

"Nobody has to be withdrawn. I'll execute the attack with a unit of nineteen men. The road to Antonovka is clear, and my guess is that all we'll find in the village will be the horses and equipment carts, along with the mine launchers."

The three Soviet partisans looked at Uncle Misha in astonishment.

"I can't order you to undertake such a mission. You'd be walking into certain death," Mirkovsky told him. "But if you want to sacrifice yourself to save your helpless comrades, then I'll shake your hand and tell you that your name will be eternalized in the history of our detachment."

Uncle Misha handpicked nineteen fighters from his Jewish Group and made sure they were fully armed with submachine guns and hand grenades.

Lionka was upset to learn that his father was planning to leave him behind. "I'm not letting you go by yourself. I have to go with you," he protested. "We've been fighting, shoulder to shoulder, this whole time, and now, when you're heading into such danger, you want me to stay behind? No, I'm going with you."

Uncle Misha begged Lionka to remain in the camp. It was not until Mirkovsky put his hand on Lionka's shoulder and urged, "Stay here, young man, because if your father doesn't return, at least someone will remain to avenge him," that Lionka finally relented.

Uncle Misha handed his diary, his photographs, his documents, and his copy of *Freedom's Songs* to Lionka for safekeeping. Lionka's hand trembled as he placed them in his breast pocket and steeled himself for his father's departure.

When news of Uncle Misha's dangerous mission reached the Sanitary Battalion, they all called him over. Dozens of hands were extended for Uncle Misha to shake. With tears in their eyes, they wished him success in various ways and in various languages. The last wounded partisan that Uncle Misha visited was Boris, who squeezed his hand and thanked him for his friendship. With tears in his eyes, Boris quoted to Uncle Misha the last words purportedly spoken by Zionist icon Joseph Trumpeldor after he was mortally wounded during an Arab attack on one of the first Jewish settlements in Palestine in 1920: "It is good to die for our country."

With those words ringing in his ears, Uncle Misha led his men out of the camp and toward Antonovka, staying close to the road. As they crept along, Uncle Misha reminded himself that a successful mission would protect the honor of the Jewish nation, avenge the murders of thousands of Jews, and take the fight to those who considered the People of the Torah and of Wisdom to be an inferior race. The thought filled him with so much pride and courage that he felt as if he were leading not a group of nineteen Jews, but the entire Jewish nation.

Within an hour, Uncle Misha and his Jewish fighters reached the frozen creek that encircled Antonovka on three sides. They slid down the sloped creek bank and onto the ice. Quickly crawling on their hands and knees, they reached the wall of snow on the other side. Above them, close to the creek, long stables formed the back of the village. They heard shouts in German, the neighing of horses, and, periodically, the banging of mine launchers being loaded, followed immediately by the characteristic whistle of shells flying through the air.

Not far from the partisans, in the middle of the creek, a rectangular hole had been cut into the ice to draw water. A young peasant woman carrying two wooden buckets climbed down the bank and stopped dead in her tracks when she saw the partisans. She dropped her buckets on the ice and stood there, as motionless as a statue. Uncle Misha gestured with his finger for her to come closer.

"How many Germans are in the village, and where are they?" he asked.

In a scared voice, she replied that thousands of Germans had arrived the previous night, and had gone out to fight the partisans in the morning. As Uncle Misha had predicted, the Germans had left the horses and equipment carts in the courtyard. Twenty Germans who had stayed behind to defend the horses and carts were going door-to-door, demanding eggs and butter. The peasant woman also told them that near the bridge leading to the forest, there were two mine launchers being operated by six or seven Germans. Another German was sitting on a chair next to them, transmitting orders from a telephone.

"Now tell me, dear girl," Uncle Misha pressed, "are the mine launchers far from the courtyard where the horses and equipment carts are located?"

"No, perhaps a hundred steps. A small street leads directly from the courtyard to the bridge."

"Now, dear girl, stay here for a little while. Don't leave. There might be a shoot-out, and I don't want you to get hurt."

In truth, Uncle Misha was not as concerned with the young woman's safety as he was with the prospect of her entering the village before him and warning the Germans.

THE PARTISANS PEERED down the narrow path that led to the courtyard. About a hundred steps away, they saw several tall German horses, covered with gray saddle blankets and hitched to equipment carts.

Uncle Misha quickly formulated a plan. He ordered ten partisans to throw grenades toward the courtyard. The explosions spooked the horses, and they took off running in a cacophony of whinnies and crushed carts. Some of the horses ran down the path to the creek, but the partisans shot bullets in their direction until they turned around and galloped in the only other direction, toward the bridge. The partisans rushed after them. The air was filled with the clamor of dozens of horseshoed hooves clopping on the frozen planks of the bridge and the wild cries of the German mortarmen getting trampled. The German with the telephone tried to grab the handset, but a burst of gunfire from the submachine guns mowed him down. Three mortarmen lay on the ground, having been stomped to death. The other mortarmen had run off.

Uncle Misha ordered his partisans to guard the street leading to the bridge. He picked up the telephone and heard a German cursing on the other end.

"An attack by many partisans! Quick! Help!" Uncle Misha shouted into the handset in German.

"What? What? Damn it!" came the nervous reply.

In a play on the common Nazi chant "Heil, Hitler! Death to the Jews!" Uncle Misha yelled, "Heil, Jews! Death to Hitler!" He dropped the telephone onto the frozen ice.

"Comrades, we're done here," Uncle Misha announced. He started heading back to camp.

"Uncle Misha, let me lob a few shells," asked Sasha Adeser. "After all, that's my specialty." Uncle Misha remembered that Sasha had not been armed when he had joined the Jewish Group. When Uncle Misha had asked where his weapon was, Sasha had replied that he did not have one, because he had been serving as a mortarman, and before that as a butcher.

After receiving Uncle Misha's permission, Sasha walked over to a mine launcher that was already loaded and started making preparations to fire it. "What am I doing? These were surely aimed at our camp," he suddenly realized. "I don't have a range correction."

"Aim them around one thousand yards closer than where they are currently aimed, and you'll surely hit the right spot," suggested Uncle Misha.

Delighted, Sasha fired two shells from each mine launcher, after which the partisans rolled the mine launchers off the bridge and started running back across the frozen creek.

When they were a little over four hundred yards from the bridge, the partisans heard gunfire. Bullets whistled over their heads and burrowed into nearby trees. The partisans sprinted another thousand yards into the dense forest of intertwined trees. As they pushed forward, the prickly leaves of the young pines tore their pants.

"We'll have to hide here and wait until dark," Uncle Misha explained. It was about an hour until nightfall. "We don't know which German detachment will take which paths to defend Antonovka. If we leave now, we could go right into the belly of the beast. They surely have search dogs. I'm more afraid of the four-legged animals than the two-legged ones, but they wouldn't crawl into these prickly trees."

From the forest, the partisans could hear the Germans marching to the right of them, on the road to Antonovka. They heard dogs passing them on the left. Luckily, the dogs could not pick up the partisans' scent because they were downwind. They saw flares and heard shooting in Antonovka before silence finally fell.

It was completely dark by the time the partisans returned to camp. They looked around and were relieved to find no signs that the camp had been compromised. They decided to wait until daybreak to follow the tracks that the sleighs had made as they carried the wounded to safety. Afraid of being discovered, they did not light a fire.

Suddenly they heard a rustle nearby and saw a dark silhouette.

"Who's there?" Uncle Misha shouted, knowing that the Germans would be back in Antonovka by then.

"Papa!" It was Lionka. He ran to Uncle Misha, wrapped his arms around his neck, and kissed him. Lionka's eyes filled with tears of joy.

Lionka told them that one of the partisan platoons had come under heavy fire after Uncle Misha had left. The partisans had been forced to retreat to a defensive position, which had encouraged the Germans to start attacking even more aggressively. The situation was growing dire when confusion had suddenly broken out among the Germans. As the Germans had started to retreat, four mines had exploded right in the middle of them. They had panicked and had run off in the direction of the road leading to Antonovka.

After things had calmed down a bit, Mirkovsky had sent Lionka and another partisan to see if the passage was clear. They had arrived at the road just as the last group of Germans was coming out of the forest. The last one had been tall, with a Czech machine gun on his shoulder. It had occurred to Lionka that the machine gun could be of use to Uncle Misha's Jewish Group, so he had shot the German dead. The gunfire had only increased the panic, and the remaining Germans had scampered away without even looking at their fallen comrade.

"I picked up the machine gun, and didn't forget about you, either," Lionka explained. "You now have in your leather satchel, among your documents, a German map of the region of Zhytomyr that I took from a dead German officer whom they left lying on the road."

"Why are you here?" Uncle Misha asked.

"I asked Mirkovsky to let me stay here to wait for you. Had you not come...I would have gone to Antonovka tomorrow night...to find your body."

Uncle Misha, Lionka, and the other Jewish partisans caught up with Mirkovsky the next afternoon. The partisans were overjoyed to see them alive and healthy.

Nobody was happier than Boris. "I told you," he shouted triumphantly to the other wounded partisans. "German bullets can't touch Uncle Misha!"

AT FIVE IN the evening on March 19, an emaciated horse slowly pulled a dilapidated farmer's wagon down the road toward Aleksandrovka, a village twenty-five miles south of Naroulia. The wagon was loaded with sacks, on top of which lay a man with a long beard who appeared to be sleeping. It was a Jewish partisan from Odessa named Moshe Milrod, whom the other partisans called "Popov" because his long beard made him look like a *pop*— Russian for "priest." Popov was the perfect partisan for an undercover operation. He looked like an ethnic Ukrainian, spoke Ukrainian flawlessly, and knew all of the Ukrainian customs. Just before he reached the village, Popov hid his hat underneath the sacks, wrapped the reins around his hands, and stretched out as if he had passed out drunk.

Aleksandrovka was home to a garrison where 250 well-armed German military policemen were stationed. According to partisan intelligence from early February, several of the military policemen had no interest in fighting the partisans. "Why should I shoot at a partisan? What did he do to me?" they asked. "He walks around in the forest. Let him walk." But the majority of the military policemen were loyal Nazis who had dug trenches and posted guards in anticipation of a partisan attack.

By the middle of March, the military police in Aleksandrovka had surrounded the garrison with a thick wall constructed of two rows of wooden beams with a layer of clay between them. At each corner, two military policemen armed with machine guns stood guard, night and day, in small wooden towers. The only entrance was a heavy gate that was defended by Germans with fierce watchdogs.

When Popov's wagon was just a few yards from that gate, he pretended to suddenly stir. He stopped the wagon and started looking around frantically.

"Keep driving, Ukrainian swine," ordered the military policeman standing guard at the gate.

"I lost my hat," Popov explained in flawless Ukrainian, pointing to his bare head with a confused look on his face. He climbed down and pretended to rearrange the sacks in a futile attempt to find his hat.

While Popov was rooting around in the wagon, he snuck a length of rope from under the top sack. The rope had an iron hook attached to one end. The other end was tied to the firing pin of a detonator that Popov, an ingenious bombmaker, had rigged to a mine. The mine was hidden at the bottom of the wagon, underneath a sack of explosives. Popov turned to the front of the wagon and, in the blink of an eye, attached the hook to a spoke in one of its wheels. He nonchalantly laid the reins on the horse's back and walked back in the direction from where he had come, still appearing to be looking for his hat.

After walking about a hundred yards, Popov could still hear the German guard shouting at him. He disappeared into the pine forest without looking back. Within ten minutes, he joined Uncle Misha and the other partisans hiding in the thick underbrush that surrounded Aleksandrovka.

A loud explosion shook the forest. As the partisans had expected, the Germans had tried to move the wagon. When the front wheels had turned, the rope hooked to the spoke had stretched until it had pulled the safety pin out of the detonator. The explosion had blown up the horse and wagon, blasted a hole in the wall, and set the garrison on fire.

Just as a partisan lookout who had climbed a tall pine tree was reporting that billows of black smoke were rising from the village, the partisans heard several additional explosions and the bursting of bullets as ammunition ignited in the burning buildings. The only part of the garrison that was not engulfed in flames was the school building at the other end of the courtyard, which the military police had commandeered as their headquarters.

Uncle Misha divided his group of seventy partisans into two squads: one was led by him, and the other was led by Lionka. After severing the telephone and telegraph cables to cut the village off from the outside world, Lionka's squad attacked the garrison courtyard through the hole in the wall. Uncle Misha's squad breached the gate at the exact same time. At first, the partisans had to fire carefully to avoid hitting the villagers who were carrying wooden buckets of water to extinguish the fire. But after the first few shots, the villagers ran off, shouting.

The Germans were caught so flat-footed by the attack that they preoccupied themselves with putting out the fire. By the time they remembered to grab their weapons, it was too late. Within a matter of minutes, the ground of the garrison courtyard was covered with dead and wounded military policemen.

While Lionka's squad hunted down the Germans who were running away in terror, Uncle Misha's squad attacked the school building, where several Germans had barricaded themselves. The partisans were driven back by a hail of gunfire from the windows. During a second attempt to cross the twenty yards to the school, three partisans were wounded and the squad was again forced to retreat. They took cover behind two trucks and started formulating a new plan of attack.

"I'll run out and throw a couple of grenades through the window," suggested Sasha Adeser.

Without waiting for Uncle Misha's approval, Sasha jumped from behind the trucks and started sprinting toward the school building. After a few steps, he raised from his crouched position and lobbed two grenades toward the school. In that instant, several shots rang out from the windows. Sasha fell to the ground.

The sound of the grenades exploding inside the school building was followed by the wild cries of wounded Germans. The partisans stormed into the building. They were as angry as Uncle Misha had ever seen them. They attacked the Germans like wild animals, shouting, "Revenge! Revenge!" After smashing the furniture, they piled all of the books and magazines in the middle of the hallway and set them on fire. Within minutes, the building was engulfed in flames.

As Uncle Misha's squad left the school building, they saw Lionka's squad loading sacks of sugar and flour onto a large German wagon hitched to several well-fed Belgian horses. The partisans also captured eighteen rifles and one thousand bullets, and confiscated the personal property of the village *starosta* and the military policemen. The two squads left the village together, with the bodies of two partisans who had been killed, five wounded partisans, and Sasha, who had only received minor injuries to his feet.

On their way out, the partisans grabbed the *sołtys* of Aleksandrovka, who was notorious for his devotion to the Germans. Uncle Misha left a letter with his wife addressed to the garrison commander, who had fled to Ovruch as soon as the bomb had exploded.

The note said: *Baron von Hellman, Hitler will not destroy the entire Jewish nation. However, I have destroyed the Aleksandrovka garrison.* He signed it: *Commander of the Jewish Partisan Group, the Jew Uncle Misha.*

CHAPTER 10

"The 'Youth' Oath"

Be brave, brother, never let go of the sword!
The road will be rocky, but fear not, "Youth" brother!
Freedom has to be fought for to the last drop of blood!

—LEYB MALAKH, "THE 'YOUTH' OATH"
(JOSEPH GLADSTEIN, *FREEDOM'S SONGS*, P. 49)

IN ADDITION TO THE OLDER men and women who served in Uncle Misha's Jewish Group in noncombat roles, such as doctors and nurses in the Sanitary Battalion, or as cooks, tailors, shoemakers, and barbers, the entourage included a few children. One was Sonya Zorin's son, Kostik. Another was a twelve-year-old boy who called himself Mitka, whom Uncle Misha had taken under his wing shortly before leaving Volhynia.

Lionka and five other Jewish partisans had been out on patrol one night when they had stopped at an abandoned wheelwright's workshop. The shelter was located in a dense forest of oak trees, far from any villages, and the partisans had often paused there to rest on their way to and from missions. As they approached the old workshop, Lionka noticed a figure on the ground. "There's someone there," he whispered. "Ready your weapons!"

Holding their submachine guns, the partisans crept up to the structure, where they discovered a young boy sleeping by a smoldering fire. He was wearing shabby clothes, which were several sizes too large, and clumsy, oversized boots. He was lying on top of a few dry branches, with his head resting on a long black box.

"Where did this little boy come from?" one of the partisans asked.

"He must have gotten lost in the forest," Lionka guessed. "He's probably hungry, too. Let's let him sleep for now. We'll wake him up when the soup is ready, and he can tell us who he is then."

The partisans built a large fire, put some snow in the aluminum cups they each kept tied to their belts, and held the cups over the fire. After a few minutes, the snow in the cups began to melt. They poured some grain and a piece of frozen meat into each cup, and the night air quickly filled with the smell of the partisan soup.

"Wake up, young man!" Lionka said, gently rubbing the boy's arm. "You shouldn't sleep so soundly in the forest."

The boy's eyes cracked open and quickly closed again. He rolled over to his side and went back to sleep. Lionka grabbed him by the shoulders and sat him up. The boy opened his eyes again. Seeing the armed strangers, he quickly stood up and started to run away.

Lionka grabbed his hand. "Don't be scared, little boy," he said kindly. "We're not going to hurt you. We're partisans. Do you know what partisans are?"

"I know, I know! I've been looking for you for the past three days!" he cried out happily. "Dasha sent me to you."

"Who's Dasha?"

"Dasha...someone who worked with me for the same landowner...She told me—"

"First, eat," Lionka interrupted. "You can tell us after that." He gave the boy a cup of soup and a spoon.

The boy gobbled down the soup.

"What have you been eating during the three days that you've been in the forest?" one of the partisans asked.

"Up until lunch today, I still had some bread that Dasha stole for me, which I ate with snow."

When everyone was finished eating, the partisans added some dry branches to the fire. Sitting down comfortably, they lit their cigarettes.

"What's your name, boy?" Lionka asked.

"They call me Mitka."

"Tell us, Mitka, how did you end up in this forest on such a cold night?"

"I'm from the village of Krasnovka, in Volhynia," the boy began.

"You're from Volhynia? We're practically neighbors!" Lionka exclaimed. "I know where Krasnovka is. How long have you been away from there?"

The boy explained that he had escaped from the village early the previous spring—right after his parents, his little sister, and many other peasants had been shot in retaliation for the burning of a German grain warehouse. He had run away to the forest, where he had survived the summer by eating mushrooms, wild berries, and potatoes that he had stolen from peasant gardens. In the autumn, when the cold rains had started to fall and he could no longer find anything to eat in the forest, he had gone into the nearest village and gotten a job as a shepherd for a wealthy peasant. The landowner had treated the boy well, but his wife had been a very cruel woman who had repeatedly beaten the boy for the smallest of infractions.

Once, after a wolf had dragged away one of the sheep the boy was tending, the landowner's wife had beaten him almost to death. He had decided to run away, and his only friend—a fourteen-year-old servant named Dasha—had urged him to join the partisans. One night, when the landowner and his wife were at church, the boy had taken a sack of bread that Dasha had prepared for him and had fled to the forest, but not before setting fire to the landowner's home. He had spent the last three days roaming the forest, looking for partisans.

"You're quite the partisan yourself!" Lionka exclaimed. "And what do you have in that box?"

"That's my violin!"

"You must be the son of a rich peasant if you were taught to play the violin!"

"No, my parents were very poor. But I spent a couple of years in our landlord's palace, where I was taken in to play with the landowner's sick son. The teacher who taught music to the landlord's children noticed my talent and taught me to play as well."

"I like you, Mitka!" Lionka declared. "We'll take you with us. You'll be in Uncle Misha's Jewish Partisan Detachment.

"But aren't you afraid of being around Jews? In Volhynia, the Ukrainian children are scared of being called *zhids*," Lionka continued, invoking a Russian epithet for Jews.

"I'm not afraid of Jews," the boy responded, turning his head to the side and wiping away a tear with his sleeve. "They're people, just like everyone else."

AFTER ABANDONING THE camp near Antonovka, the 1st Stalin Partisan Detachment had established a new base camp roughly three miles east of Luben, a village eighteen miles southwest of Naroulia. When a unit of Hungarian troops arrived in Luben, Uncle Misha grew concerned. The majority of the partisans were away on various assignments, leaving behind only forty partisans to guard the camp, along with the Supply Squad and a few partisans who were sick and wounded.

Uncle Misha dispatched Mitka to find out how many Hungarians there were, how well they were armed, and what they were doing in Luben. Barefoot and dressed in short linen pants, with a bag over his shoulder and a long whip in his hand, the boy easily passed for a shepherd.

"What are you going to say if someone stops you and asks who you are?" Uncle Misha asked.

"I'll say that I'm from the village of Khrystynivka," Mitka responded quickly. "And that I'm looking for a white cow, with red spots and a broken right horn, that separated from the herd and headed toward Luben."

A few hours later, the boy came running back to the camp, sweaty and beaming with joy. He related to the partisans that he had walked into the village without anyone noticing him. In the middle of the village, he saw six large German wagons. Beside the wagons, under an old pear tree, there was a field kitchen on a two-wheeled cart. A fat cook was sitting on a bench next to the tree, reading a newspaper. Despite the language barrier, Mitka earned the Hungarian cook's trust by helping him chop wood and stir the soup. When the cook had fallen asleep, the boy had stolen his pistol.

"Come, Lionka," the boy cried excitedly, triumphantly pulling a Belgian Colt from his bag. "You can teach me to shoot on the other side of the swamp!"

"Hold off on learning to shoot!" Uncle Misha ordered. "You haven't reported to me what you saw during your reconnaissance mission. After all, I sent you to Luben to find out how many Hungarians are there and how they're armed, not to steal pistols from sleeping cooks."

Mitka's face turned red with anger. "I told you that there are six wagons," he retorted. "Assuming that a maximum of five of them travel on each wagon, there are thirty Hungarians there. The cook is the thirty-first, and the groom makes thirty-two.

There can't be more, because the Hungarians aren't partisans who travel ten to a wagon.

"They only have one heavy machine gun, similar to our Maxim," he continued. "I saw it sitting on a wagon, covered with a green camouflage net. Judging from the new German sacks with painted swastikas I saw on one of the wagons, it looks like they came to Luben to confiscate grain."

An hour later, acting on the intelligence Mitka had gathered, Uncle Misha's Jewish Group carried out an attack on Luben. They killed thirty Hungarians and took the wagons. When Timke the Cook whipped up some soup in the looted field kitchen for the first time, Mitka stood next to him, proudly showing him how to use the pressure cooker.

NOW THAT MITKA had proved to be adept at espionage, Uncle Misha dispatched him on a sabotage mission similar to the one they had devised for Moshe "Popov" Milrod in Aleksandrovka. Popov had been a pyrotechnician before the war. As a partisan, he had established himself as the Jewish Group's chief bomb-maker. Popov had assembled a team of partisans who would scavenge unexploded mines and ordnances that he would carefully disassemble to create new bombs. He was particularly fond of building what he called "presents"—mines specially rigged to be triggered by the Germans.

On a sunny spring morning, an old peasant cart traveled down a forest path leading to the village of Bielki. The cart was loaded with large linen bran sacks. The emaciated, mangy horse pulling the cart stopped after every couple of steps. It was trembling with every heavy breath.

Mitka sat on top of the sacks, using his long whip to repeatedly beat the horse across its bony body. He prodded the horse along, cursing at it with Polesian epithets. As soon as he started glimpsing houses through the century-old oaks and pines that formed a green wall around the village, Mitka let the horse take a quick break. He climbed down from the cart, took out a large wrench from under a sack, and unscrewed the nut that was securing the right wheel. Looking around to make sure nobody was watching, he tossed the nut into the bushes and drove off.

Between the boy's frantic shouting, the cracking of the whip, and the loud screeching of ungreased wheels, the cart made a loud entrance. It rolled noisily into the village and past the squat peasant huts with straw roofs that lined the street. The cart made its way to the middle of the village, where a large wooden house with a glass front porch stood on a high brick foundation. The building housed a strong police force, with forty Ukrainian auxiliary policemen and six German military policemen stationed there.

When the boy reached the police station, he stopped whipping the horse. The exhausted animal understood this to be permission to halt. It stood there with its head bowed down.

"Move!" Mitka wailed. "Go!" But the horse did not budge.

Hearing the boy's desperate cries, six Ukrainian auxiliary policemen came out of the station. They observed with curiosity the dilapidated cart, the mangy horse, and the boy in tattered clothes. The clean-shaven face of a well-fed German military policeman appeared in one of the windows. He broke out in laughter and called over a fellow military policeman to take a look at the dumb Ukrainian's primitive transportation.

The boy climbed down from the cart and inspected the right wheel.

"I lost the wheel nut!" he exclaimed in a heartrending cry. He started hitting himself in the head. "What am I going to do now? My stepfather is going to kill me!"

The policemen stood there, laughing at the pathetic peasant boy.

"All of the nuts were still there just a little way back in the forest," the boy kept crying. "How am I going to go on?

"Please, sir, hold my horse for a few minutes," the boy asked, handing the reins to one of the policemen. "I'll go look for the nut." He started walking back down the road with his head bent down. He kept squatting down and combing through the dirt with his hand, pretending to be searching for the wheel nut.

When the forest became dense again, he quickly turned off the road and started running as fast as he could. After sprinting for about five hundred yards, he stopped, put two fingers in his mouth, and whistled loudly. One long whistle, followed by two short whistles and another long one—the signal Lionka and Mitka used whenever they got separated. An identical whistle responded nearby, and Lionka and two other partisans emerged from the forest.

"Did you deliver the present?" Lionka asked.

"I delivered it not only to the police station, but also to six Ukrainian auxiliary policemen and two German military policemen who were guarding it," Mitka bragged. "Oh, how I fooled them!"

An informant in the village later told Uncle Misha that after Mitka had wandered off, the policemen had stood next to the cart for a long time, cracking jokes about the mangy horse and the foolish driver. When the boy did not return, they decided to bring the horse and cart into the courtyard of the police station. But neither loud shouts nor heavy blows to its mangy rump could convince the horse to do anything but stubbornly flick its balding tail. One of the policemen concluded that it would be easier to get the horse to move if they reduced the amount of weight it was carrying, and started removing the sacks of bran from the cart. He had taken off two sacks and had just grabbed a third one when there was a big explosion. Popov had placed a mine and a detonator at the bottom of the cart, and had tied the safety pin to the sack that the policeman had just yanked.

The explosion took out the sacks, the cart, and the horse, along with four of the Ukrainian auxiliary policemen. The other two were severely wounded by shrapnel from the cart. They fell to the ground and started thrashing about in agony. The German military policeman in the window was hit by a piece of wood that gouged out one of his eyes and knocked out all of his teeth.

As the peasants came running out of their houses, the air filled with slips of white paper that had filled the sacks under thin layers of bran. The paper floated gently back down, covering the road, the rooftops, and the yards like fresh snow. Some of the peasants picked up the pieces of paper, read them, and cautiously slipped them into their pockets. They were leaflets that the Soviets had airdropped a few nights earlier, reporting on massive German defeats on the Eastern Front.

The Red Army's victory in the Battle of Stalingrad a few weeks earlier had signaled a major turning point in the war, both militarily and psychologically, and the Soviets were eager to capitalize on the success through printed propaganda. The leaflets, which spread across the ground, warned the Ukrainians who were collaborating with the German occupiers to cease their traitorous activities. The Red Army was advancing, and their Day of Judgment was looming.

THROUGHOUT THE SPRING, the partisans kept hearing stories of entire police forces abandoning their posts and joining the partisans in the forest, like rats fleeing a sinking ship. The Red Army was gaining the upper hand in the war, and the local policemen knew that they would soon have to answer for having collaborated with the Germans. They hoped to whitewash their crimes by joining the partisans.

When an informant told Uncle Misha that a large group of policemen in Ovruch was prepared to surrender themselves and their weapons to the partisans, he decided to dispatch several partisans to the city as spies. He wanted them to infiltrate the townspeople and find out what the military government was up to. He was also toying with the idea of staging an assault on Ovruch, to blow up the train station, along with the bridge on the main highway that ran through the city.

Uncle Misha sent Mitka along with the spies, to keep an eye on them from afar and report back immediately, should anything happen to them. Mitka would pose as a street performer who was passing through Ovruch on his way to the city of Zhytomyr, where he had heard his father was being held in a prisoner-of-war camp. Mitka left the partisan camp with his violin and paperwork that had been masterfully forged by a partisan who had been a stampmaker, showing that he was Dmitry Rubina, the son of Ivan Rubina, from the village of Lystvyn, a town less than twenty miles west of Ovruch.

When Mitka got into town, he purchased a clay bowl from the local market and walked over to Saint Basil's Convent. Taking his place alongside two rows of beggars and buskers in front of the entrance to the church courtyard, he sat down with the bowl between his legs. He took out his violin and started singing and playing one of the Ukrainian songs he had learned while growing up in Krasnovka.

Despite Mitka's attempts to blend in, the talented boy was no ordinary street performer, and a crowd gathered around him. When he finished his first song, they threw coins into his bowl.

As Mitka continued to perform, he became so engrossed with singing and playing that he did not notice a commotion in the crowd. People started jostling each other to make way for a German officer. After listening to the boy for a few minutes, the officer tapped Mitka on the shoulder with his walking stick to get his attention. Seeing the officer's uniform, Mitka jumped to his feet and gave a reverential bow.

"Come with me," the officer commanded in German.

Mitka felt his breast pocket to make sure he still had his forged documents. He calmly returned the violin to its case, retrieved the coins from the little bowl, and left with the officer.

After walking down several blocks, they arrived at a one-story building guarded by a German soldier and flanked by several limousines and motorcycles. They walked up a short flight of stairs and entered a large, brightly lit canteen, where German officers were eating, drinking, and talking loudly. In one corner, an elderly gentleman with long gray hair and a black tuxedo sat at a piano. The officer led Mitka to the pianist and exchanged a few words with him.

"Can you read music?" the pianist asked the boy in Russian.

"Yes."

The pianist selected Ignacy Jan Paderewski's Minuet in G major from a pile of sheet music lying on the piano and placed it in front of Mitka as a test. The old man listened attentively as Mitka started to play. He accompanied quietly, at first playing only the bass line and harmony in his left hand, and then adding his right hand once he grew confident in the boy's abilities. As they played, the canteen grew quieter and quieter, until everyone had stopped talking to hear the music. When the minuet was over, the room resounded with applause.

Smiling warmly, the German officer offered Mitka a job playing at the canteen for two hours at lunchtime and from seven to eleven in the evenings. Sticking to his cover story, Mitka replied that he had to keep searching for his father. He had left a sick mother and three younger siblings at home, he explained, and he was the only breadwinner. The officer promised to write to the commandant in Zhytomyr. If the boy's father was indeed in the prisoner-of-war camp there, he would be transferred to Ovruch. Mitka had no choice but to accept the position.

Mitka immediately went to Uncle Misha's informant Keril and asked him to tell Uncle Misha what had happened. The partisan commander responded with an order for Mitka to stay in Ovruch and report everything he saw through Keril.

———

THE CANTEEN WAS one of many restaurants that the Germans had commandeered on the road to the Eastern Front. It was a place where soldiers could pay next to nothing for gourmet food and French wine, served to them by pretty Ukrainian waitresses. As Mitka entertained the guests, he took note of the sizes of the units and the types of uniforms worn by the soldiers on their way to the front. He eavesdropped on the conversations of the few who returned. During his afternoon breaks, he walked the streets of Ovruch, reading the notices posted by the military administration and noting what was happening on the streets. He passed on to Uncle Misha everything he read and heard through Keril.

Over the next several weeks, Mitka became something of a fixture at the canteen. The commandant who dined there every evening went so far as to have an army tailor sew, out of the same material as German uniforms, a pair of pants, a jacket, and a side cap for the young violinist. The pianist and the rest of the canteen staff were delighted when Mitka arrived a few days later dressed as a little German soldier.

Mitka received two reichsmarks a day for playing at the canteen, plus lunch and dinner in the basement kitchen. One day, after eating his lunch, he peered down a dark hallway and noticed a door that had been left open. Out of curiosity, he peeked inside. By the dim light coming from a small grated window, he saw a large cellar packed with empty wine cases, old herring barrels, and other discarded restaurant supplies piled in disarray. There was a crack climbing up the wall across from the door, presumably damage from a bomb exploding nearby during the German occupation.

Mitka, who had always listened with rapt attention to the partisans' stories of heroic sabotage missions, stopped dead in his tracks. He realized that if he could plant a bomb in the crack, he could demolish the building with the Germans inside. Mitka was instantly obsessed with the scheme. Every time he walked down the hallway, he would peek into the cellar and imagine avenging the murders of his parents and little sister with a sabotage mission of his very own.

Mitka passed his idea along to Keril. Uncle Misha approved the plan, and assigned Popov to go over all the details with Mitka. The bombmaker met with the boy at a rendezvous point a little over three miles away. He quizzed Mitka on details, such as the thickness of the walls, whether they were made of brick or stone, and how much time the boy would need to escape. Popov calculated that the mission would require forty pounds of TNT.

When they met again a few days later, Popov brought a sack of TNT and taught Mitka how to assemble the explosives. Mitka had watched Popov show other partisans how to make mines, and was a quick study.

Mitka had a plan for smuggling the explosives into the canteen. Every night for the next several evenings, after finishing his dinner and saying good night to the cook, he crept down the hallway with his violin in its case. He darted into the cellar, hid the instrument in a barrel, and calmly walked out of the canteen with an empty violin case. The next day, he returned to the basement for his lunch—with a few pounds of TNT hidden inside the case. He ducked back into the cellar and swapped the explosives for his violin. After taking several days to sneak all forty pounds of TNT into the cellar, he slipped back in a few times to remove several stones from the wall to make a larger nest for the mine. He assembled the TNT as Popov had taught him, inserted a detonator with a long fuse, and hid everything behind some old wine cases and herring barrels.

Mitka and Keril used every spare moment to finalize the details of the mission. Every day, they would visit the river that runs along the south of Ovruch. They would act as if they were going there to fish or bathe, but they were secretly planning the escape route that Mitka would take after the explosion. They figured out which streets and orchards he would pass through on his way to the river and found a spot where the river was shallow enough for the boy to cross.

A FEW DAYS after planting the explosives, Mitka reported to the canteen to find it buzzing with the news that a division of the SS would be coming through town. The partisans had been so successful in disrupting rail travel that the division had been transferred from railcars to cargo trucks, cars, and motorcycles in Korosten, and was now heading toward Ovruch on their way to the Eastern Front. The quartermasters had already arranged housing for the night, and the officers would be eating dinner in the canteen.

SS officers started arriving at the canteen in their formal dress uniforms at three in the afternoon. The dining hall was soon filled with the sounds of loud laughter, the clinking of wineglasses, the tinkling of dishes, and, loudest of all, Mitka playing his violin, to the accompaniment of the piano. Thoroughly enjoying themselves, the officers sang along to the music. From time to time, the howls and singing were interrupted by the shrieks of the Ukrainian waitresses who were subjected to the officers' indecent behavior.

As the evening wore on, the Germans requested tangos and waltzes to which they danced. Drunken officers would stagger over to the musicians and demand that they play their favorite song. One officer sat at a table shouting wildly, "Fiddler, play 'Volga, Volga.'" Standing in the middle of the dining hall and hugging a bottle of cognac, another swayed back and forth while tearfully singing the nineteenth-century German ballad "Forest Joy": "'My father doesn't know me, my mother doesn't love me, and I don't want to die; I'm still so young.'"

By ten o'clock, Mitka's fingers ached from so much nonstop playing. His eyes stung from the cigar smoke. "I'm playing for you for the last time," he thought, as he smiled at his drunken audience every time they applauded. "Eat, drink, and be merry, you damned Germans. These are your final hours. Tonight I'm going to play you a song that will blow you to bits while dancing."

At eleven, the elderly pianist convinced the canteen manager to allow the musicians to retire for the evening. German officers who could play the piano took over, and the merriment roared on. As usual, Mitka went down to the basement after his shift for his dinner, but he was too nervous to eat. As an excuse, he told the cook that he was exhausted after playing for eight hours straight, and would just head home.

But, instead, he tiptoed into the cellar and quietly closed the door behind him. Sneaking around in the darkness, he located the fuse and ignited it. His heart pounded as he ran out of the cellar and down the hallway. Slowing to a walk as he calmly approached the German soldier guarding the canteen entrance, he stretched out his right arm in the Nazi salute and shouted a sarcastic "Heil, Hitler!"

The guard, familiar with the affable young violinist, laughed and retorted, "*Ach*, you little Ukrainian swine." And Mitka vanished into the darkness.

After running for two hundred feet, he felt the ground shake. He heard a loud explosion behind him, quickly followed by windows shattering in nearby houses. A few moments later, the air filled with the sounds of police whistles and sirens. Three flares went up, illuminating the city in bloodred light. Pressing his body against walls to hide from view, Mitka made his way toward the river and plunged in, holding his violin above his head with both hands to protect it from the cold water, which reached all the way to his neck. When he reached the middle of the river, he looked back and saw a great fire engulfing the city.

When Mitka reached the other side of the river, five partisans pulled him into a wagon. The horses took off in a wild gallop, and the partisans quickly disappeared into the dark forest.

For several moments, Mitka was silent, stunned by the over-whelming success of his mission. Then, raising a clenched fist to the red sky, he proclaimed in a trembling voice, "That is for my parents and my little sister."

CHAPTER 11

"Never Say That You Have Reached the End of the Road"

Never say that you have reached the end of the road,
Though leaden skies blot out the light of day.
The hour that we have been longing for will indeed
    come,
When our steps will beat out: "We are here!"

—HIRSH GLIK, "NEVER SAY THAT YOU HAVE
REACHED THE END OF THE ROAD"

SEVERAL MEMBERS OF UNCLE MISHA'S Jewish Group were relaxing on a hillside, enjoying the sunny spring day. Boris Goldfarb was lying on his back, staring up at the blue sky. "Mottel of Berezhnytsia" and "Sasha of Odessa" were arguing, as they often did, over whether the world would recognize the Jewish claim to the Land of Israel after the war. Sasha contested that Jews would be able to restart their lives wherever they ended up. This angered Mottel, who felt strongly that a nation without a state is no nation at all.

Mottel never missed an opportunity to express his regret over not having immigrated to the Land of Israel before the war.

He never forgave his parents for having discouraged him from leaving. They ended up in a mass grave on the outskirts of Sarny; he ended up in the forest. But Mottel was proud that he had become a partisan and was taking revenge on the Germans, and he never lost hope that he would someday reach the land of his biblical ancestors.

All of a sudden, everyone was distracted by the honking of wild geese flying overhead, in formation on their way back from warmer climates. Two geese flew high in the sky, making large circles over the forest.

Lionka followed their flight attentively. "They'll find their nest soon," he said with a sigh. "Even they have a home." Everyone fell silent.

The wistful mood was interrupted by the arrival of Zaidel Green, who was returning from an assignment with Ivan Shitov's Khrushchev Partisan Detachment. Holding a submachine gun in one hand and a slice of bread in the other, Zaidel sat down next to Uncle Misha.

"Uncle Misha," he said. "I have some interesting news for you." While he was with Shitov's partisan detachment, Zaidel had learned that the Jews in the Warsaw ghetto had launched an uprising.

The Germans had entered the Warsaw ghetto in January 1943 to transport thousands of Jews to labor camps. After encountering resistance, they had reentered the ghetto on April 19 with two thousand soldiers and policemen, supported by tanks and artillery. The Jews were fighting back with pistols, a few rifles and automatic weapons, and homemade grenades. What the Jews lacked in weaponry and military training, they were making up for in courage, engaging in guerrilla warfare and fighting in hand-to-hand combat. They were familiar with every inch of the ghetto, and were able to strike quickly before disappearing into underground tunnels and bunkers. They were fighting valiantly, knowing full well that they had little chance of survival.

In the end, the German military would indeed overpower the Jews. The Germans would advance through the ghetto, block by block, razing buildings to the ground along the way. At least seven thousand Jews would be killed, and another seven thousand would be captured and sent to the Treblinka killing center. Approximately 42,000 would be deported to labor camps or the Majdanek concentration camp. By May 16, what had once been Warsaw's Jewish Quarter would be in ruins.

Uncle Misha had Zaidel repeat the story to the entire unit, who listened with great interest. "A fierce battle is raging in the Warsaw ghetto. The youth have organized themselves and are putting up a valiant resistance. The Germans are fighting back with every weapon at their disposal. The ghetto is burning from all sides. But in the flames of the fires, under the hail of artillery shells, the Jews of Warsaw are defending themselves heroically in the ghetto," he informed them. "The Jews know that they have no chance of winning the battle, but they keep fighting, because they have nothing to lose."

"The Warsaw ghetto fighters have awakened the spirit of the Maccabees!" Boris exclaimed. "They're fighting not for victory, but for the honor of the Jewish nation."

"It's too bad that Warsaw is so far away," Lionka remarked. "We could have helped them with weapons and ammunition, now that we have such a large supply." By then, the partisans had such a large stockpile that they had hidden weapons underground in several places.

"What can we do to help our heroic brothers and sisters in Warsaw?" "David of Yarevysche" asked.

"We can't help them directly," Uncle Misha replied. The best way to respond would be to keep fighting. "This will be how we express our solidarity with the ghetto fighters: an act of revenge for those who have fallen in this war of the few against the many."

———————

UNCLE MISHA'S JEWISH Group was not alone in being galvanized by the news of the uprising in Warsaw. As soon as the fighting started, a report was broadcast by the radio station of the Polish underground resistance movement.

"Hello! Hello!" the dispatch announced. "The remaining Jews in the Warsaw ghetto have started an armed resistance against the Nazis. The ghetto is in flames!"

There was no information beyond those few lines, but the Jewish partisans in the Vilna ghetto, some 250 miles northeast of Warsaw, were immediately inspired by their brothers and sisters who had taken up arms in defense of Jewish honor. "The news of the uprising lifted our spirits and made us proud," partisan and musician Shmerke Kaczerginski later recalled. "We felt as if we had grown wings."

On May 1, as a surreptitious celebration of May Day, the Jews of the Vilna ghetto organized a cultural evening around the theme "Springtime in Yiddish Literature." Every speech and every song was infused with the excitement over the uprising in Warsaw. "As we celebrate this first of May as a community, the Warsaw ghetto is engaged in combat. Glory to the fighters! Glory to the fallen!" the evening's host called out as the hundreds in attendance rose as one.

At one point in the evening, partisan-poet Hirsh Glick quietly walked up to Shmerke.

"Well, what's going on with you, Hirsh?" Shmerke asked.

"I've written a new poem. Would you like to hear it?"

"Right now? Okay, read it!"

"Not now. I'll come by tomorrow morning," Hirsh responded, adding, "It's a poem to be sung."

Bright and early the next morning, Hirsh paid Shmerke a visit. "Listen closely," Hirsh said. "Here it goes."

Hirsh started singing, quietly at first, but his voice grew stronger as he continued. His eyes twinkled and one foot stamped along, as if he were marching as he sang the words he had written to a prewar Soviet melody. The first and final verses urge Jewish fighters never to give up, regardless of how dire the situation has become. "The hour that we have been longing for will indeed come," the song promises. "When our steps will beat out: 'We are here!'"

Hirsh's song "Never Say That You Have Reached the End of the Road" spread like wildfire to other ghettos, to the labor and concentration camps, and even to partisan detachments in the forest. The "Partisan Song," as it came to be known, served as a great inspiration to Jews who were resisting the Nazis.

"In moments when it seemed as if the single, inevitable conclusion was death, the words of our young partisan-poet Hirsh Glick resonated in our souls," Shmerke would later write. "We sang. Even if we sang a sad tune, the sadness fostered hate and rage within us—healthy feelings that called for action, for revenge!"

UNCLE MISHA WAS on the editorial staff of the 1st Stalin Partisan Detachment's magazine, *Stalinets*. The first issue had been published on February 23, 1943—the Red Army's twenty-fifth anniversary—and had been read with great interest by partisans in not only the 1st Stalin Partisan Detachment, but also other detachments in the area.

The second issue of *Stalinets*, published on May Day, was even more popular. It was even reviewed in the Moscow newspaper *Labor*, earning the detachment a letter of congratulations from Timofei Strokach, the head of the Ukrainian Staff of the Partisan Movement. The issue includes three articles by Uncle Misha. The first, titled "The Misfortune of First Lieutenant Knot," is a farcical story about a bungling German police chief who tried unsuccessfully to take on the partisans. The third is an interview with a partisan named Tadeusz Ciechanowski, who had joined the detachment two weeks earlier, about his recent experiences in Lviv.

The second article, titled "Revenge," tells the story of a peasant boy named Iliusha Gusevik, which is obviously a pseudonym
for Mitka. Iliusha's father was hanged by the Germans for having been the kolkhoz chairman, but the rest of Iliusha's family
was murdered after the German granary mysteriously burned
down, just as Mitka had told Lionka when they first met. From
then on, Iliusha's story is identical to Mitka's. Iliusha escapes to
the forest, where the partisans discover him sleeping. A few
months later, Iliusha infiltrates a town anonymized simply as
"R," where he is hired to play the violin at a German canteen. He
sneaks TNT into the canteen in his violin case, and detonates the
explosives during a visit of the SS division staff.

Uncle Misha anonymized as much as he could about the
identity of the protagonist, apparently out of concern that
Mitka could be captured by Germans and connected to the
bombing. In addition to also masking the location, he obscured
the date, suggesting that it had taken place the previous August
or September. In a brief epilogue, Uncle Misha even claimed that
the boy was in a different detachment, and that he had only met
him long enough to hear his story before they parted ways.

ON JUNE 7, 1943, Uncle Misha looked at the primitive calendar
he had kept with him since leaving Korets and noted that the
next day would be the Eve of Shavuot. This would mark the first
anniversary of the Aktion in which his wife, Golda, and their
daughter, Feigela, had been murdered.

He thought back to that day, when crazed Nazis had broken
down his door and led him and his family to the local administration building. He could still see the sadistic faces of the murderers.
He could still hear their wild screams, as well as the sounds of sav-
age beatings and the heart-wrenching cries of men, women, and
children. He remembered Golda and Feigela being led away, and
the peasant carts later returning, filled with the clothes of the
Jews who had been murdered. He would never forget the mo-

ment when he, his son, and his nephew had recognized the coats Golda and Feigela had been wearing just hours earlier.

Now, a year later, he was the leader of a successful partisan unit. He was sitting on a tree root in a thick forest, surrounded by his sisters- and brothers-in-arms. Some of the partisans were singing to themselves while cleaning their weapons. Others were talking to each other. The sound of their murmuring was occasionally punctuated by carefree laughter. Everyone seemed so calm and happy. Their spirits were lifted by the sunny day in the beautiful green forest.

His thoughts were interrupted by joyous shouts coming from all around him. "The circus is here! The circus is here!"

Mitka rode into the clearing in the middle of the camp on Lionka's horse, Ginger. Mitka was wobbling from side to side on Ginger's back, while holding the horse's mane in his left hand. Lionka was walking in front of them with his sleeves rolled up and holding a long whip.

Uncle Misha had often reflected on the strong bond that had formed between the two boys. Mitka, in particular, had grown quite attached to Lionka. At the same time, Uncle Misha could not shake the feeling that Mitka was hiding something from them. The boy seemed too sophisticated to have been raised by peasants. When Uncle Misha had shared his suspicions with his son, Lionka had waived him off, noting that Ukrainians could be very smart, and theorizing that Mitka had received an education during the years he had spent living in his landlord's home, when he had also been taught to play the violin.

All of the partisans gathered around Lionka and Mitka. Even Timke the Cook left his simmering pot and walked over with a large ladle in his hand.

Lionka stood in front of the horse. He cracked his whip twice and commanded, "Ginger! *Révérence!*" He tapped Ginger's feet with the handle of his whip, and the horse responded by bowing, lowering one knee to the ground. Mitka lost his balance and toppled over the horse's head. He sprang back to his feet and was sitting on the horse again within the blink of an eye.

"Now rear up!" Lionka ordered. The horse stomped its front right foot, flicked its ears, and finally raised his front legs in the air. As Ginger stood on its hind legs, Mitka held on to its neck with both hands and laughed loudly. The partisans around them applauded and shouted, "Bravo!"

"And now, for our final number," Lionka announced, raising his hands into the air, "Ginger will root out a German spy!"

Ginger stuck his thin muzzle into the pocket of Lionka's coat. He pulled out a piece of dry bread and started to chew it.

"Keep searching!" Lionka commanded, lining up his other pocket underneath the horse's muzzle. Ginger nuzzled in and came back out with a piece of paper that had been folded in quarters. He held the paper in his mouth.

"Ginger asks that someone read this German document to him, because he hasn't yet learned how to read," Lionka joked.

"If you were able to teach him all these tricks," one of the partisans remarked, "you should also be able to teach him to read German."

"When I teach him how to read, I'll make him the editor of the *Khabno News*," Lionka responded. The *Khabno News* was a Nazi propaganda newspaper. "He's smarter than the current editor, and does everything I order him to do, just like that editor writes everything the Nazis tell him to write."

The partisans were delighted with the joke, and overjoyed by the entire skit.

"The circus is over!" Lionka declared as the partisans applauded loudly.

A FEW MINUTES later, Lionka and Mitka walked up to Uncle Misha. "You know what, Papa?" Lionka asked. "We've decided that if we survive this war, we're going to ride Ginger to Moscow and introduce ourselves to Voroshilov." Kliment Voroshilov was the commander in chief of the Central Staff of the Partisan Movement.

Noting his father's somber face, he quickly asked, "Why are you so sad?"

"Tomorrow is the Eve of Shavuot," Uncle Misha answered quietly.

Lionka's face immediately darkened. He lowered himself to the grass and sat next to his father. He gazed off into the distance, mindlessly tapping his boots with the handle of his whip as he relived that horrific day.

"I've decided to pray publicly, and recite the Kaddish," Uncle Misha informed his son. "We'll gather in the pine forest on the other side of the swamp. Find some wax and make a few candles. I'll gather a minyan." Jewish custom requires a minyan—a quorum of at least ten men—for public prayer.

The rays of the setting sun were still glistening in the tops of the tall pine trees when twelve Jewish partisans, with rifles on their shoulders and grenades hanging from their belts, left the camp. Following a narrow path that wound between the trees, they headed toward the large swamp. As they walked down the path, Uncle Misha glanced over his shoulder and saw that Mitka was following them.

"Go back to the camp," he ordered. "We're going to go pray."

"What holiday is it?" the boy asked.

"Today marks a year since the Germans murdered our family members."

"My family was killed by the Germans, too," the boy reminded him.

"But we're Jews, and we're going to pray to our God."

"My father taught me that everyone has the same God. I won't bother you. Please let me come with you."

Uncle Misha relented.

By the time the partisans arrived on the other side of the swamp, the sun had already set, and darkness had fallen over the forest. They set the candles in two rows on the wide trunk of a fallen tree and lit them.

David of Yarevysche pulled a prayer book out of his leather satchel. As he read the evening prayer service, everyone repeated the words quietly. They all thought back to their hometowns. They recalled the moments that their neighbors, friends, and family members had been violently murdered.

At the end of the service, everyone said the Kaddish, fighting back their tears. After they recited the last line, "May He bring peace to us and to all of Israel, and let us say Amen," they heard a high-pitched voice behind them, slowly repeating the Hebrew words. They turned to find Mitka standing there, large tears rolling down his cheeks, holding his own prayer book. They stared in astonishment as the boy ran up to Uncle Misha, wrapped his arms around the partisan commander's neck, and tearfully cried, "Uncle Misha, I'm Jewish, too!"

As the boy would share with the partisans that night, his life had closely resembled the story he had told Lionka when they had first met. He was indeed from Krasnovka, a village in Volhynia that was less than twenty-five miles away from Korets. But he was not the son of ethnic Ukrainians, as he had led the partisans to believe, but of Jewish miller Burtzik Schlein and his wife, Chana. After the Germans had murdered his parents and his little sister, Batyale, the previous summer, the boy had escaped to the forest, taking with him his father's prayer book and his most prized possession: his violin.

The boy's story about spending the summer in the forest was true, as was his tale of being hired as a shepherd by a kindly landowner and his wicked wife. That winter, after finding the boy's prayer book, the landowner's wife had made plans for their son, who was a Ukrainian auxiliary policeman, to interrogate the boy the next day to determine whether he was Jewish. That night, after the landowner and his family had left for church, the boy had set their home on fire and had run off. Three days later, Lionka had discovered him sleeping in the forest.

Now that he knew Mitka was Jewish, Uncle Misha finally understood how the boy had developed such a strong bond with Lionka. What Uncle Misha could not figure out was why the boy had kept his Jewishness a secret for so long. After all, the partisan unit included many Jews, its leaders were all Jewish, and it even went by the name Uncle Misha's Jewish Group.

Lionka felt betrayed that his young friend had not trusted him enough to share such an important detail. "First of all, tell me what your Jewish name is," he demanded. "And second of all, why didn't you tell me that you're Jewish? Do you think it's better to be a Ukrainian?"

"My real name is Motele, and I want you to call me that from now on," the boy replied. "And I didn't tell you that I'm Jewish because ever since the first day the Germans arrived, I've lived through so much as a Jew that even among friends I felt safer as a non-Jew. Also, it seemed to me that I would have more opportunities as a Ukrainian to avenge the murders of my parents and my little sister."

WHEN BORIS GOLDFARB opened his eyes, he was lying on the floor of a large, unfurnished room.

"Where am I?" he wondered.

His eyes scanned the room's gray walls, finally stopping on a portrait of Hitler that hung in an ornate frame. Two menacing, evil eyes stared back at him.

Thinking that he might be dreaming, Boris closed his eyes again. He felt a dull pain in his left hand. When he tried to sit up, he found that his hands and feet were bound. "I'm being held captive by the Germans!" he realized. He could not recall how he had gotten there.

As he wracked his brain, scattered flashbacks started to emerge from the fog of his memory. The partisans were cautiously leaving the forest, scampering across a road toward a stack of felled trees on the other side. They heard gunshots coming from behind them, but by then they had already taken up defensive positions behind the log pile. The Germans kept coming closer, growing more aggressive by the minute. Boris, who was leading the squad, instructed the partisans to shoot sparingly, as they were running low on bullets. Just as Boris was giving an order for the partisans to ready their grenades, the Germans jumped out from behind the trees and started running across the road to attack the partisans.

The partisans threw their grenades and raced through a field toward another log pile, behind which loomed the dense forest. Boris was bringing up the rear. All that separated him from safety was a large oak lying on the ground. He slowed down to climb over it. Just as he had thrown one leg over the felled tree, he felt a sharp pain in his left hand.

That was the last thing he remembered. The partisans must not have realized he was injured. Otherwise, they would have never left him behind to be captured.

Boris's thoughts were interrupted by the sound of heavy footsteps. A German military policeman holding a submachine gun walked over and stared at him for a few seconds. Seeing that Boris was awake, he smirked, made an about-face, and left the room.

A few minutes later, a German officer entered the room with a young woman and two armed military policemen. The woman had a pale, kind face. Her almond-shaped eyes looked at him with compassion. The officer was tall and bony, with a long, narrow face and piercing gray eyes.

"Untie him!" the officer commanded. The military policemen stood Boris up and freed his hands and feet.

"Ask him what his name is," the officer instructed the woman in German. She translated the question into Ukrainian.

Boris did not respond.

"Whose detachment is he in?" came the second question.

Boris did not respond.

"Tell him," the officer said, turning to the interpreter, "that I have other ways of making him talk."

Boris remained silent.

"You're still young. You can and should stay alive, and contribute to your people. You let yourself be misled by the Judeo-Communists who wanted to turn your Ukraine into a testing ground for Stalin's wild ideas," he addressed Boris through the interpreter. "Now our Führer has liberated your country from the Bolshevist plague, and with the help of your people, he'll establish an independent, sovereign state."

Boris smiled to himself. "He doesn't know that I'm Jewish," he realized. The officer assumed that Boris was a Soviet partisan.

"Lie back down," the officer continued. He turned back to the Ukrainian woman and ordered, "Have the nurse rebandage his wound, give him something to eat, and then bring him to my office for questioning."

After they left, Boris walked over to the window and peered out. The room was on the fourth floor of a brick building that looked like an old castle or monastery. A splendid orchard stretched as far as he could see. Tall German horses were grazing among the trees.

The interpreter returned with a young German nurse with expressionless gray eyes. Without saying a word, the nurse went over to Boris and took the bandages off his injured hand. Boris was glad to see that the wound was not too bad. The bullet had passed through the soft tissue without breaking any bones.

The Ukrainian woman held him by the elbow and gently rebandaged his hand. She made Boris feel at ease, and he was surprised that she was not triggering the contempt that partisans typically felt toward Ukrainians who collaborated with the Germans. They usually considered the *starostas*, the Ukrainians who ran the depots, and the interpreters to be even worse than the Germans.

A military policeman brought a bowl of soup and a large piece of bread. The sight of the food reminded Boris of how hungry he was, but he refused to touch it.

"Why aren't you eating?" the interpreter asked.

"I don't need food anymore," Boris answered bitterly. "I know that the only reason you want me to regain my strength is so I'll be able to endure the torture longer."

"Don't be so pessimistic," the woman whispered. "It could be that you need your strength not to endure the torture, but to avoid it."

"What did she mean by that?" Boris asked himself after the two women had left. The Ukrainian woman's kindness gave him a sliver of hope, but he quickly reminded himself that women often played a significant role in German interrogations. He could not let down his guard for someone who was likely a skilled German agent.

A FEW MINUTES later, two armed military policemen escorted Boris down a long corridor to a door marked MILITARY POLICE COMMANDANT. Inside, the officer from before sat behind a heavy oak desk covered with stacks of papers. Boris looked at the officer, and then at another large portrait of Hitler. There was a placard underneath it that read in Ukrainian: HITLER, THE LIBERATOR. At a small table to the side, the interpreter was nervously biting the tip of her pencil. When Boris caught her eye, she blushed and looked down.

Finally the commandant turned to the Ukrainian woman and said, "Ask him how he's feeling."

She translated the question into Ukrainian.

"I'm feeling strong enough to withstand your worst torture and still not betray my friends," Boris replied.

"He says that he's feeling much better, Herr Commandant," she answered in German. "And he thanks you for sending the nurse."

Boris, who was fluent in German, was dumbfounded.

"Tell him that if he answers all of my questions truthfully, I'll only hold him captive for a short time, and then I'll release him," the commandant continued.

Before the interpreter had the chance to translate, Boris cried out in Ukrainian, "Your words are all in vain! You can tear my flesh and break my bones, but remember this: An even worse fate awaits you in the near future!"

"What did he say?" asked the commandant.

"He says that he still feels very weak and exhausted. He asks that you let him rest for a day or two, and then he'll give you the information you want."

Boris wanted to exclaim that this was not at all what he had said, but an inner voice told him to hold his tongue. He looked at the Ukrainian woman in astonishment.

"I'll let him rest for a few days, but first he has to answer the following question," the commandant proposed. "Does he know which partisans were responsible for the bombing of the movie theater in Naroulia during the celebration of the second anniversary of the war?"

"Uncle Misha's partisan unit," Boris replied through the interpreter.

"Who are his contacts within the local population of Naroulia?"

"I don't know."

"Can you tell me where Uncle Misha's unit is now?"

Boris did not respond.

"Answer quickly!" the Ukrainian girl urged, turning to Boris. "It doesn't matter what you say, just say something.... Speak for your own sake.... Trust me, I'm your friend. I'll prove it to you later."

Boris remained silent.

The commandant sprang from his chair, ran over to Boris, and angrily slapped him twice in the face. Boris felt the room spinning. He staggered backward and blacked out. The military policemen caught him under his arms before he hit the floor.

When Boris regained consciousness a few minutes later, blood was streaming from his nose, down his jacket, and onto the polished parquet floor.

"I'll make you talk, you communist swine!" the commandant shouted.

"Why get so worked up, Herr Commandant? It's bad for your health," the interpreter coaxed in a friendly voice. "You know full well how stubborn these bandits can be. You won't get anything out of them through anger." Her gentle words managed to calm the officer's nerves. He sat back down with a guilty smile.

"I can't control myself when I see these wild forest dwellers who refuse to understand the good that the German Army brought them. Instead of helping us realize the grand plan of the new European order, they get in our way."

"They let themselves be provoked by communist agitators who mingle with the people and sow blind hatred toward their liberators," the interpreter added.

The telephone rang, interrupting their conversation. After a short exchange, the commandant put down the handset and turned to the interpreter. "All right," he conceded. "Arrange for a mattress and some food to be brought to his room. We'll resume the questioning tomorrow."

THAT NIGHT, BORIS was sleeping when the interpreter came into his room with an armed military policeman.

"Here. Take this blanket," she whispered. "Wait until we leave before unfolding it. Go to where the orchard ends. I'll be waiting there for you on the dirt road." She put a bundle on the mattress and left the room with the military policeman.

Boris reached down and grabbed the blanket. He was shocked to discover a pistol hidden inside the folds, along with rope and a knife. He quickly hid the knife and the rope under his mattress and put the pistol in his pocket.

"I can't even think about escaping until everyone's asleep," he told himself. To avoid suspicion, he lay back down on the mattress, covered himself with the blanket, and pretended to sleep. He lay motionless for a long time, listening carefully to everything around him.

When the time was right, he got up, tiptoed over to the window, and quietly opened it. He saw nothing but darkness. He tied one end of the rope to the window and started sliding down the wall, holding the rope with both hands. A few seconds later, he was lying in the moist grass.

He listened for a few moments. Everything was quiet. Nobody had noticed his escape.

He cut off a length of rope and started crawling toward the silhouette of a horse. He had grown up in a village, and knew his way around horses. He stood up and gave the horse a few friendly strokes on its neck. He fashioned a bridle out of the rope and cut the rope that was binding the horse's front legs. He cautiously led the obedient horse forward.

After a few minutes, he reached the edge of the orchard. He stopped and looked around. His eyes had acclimated to the darkness, and he was able to see his surroundings clearly. In front of him was a wide country road, and then a field, and on the other side of that was the forest.

Just as Boris was about to step out of the orchard, he noticed a shadow approaching from his right. He quickly drew his pistol and remained frozen in place, ready for anything. When the shadow came closer, he realized that it was a military policeman on patrol. As the patrolman walked in his direction, Boris saw a second figure appear from the darkness and start to follow the German.

The military policeman was just a few yards away from Boris when a loud whistle pierced the air. There was shouting from the direction of the brick building. A red illumination flare flew up in the sky.

"They figured out that I escaped," he realized. "I'm doomed."

The patrolman switched on a flashlight and started pointing it toward the orchard. Boris aimed his pistol at the German, but before he could pull the trigger, two shots rang out and the military policeman fell to the ground. The Ukrainian interpreter emerged from the shadows with a pistol in her hand. "Quick, let's get out of here," she urged nervously.

They helped each other onto the horse and cantered toward the forest. Riding in front, Boris wrapped his arms around the horse's neck and whistled for it to gallop. The interpreter wrapped her arms around him as they hurried away. After a few minutes, the woman asked, "What's your name, partisan?"

"Boris Goldfarb. I'm a saboteur from Uncle Misha's Jewish Group." It seemed to Boris that she trembled a bit as he said it, and clung to him even tighter.

Later, when they stopped to rest the horse, Boris took her by the hand and thanked her. "I'll never forget how you rescued me from certain death," he said. "Tell me who you are, where you are from, and what your name is. I want to know who it is that I owe my life to. I'd like to know the name of the person I'll always carry in my heart."

"It's not you who needs to thank me. I'm grateful to you for giving me an excuse to pull myself out of the hell that I'd found myself in for the past year and a half, to end the role I had to play. As I'm sure you've already figured out, I had to perform that role as part of the underground resistance movement. I wanted to stop a few months ago, but I couldn't find the right opportunity," she responded. "You ask me who I am? I'm the daughter of a poor Jewish tailor from a small village on the Dnieper." The Dnieper is a major river that flows from Russia and Belarus through Kyiv before flowing into the Black Sea. "My name is Reizele Osterman."

CHAPTER 12

"Brave in the
Face of the Enemy!"

Let the one who acts simply stand,
Brave in the face of those who oppress
His brothers and companions—
Brave in the face of the enemy!
—MORRIS WINCHEVSKY, "THE FUTURE"
(JOSEPH GLADSTEIN, *FREEDOM'S SONGS*, P. 47)

ONE EVENING WHILE THEY WERE operating near the city of Korosten, Uncle Misha's Jewish Group was returning from a mission when a young woman ran toward them. She was short, around seventeen or eighteen years old, and was wearing an old, dirty shawl. Her clothes were torn, and her small, bare feet were caked in mud. She looked as if she had been on a long and difficult journey.

"Finally I've met some real partisans," she said to Uncle Misha, who was riding in front. "I can tell that you're the one in charge. Take me with you. I have nowhere to go, and nobody left in this world. I want to become a partisan." Her big black eyes stared at Uncle Misha pleadingly.

"Who are you?" Uncle Misha asked. "And how do you know the forest so well?"

"I'm from the village of Mikhailovskii. I came here from Munich." Mikhailovskii is in the Bryansk region. Munich is, of course, in Germany.

Noticing the confused glances that the partisans were exchanging, the girl took off her shawl and revealed a large OST patch sewn onto her clothing. The patch designated her as an *Ostarbeiter*—German for "Eastern worker"—a forced laborer deported from Eastern Europe to work in Nazi Germany. The girl explained that the previous fall, a large punitive expedition had entered the Bryansk Forest looking for partisans and their collaborators. The Germans had burned down several villages, including Mikhailovskii, and had murdered the old men and women. They had taken the young men and women to the train station, locked them in boxcars, and sent them to Munich.

The girl had performed manual labor for six months in an underground factory, where she had grown sick from working in difficult and unsanitary conditions. After she was hospitalized for six months, the camp administration had decided that she was no longer useful. She handed Uncle Misha a piece of paper that read: *This* Ostarbeiter, *the Ukrainian Luba Androsova, has been deemed by the camp commission to be unfit for physical labor and is allowed to return to her place of residence, the village of Mikhailovskii in the Bryansk region.*

The girl had boarded a cargo train heading east. She had gone looking for partisans after learning from a peasant woman that there were some in the forest near Korosten. She had been wandering around for a week, hoping to find them.

The partisans scrutinized the pitiful girl, who looked as weak and helpless as a small child.

"I'd sure hate to be the Germans if a 'strong' partisan like you showed up in the forest," one of the men quipped sarcastically. They called him "Thälmann" because he looked very German, reminding them of imprisoned German Communist Party leader, Ernst Thälmann.

Luba sized him up with an angry glance and retorted, "I've read many stories about the partisans during the Russian Civil War. Based on those tales, I know that their successes were mostly the result of their brains rather than their brawn. So my guess is that I'd be more useful than you are."

Thälmann's face flushed with embarrassment. "And did you bring a pacifier?" he asked the young girl.

"I wasn't aware that partisans needed them," she quickly replied. "Had I known, I would have brought a dozen pacifiers just for you."

Thälmann spat on the ground angrily, while everyone else laughed.

Uncle Misha took an instant liking to the quick-minded girl. Although he was worried that she could be a double agent, like Piotr Tsukanov, he decided to take her in. If she were a spy, he reasoned, it would be better for her to be with his partisan unit. Uncle Misha's Jewish Group now had experience with double agents, and was better equipped than other units to expose and neutralize her. A spy could do serious damage to a different group.

As Uncle Misha and Luba rode together back to the camp, he continued the conversation. "It would be better for your poor health if you lived in peaceful conditions in a village, rather than in a forest, where one often goes hungry, sleeps without a roof over their head, and lives in constant fear," he told her.

"I can't do that, for several reasons," she responded. "First of all, I can't stand to look at the German murderers who have caused me so much suffering. Secondly, I want to avenge the murders of my parents. And third...third is a secret that I'm keeping to myself."

WHEN UNCLE MISHA and Luba reached the outpost of the partisan camp, they hopped off the horse and led it by the reins to two Jewish sentries: "Srolke the Machine Gunner" and Zaidel Green.

"Any news?" Uncle Misha asked in Yiddish.

"Everything's in excellent order," Srolke the Machine Gunner replied. "We're looking forward to the changing of the guard. I can smell the latkes frying in hemp oil from here." Timke the Cook had recently learned how to make the potato fritters. "They're just as good as the ones my mother used to make for Hanukkah. All that's missing is a few goose cracklings."

Luba was standing nearby, listening to the conversation with a look of surprise. Suddenly she grabbed Uncle Misha's hand. "You're Jews? How lucky I am!" she called out in Yiddish. "This is the secret I was afraid to tell you." There were tears in her eyes.

When he recovered from his shock, Uncle Misha asked, "Was the whole story about Germany made up?"

"No, it was all true." As she would later explain to the partisans, the girl who was now calling herself Luba Androsova had been born Sarah-Liba Zigman, to a Jewish family in Lviv. From an early age, she had demonstrated a talent for both music and dance. In May 1941, when she was sixteen, she had moved to Moscow to study singing at the conservatory. She had lost contact with her family after the Germans had occupied Lviv on June 30, and had read in horror the news of the atrocities the Germans had committed against the Jews in occupied Ukraine.

When the harvest had begun that autumn, the Minister of Education had canceled schools and had sent the students to kolkhozes to replace the young men who had been conscripted into the Red Army. Luba had been sent to a kolkhoz near Mikhailovskii, where she had stayed with a kolkhoz worker named Piotr Androsov and his wife, who had three sons in the Red Army. That winter, when gangs of armed Germans had come to the kolkhoz to commandeer food, the Androsovs had obtained a certificate from the village council showing the girl to be their daughter, Luba. They had given her old clothes that made her look like a peasant girl, and she had continued to work in the kolkhoz.

In October 1942, with the Soviet partisans gathering in the Bryansk Forest, several divisions of the SS had arrived to drive off the partisans and punish the local population for having lent aid to them. One of the punitive expeditions had surrounded Mikhailovskii. They had corralled every adult man and woman into a wooden barn and burned them alive. Then they had loaded the youth into boxcars and had sent them to Munich as *Ostarbeiters*.

Since Luba was fluent in Ukrainian and German, Uncle Misha assigned her to assist Reizele Osterman, who was now serving as the "Minister of Propaganda" for Uncle Misha's Jewish Group. Reizele, who spoke English, German, Russian, and Ukrainian, typed up flyers in which she translated communiques from the English and Soviet headquarters into German and Ukrainian, adding her own commentary. A team of young peasants she had recruited would paste the flyers in prominent places in nearby villages. The Germans and their Ukrainian collaborators, who worked very hard to keep the news of German defeats from the local population, were often shocked to learn that the villagers knew what was happening on the Eastern Front on a day-to-day basis.

After a week of resting in the camp and regaining her strength, Uncle Misha hardly recognized Luba when she stopped by the staff *kibosh*. She wore clean clothes and a white kerchief made of parachute fabric. She smiled politely, and Uncle Misha saw for the first time how beautiful she was.

"Uncle Misha, where did you find such a gorgeous girl?" an elderly partisan named Sizov called out in surprise. Luba broke out into a ringing laughter.

Luba quickly became a valuable member of Uncle Misha's Jewish Group. She approached every job, no matter how difficult, with a smile on her face, often joking, singing, or dancing. In her free time, she visited the Sanitary Battalion to help the nurses or to sit with the wounded partisans, talking or reading books to them.

Luba was also a gifted dancer. Now that the weather was warm and they were no longer confined to seeking warmth around the campfire, the partisans would hold social events every evening, dancing to the accordion until midnight. After Luba ran all of her potential suitors ragged in the group dances, she would dance Russian folk dances, such as the *kamarinskaya* or the *yablochko*. She danced with such lightness and grace that it seemed as if she were floating on air.

The beautiful and charming Luba captured everyone's heart. Not surprisingly, all of the single men in the unit competed for her affection. She considered them all to be friends, and responded to their overtures with kind laughter.

THE ONLY BACHELOR who did not attempt to woo Luba was a young man the partisans called "Yossele the Monk" because he was a quiet and serious person who was always deep in his own thoughts. He would lay for hours on his back with his hands behind his head, staring off into the sky. In the evenings, when all of the other partisans were socializing, Yossele would sit by himself in his *kibosh*, reading books by candlelight. Yossele was just as attracted to Luba as everyone else, but he was too shy to express his affection.

The partisans knew little about Yossele the Monk's background beyond the fact that he was from a small Jewish town in Polesia, and that he had been led to the mass graves with his parents during an *Aktion*. Just as they had done elsewhere, the Germans had made the Jews strip off their clothing and line up in rows of six at the edge of a deep pit. Yossele had watched his parents get shot, and had calmly awaited his own death. The Germans had shot him and the five other men in his row, and they had all fallen into the pit. But Yossele had only suffered a minor injury. When the *Aktion* was over, he had dragged himself out from under the bodies of those who had been shot after him and the thin layer of dirt the Germans had tossed onto the pit. Wearing only torn underwear, he had escaped to the forest, where he had lived on wild berries and mushrooms for several weeks, before Uncle Misha had found him sleeping under a tree.

Yossele took his duties as a partisan very seriously. He prepared carefully for every mission, carried out his tasks diligently, and never did anything reckless. But his disheveled appearance and detached personality reflected the scars of the trauma he had endured during the *Aktion* in his hometown.

It was Luba's presence in Uncle Misha's Jewish Group that finally coaxed Yossele the Monk out of his shell. He started combing his long hair and shining his boots. Then, one night, he emerged from his *kibosh* and walked over to the central square across from Uncle Misha's *kibosh*, where the other partisans were playing the accordion and dancing. He leaned against a tree and stood there for the rest of the evening.

From then on, Yossele would watch the partisans every night, but he would never participate. When there was a group dance, such as a Belarusian *lyavonikha* or a Polish polka, the partisans would try to drag Yossele into the circle, and he would resist with all his might. But when Luba would enter the center of the circle for a solo dance, the stoic indifference would disappear from his face. His dark gray eyes would sparkle and his mouth would fall open as he watched her dance.

One time, Luba grabbed his arm and tried to pull him into the circle, but he still refused to budge. Worried that she had embarrassed Yossele with her attention, she blushed and lightly squeezed his strong hands.

The next day, Luba stopped by Yossele's *kibosh*, where he was lying on the ground reading.

"What are you reading, Yossele?" she asked.

"I'm reading a Ukrainian book, but it's not very interesting," he answered, standing up.

"I got my hands on a copy of Lion Feuchtwanger's *Josephus*. If you come to my *kibosh*, I'll give it to you." She peered inside

Yossele's *kibosh* and saw a tin bowl with some leftover soup next to a dirty footwrap. "Your *kibosh* looks like a widower's room, and your shirt's not particularly clean. If you want, you can give it to me and I'll wash it."

That evening, Luba returned Yossele's shirt, cleaned and ironed. She visited with him for a little while, and they had a pleasant conversation.

Every night from that point forward, Yossele would wait for Luba to come to his *kibosh* on her way to the square, and they would walk together to and from the evening festivities. The other partisans were initially surprised to see Yossele the Monk in the role of a suitor, but they eventually attributed it to Luba's magical powers.

ONE NIGHT, THE evening festivities were just winding down when Uncle Misha suggested that Luba perform one more dance.

"They're fed up with all of my Russian dances, but I'd gladly dance a *khosidl*," she replied. A *khosidl* is a slow dance in Hasidic style that is frequently performed at Jewish weddings. "In our family, I was famous for my *khosidl* when I was just six years old. When any of my relatives got married, they would pay extra for the fiddler to play for me. I'd dance, and my dear parents would be filled with joy. Oh, where has my beautiful childhood gone?"

"If that's what you want, then dance a *khosidl*," Uncle Misha said. "I, for one, would love to see it."

"But who'll play for me? Vasily doesn't know how." Vasily Vasilievich was the Soviet partisan who played the accordion every night.

"Sing it to him a few times. He's talented. He'll figure it out in no time."

It took Vasily a little while to understand what Luba wanted, but when she finally started to sing, he started picking out the tune. After a few times through the melody, he was able to play it by himself.

"It just doesn't speak to my soul," Luba cried out, wringing her hands. "It doesn't feel Jewish!"

Yossele, who had been standing nearby, turned to Uncle Misha. "Bring me your violin," he said. "I'll play a *khosidl* for Luba!"

"You can play the violin?" Uncle Misha was astonished. "You never told us that."

"I come from a family of musicians. My father was the concertmaster of the local Jewish orchestra. My grandfather was an even better violinist. He played not only at Jewish weddings, but also the weddings of the wealthiest aristocrats. They started teaching me to play the violin when I was eight years old. I was very talented, and my father was convinced that I would take over his position as the concertmaster."

Uncle Misha sent a partisan to his *kibosh* to retrieve his violin. Meanwhile, Luba prepared for her dance. She tucked her thick hair under a hat, leaving out only two sidelocks, which she twirled with her fingers. When she stuffed her hands into the sides of her velvet vest, she looked just like a Hasidic boy.

Yossele tuned the violin, played a few notes, and then rested the bow on the strings. He stared off into the night, as if conjuring up images from his past that he could turn into music. The partisans surrounded him, curious and impatient for him to start playing.

"First I'll play a tune by my father, which he used to play at weddings while the bride was being seated. Then I'll play the *khosidl*."

Yossele drew the bow across the strings, and soft notes began to flow out of the violin. He fell into a trance, and the violin followed. It sang, it wailed, it dreamed, and it conveyed his every emotion through sweet melodies. In the middle of a dense forest, miles and miles behind enemy lines, a Jewish boy who had been saved from the hands of German murderers only by a miracle brought back to life, through music, Jewish traditions and Jewish customs—centuries-old moments of merriment in which joy mixed with tears.

The partisans listened intently, transfixed by his playing. They forgot that they were standing on a moonlit meadow surrounded by centuries-old pine trees. In their minds, they were transported to a Jewish wedding in a small Ukrainian town. Instead of the sunburned faces of partisans dressed in a hodgepodge of ragged uniforms, they saw the shining faces of the happy couple's relatives wearing silk belts, satin coats, silver kerchiefs, and their best jewelry.

As Uncle Misha listened to the plaintive wailing of the violin, he imagined the officiant in a big velvet hat, a red scarf in his hand, standing on a bench in the middle of the room, reciting his rhymes. He saw the bride sitting in a chair that her friends were lifting up in the air. He looked through her translucent veil and saw a pale face and dark eyes that were damp with tears. As Uncle Misha watched Luba standing next to Yossele, tears flowing down her face, he imagined her as the bride.

Yossele never took his eyes off Luba. It seemed as if he were playing just for her, conveying through melodies the powerful emotions that he lacked the courage to express in words. The other partisans who stood there, breathlessly listening, sensed both the mourning of Yossele's pained soul and his deep love for Luba.

He ended with a high, wailing note that gradually faded away, disappearing somewhere between the ancient trees. For a few moments, everything fell silent. Then Yossele quickly drew the bow across the strings again and launched into a merry *freylekh*—a joyful dance tune.

Luba snapped out of her reverie, jumped into the circle, and started to dance. In the blink of an eye, she transformed herself from the tearful bride into a young Hasidic man dancing artfully to the sound of a Jewish *freylekh*. Her slim body and nimble legs followed each beat, melting together with Yossele's playing into the harmony of music and dance. She snapped her fingers and waved her arms. She danced around the circle, holding her side with one hand and a handkerchief with the other. "Faster, louder!" she encouraged the onlookers as they clapped their hands to the beat and sang along with the familiar tune.

Every time she danced near Yossele, who still had not taken his eyes off her, Luba would smile and wink at him, as if to signal that she was dancing for him alone. Yossele seemed to understand, and played ever more vigorously.

When Yossele drew the bow across the strings for the final chord, Luba stopped across from him, breathing heavily.

David of Yarevysche threw a glass on the ground. Mimicking the Jewish wedding tradition, he stomped on the glass with his steel-toed boots. "Mazel tov! Mazel tov!" he exclaimed. "May this be a lucky hour! Bride and groom, you may kiss each other!"

Luba wrapped her arms around Yossele's neck, and they kissed.

"Bravo!" the partisans cheered, clapping enthusiastically.

Luba leaned on Yossele's arm as they left the square without saying a word. From time to time, she drew closer to him, looking at him lovingly. When they reached Yossele's *kibosh*, he stopped, as he had every night, to tell her goodbye. But Luba did not let go of his hand.

"Today I'm your bride, and one should not leave a bride alone in the forest," she said with a smile. "You have to walk me home."

Yossele would not return to his *kibosh* until the next morning.

WHILE THE PARTISANS were near Korosten, their suspicions that Piotr Tsukanov had been a double agent were confirmed. Uncle Misha's informant in Korosten, the son of a local physician, passed along the news that Tsukanov was indeed alive. He had been awarded the Iron Cross in Berlin and had since been assigned as the chief of police for the city and district of Korosten. Uncle Misha knew that this was a high-ranking position that would only be assigned to someone whom the Germans trusted implicitly.

Shortly after Tsukanov was assigned to the Korosten district, there was a marked increase in German attempts to disrupt partisan activities there. Tsukanov knew that the partisans killed the Germans' informants and burned their businesses—not only to punish the collaborators, but also to deter others from assisting the Germans. He started using those same tactics against the partisans. In addition to arresting peasants suspected of having contact with partisans, he organized a new network of informants who were more intimidated by him than by the partisans. He recruited some informants by offering bounties, and others by making threats. In some cases, Tsukanov kidnapped children and told their mothers he would only release them if the mothers not only brought him information about the location of partisan detachments, but also served as guides for the punitive expeditions. Tsukanov focused his efforts on areas close to the railway lines, where small units of partisans carried out sabotage missions, just like the one Lionka had taken him on several weeks earlier.

When two days had passed since a saboteur squad led by Zaidel Green was supposed to have returned from a mission, Uncle Misha and his partisans grew very concerned. Luba was distraught, because Yossele had been among the eight men in that squad. She kept coming into the staff *kibosh*, asking if there was any news. Every chance she got, she would climb the hill near the camp entrance and stare at the narrow trail on which the squad was supposed to return.

Zaidel finally showed up on the third day, with five members of his squad. They were all hungry, exhausted, and dejected. Yossele and another partisan, named Chigirin, were not with them.

As Zaidel explained to the partisans, his squad had proceeded carefully, avoiding every village and settlement, and had reached the railway line without any trouble. Just a little over a mile from where they were going to lay the mine, they crossed a river and were approaching a stack of felled trees next to the railway when a dog started barking. Right after that, a red flare flew into the air.

The partisans dropped to the ground to avoid being seen, but it was too late. The Germans had spotted them and had started shooting. Zaidel ordered the partisans to drop the heavy mine and make a hasty retreat. The night was very dark, so he cautioned the partisans that returning fire would only reveal their location. As they ran, bullets flew over their heads. Suddenly Chigirin fell to the ground. Zaidel bent over him and saw that he had been shot through the head.

Zaidel and Yossele continued to run. They wanted to reach the large swamp that was nearby and rest in the tall reeds. They knew that the Germans would not follow them into the dense, foul-smelling swamp. They were just a few yards from the swamp when there was another volley of gunfire.

"I'm hit!" Yossele shouted. He grabbed Zaidel's hand and started sliding to the ground.

Zaidel caught Yossele under his arm. He urged Yossele to stay strong enough to reach the swamp, but Yossele had been hit in the leg and could not walk. Zaidel handed Yossele his weapon and threw Yossele's arm over his shoulder. A few minutes later, they were standing up to their knees in the swamp, hidden behind the tall reeds.

As the partisans had predicted, the Germans chased them as far as the swamp and stopped. They refused to enter the swamp, and instead started shooting nonstop into the dense reeds. Zaidel walked a few dozen yards farther into the swamp. The whole way, Yossele was leaning on him and moaning quietly.

"We have an hour or an hour and a half until the break of dawn," Zaidel told Yossele. "While the search dogs are resting, we should get out of the swamp and try to reach the 'bunker.' Then we'll be safe." The "bunker" was the remnant of a fortification along the old Stalin Line, a series of concrete bunkers and pillboxes that the Soviet Union had built along its pre-1939 border with Poland. The defensive structures had been abandoned after the Molotov–Ribbentrop Pact had expanded the Soviet Union's borders westward. Since then, many of the fortifications had been destroyed or booby-trapped with mines, but the partisans had cleared some, and now used them as hideouts.

After the gunfire stopped, Zaidel assumed that the Germans had left. He started slowly working his way back out of the swamp. When he could feel the bank under his feet, he laid Yossele on the ground. Zaidel had just started to bandage Yossele's leg when the shooting started again. A bullet pierced his left arm.

"Run, Zaidel.... You can't help me anymore," Yossele gasped. "Save yourself, at least."

"I can't leave you behind in this kind of danger."

"Save yourself. I won't be captured alive." Yossele removed his grenades from his belt.

Bullets were still zipping all around them. They heard shouts in German and Ukrainian getting closer and closer.

Zaidel wrapped his right arm around Yossele and tried to drag him.

Pushing himself away, Yossele shouted, "I beg you, Zaidel, save yourself! I want you to tell Luba that I died with her name on my lips."

Crawling on his hands and knees, Zaidel managed to escape and reach the bunker within an hour. He lay there all day. When it grew dark, he reunited with the rest of his squad. They went to an informant and asked him to find out what had happened to Yossele.

The informant returned the next night and told Zaidel what he had learned from one of the Ukrainian auxiliary policemen who had participated in the manhunt. After Zaidel and Yossele had entered the swamp, the joint German and Ukrainian expedition had lost the partisans' tracks. They had shot into the reeds for a while, and then had decided to stay in the area and wait

until dawn. They had fired at every suspicious movement, which
was how they had shot Zaidel. At the break of dawn, they had
gone looking for the partisans' tracks and had found Yossele,
whom they took for dead. As they approached him, he unpinned
a grenade and blew himself to pieces, along with three Germans
and one Ukrainian.

LUBA WAS IN the staff *kibosh* when Zaidel reported on the ill-
fated mission. She sat there, pale and unmoving, until Zaidel repeated Yossele's last words. Then she bit her lip, started crying,
and stormed out. She went to her *kibosh* and lay in bed for two
days. Some women partisans brought her food, but she refused
to touch it. They tried to console her, but could not find the right
words. On the morning of the third day, she returned to the staff
kibosh and sat down next to Uncle Misha.

"There's something important I'd like to discuss with you,"
she said quietly.

"Tell me what you want."

"The only person responsible for my Yossele's death is that traitor Tsukanov," she began. "So I've decided to go to Korosten and
take revenge on that lowlife. I shall become Tsukanov's Angel of
Death. This is something that I have to do, even if it costs me my
own life."

Uncle Misha was surprised. "My dear Luba, I understand
your desperation over Yossele's death. We all loved him very
much," he said. "But you're young, and I think that after all of
the difficult experiences you've gone through, it doesn't make
sense to risk your life on such a dangerous mission."

"The mission is not as risky as you think, Uncle Misha," she
protested. "I've thought out every detail of my plan, and I'd like
to present it to you."

"I'm busy now, but if you come back in a few days, I can give
you my full attention." Uncle Misha was stalling her, hoping that
with time she would come to her senses.

In the meantime, the partisans' situation was growing worse by the day. They suffered two more losses that bore the hallmark of Tsukanov's experienced hand. By then, Mirkovsky had been reassigned to another detachment, and his former chief of staff, Vasilii Ushakov, had assumed command. The 1st Stalin Partisan Detachment had been pulled out of Saburov's United Partisan Federation and had been renamed the Comrade Stalin Partisan Federation, with three detachments: the Borovik Partisan Detachment, named after a former commander; the 2nd Stalin Partisan Detachment; and the Kyiv Partisan Detachment. Uncle Misha's Jewish Group was assigned to the Borovik detachment.

One day, when Uncle Misha and the commanders of other units within the Stalin Partisan Federation were listening to the physician's son from Korosten tell them about the atrocities that Tsukanov was committing there, Luba walked into the staff *kibosh*.

"I believe that it's high time that you listen to my plan to go to Korosten to kill Tsukanov," she declared. "I'm certain of my success, because my mother came to me in a dream last night. She said, 'Go to Korosten and kill Tsukanov. I'm going to help you.' And when my mother appears in my dreams, she always brings good news."

"Now I know that it was from your mother that you inherited your bravery," Uncle Misha joked in an attempt to lighten the mood. "A dream is a weak argument for allowing yourself to fall into that lowlife's hands. You were probably thinking about Tsukanov when you were falling asleep, and that affected your dream. But I did promise to hear you out. Sit down and explain your plan."

Luba pulled a folded piece of paper from her corset. It was the German document identifying her as a demobilized *Ostarbeiter* and permitting her to move around freely in occupied Ukraine on her way back to the Bryansk region. She told Uncle Misha that her plan was to put on the torn clothes with the *Ostarbeiter* patch, which she had kept as a souvenir, and go to Korosten. She would get herself arrested, which would mean that she would be taken to Tsukanov. Luba had heard the stories about how much Tsukanov liked the ladies, and she knew he would be attracted to her. Once she got close to him, she would find a way to kill him. Just in case she failed, she would bring a dose of poison from the partisan doctor so she could kill herself if she was compromised.

"The first part of your plan is easy," said Gavriil Negrobov, Mirkovsky's former aide-de-camp, who had become Ushakov's chief of staff. "That is, you can get arrested and even brought to Tsukanov, but I doubt that you'll be able to kill him without a weapon."

"I'll just try to make Tsukanov's acquaintance, and then we'll see," Luba replied confidently. "Moreover, I'll stay in contact with you through our informant in Korosten, and I'll consult with you and keep you up to date about my situation. I therefore ask that you allow me to go to Korosten. I really do believe that I'll become Tsukanov's Angel of Death."

"We heard your plan, and we'll consider it," Uncle Misha said.

After Luba left the *kibosh*, the partisan commanders discussed her plan. The majority voted in favor of allowing her to go. They argued that she had a valid identification, that her Ukrainian was flawless, and, most importantly, that she was smart, brave, and quick on her feet.

LUBA LEFT THE camp the next morning, barefoot and in the clothes she had been wearing when she had first encountered the partisans in the forest. After loitering near the government offices for an entire day, trying unsuccessfully to attract the attention of the police, she found shelter for the night in a peasant's home. At ten the next morning, she was finally approached by a Ukrainian auxiliary policeman guarding the entrance to a government office. When he asked her questions, she mouthed off to the officer, making him so mad that he pushed her to the ground and led her to the police station at gunpoint.

She was taken to Tsukanov, who, as she had predicted, was instantly attracted to her and eager to believe that she was a dim-witted kolkhoz girl trying to get back to the Bryansk region. When she told him that she was traveling by foot, he suggested that she stay in Korosten and earn enough money to take the train. Hoping to get close to her, he offered her a job cleaning the police station.

After Luba had been in Korosten for a week, she sent Uncle Misha a note through the physician's son: *The net has been cast, and the fish will have to swim into it. In the meantime, I've decided to engage in productive work.* By "productive work," she meant "spying." This included finding out the names and addresses of villagers who were secretly informing on the partisans. As they always did, the partisans killed the traitors and burned their busi-nesses to the ground.

On one occasion, Luba eavesdropped on two policemen com-plaining that the next day they had to go to Luhyny, a village about fifteen miles northwest of Korosten. They were to re-inforce a squad of local policemen who were escorting confis-cated oxen to Korosten, where they would be shipped to the Eastern Front to feed German soldiers. As soon as Uncle Misha received that intelligence, he dispatched several squads of parti-sans, who set up ambushes along the route the police would take. The partisans took out seventeen policemen and brought back the oxen as food for themselves.

Another time, Luba got her hands on a directive from the Area Commissar to the chairmen of the village councils, order-ing them to prepare lists of young men and women to be sent to Germany for forced labor. She provided Uncle Misha not only with that information, but with a copy of the directive itself, which Reizele Osterman reproduced, alongside her commentary, and distributed throughout the nearby villages. Instead of wait-ing in their homes to be apprehended, the youth fled to the for-est and joined the partisans.

The next update that Uncle Misha received informed him that Luba had secured a new position cooking and cleaning for Tsukanov at his private residence. Three days later, she passed along yet another note to Uncle Misha: *My master will leave Korosten at ten in the morning, heading to Yemilchyne to meet the leader of a band of Ukrainian nationalists called the Polissian Sich. He'll be traveling in a small, four-seater car. The car is light blue, with license plate number 2177. I hope that you'll welcome him, Uncle Misha.*

As soon as he received the message, Uncle Misha left on horseback with a group of forty armed partisans. By midnight, they arrived at the road that led westward from Korosten to the village of Yemilchyne and started looking for an ideal spot for an ambush.

By the time dawn started to break, they were well camouflaged and waiting a few dozen yards from the road for Tsukanov. It was not until noon that they heard the sound of a car engine and saw a plume of exhaust appearing on the horizon to their right. A few minutes later, they saw a small light-blue car heading toward them. As the car passed them, Uncle Misha gave the order to fire, but only at the tires and the engine.

The car came to a quick stop. Much to the partisans' surprise, Luba jumped out. They would later learn that she had talked Tsukanov into taking her along.

"Let's save ourselves!" Luba shouted, pulling Tsukanov by the hand. She wanted to capture him alive, and was worried that the partisans would shoot him if they remained in the car.

After they ran about twenty yards, Tsukanov started dragging Luba toward the forest, in search of a hiding place.

"Stop!" Luba yelled, drawing the pistol she had stolen from Tsukanov while he was embracing her in the car. "Don't move!"

Tsukanov pounced on her with lightning speed, but before he could grab the gun, she shot him. He collapsed to the ground.

"Uncle Misha! Quick, come here!" Luba called out. "Save him! I don't want him to die just yet. There's something I have to say to him."

When Uncle Misha ran up to Tsukanov, he was lying on the ground, showing no signs of life. His face was pale, and a red line of blood was streaming from his mouth. Luba stood over him, still holding the pistol.

The partisans tied up the driver and another passenger and took them away. They doused the car with gasoline and set it on fire.

They brought Tsukanov back to the camp, where the doctor and his team got to work trying to revive him. Luba stood next to Tsukanov, staring down at him with contempt. After a few injections, he started to stir.

"Uncle Misha!" Luba exclaimed. "Come quickly. He's alive!"

Hearing her voice, Tsukanov opened his eyes. "Luba, my little Luba," he said weakly. "I don't feel so good..."

"I'm not little Luba anymore," she hissed, bending over him. "I'm Sarah-Liba Zigman, a partisan from Uncle Misha's Jewish Group. You must be surprised to be dying at the hands of a partisan woman, much less at the hands of a lady *zhid*. And here's your former commander, Uncle Misha."

"Do you recognize me?" Uncle Misha asked, kneeling over him. Judging from the terror on Tsukanov's face, he did.

"Whatever it is you want to tell him, say it quickly," the doctor urged Uncle Misha. "His minutes are numbered."

"Tsukanov, you traitor, you got the punishment you deserved," Uncle Misha taunted him, looking directly into his fearful eyes. "You can rest assured that all the other traitors will receive the appropriate punishment, just like you."

Hearing those words, Tsukanov trembled and exhaled his last breath.

CHAPTER 13

≡≡≡≡

"At the Edge of the Forest"

At the edge of the forest stands an old oak tree,
And underneath that oak tree lies a partisan.
He lies there, not breathing, as if he were sleeping,
His golden curls rustling in the wind.

—PETR MAMAICHUK, "AT THE EDGE OF THE FOREST"

B Y JULY 1, 1943, THERE were almost 30,000 partisans spread out over 17 federations and 160 independent detachments in Ukraine. The partisans were derailing trains, blowing up depots, and attacking garrisons with increasing frequency, causing significant damage in the German rear, both militarily and psychologically. "Gangs organized partly in military style are emerging in areas that have been calm before now," a German army report noted. "The impression is growing among the population that the Germans will not be masters of the situation."

In response to the partisans' success—not only in disrupting the German rear, but also in winning over the local peasants—the Germans had been intensifying their efforts to track down the partisans. The Germans started launching large-scale missions that included both regular army divisions and security forces, often with the support of tanks and heavy artillery. They also used airplanes to provide tactical support for antipartisan operations, and had recently increased the bombing and strafing of partisan-held areas. The pilots flew low over the forest, shooting everybody they saw, regardless of whether it was a man working peacefully in a field, a woman gathering mushrooms, or a young shepherd grazing cows in a meadow. In June and July 1943, the Germans launched an operation in the area between Ovruch and Mazyr during which they destroyed 807 partisan camps and killed over five thousand partisans and their collaborators.

One morning, Motele and another boy from Uncle Misha's Jewish Group were grazing horses in a dense forest less than a mile from where the Jewish Group was encamped when they spotted two Germans coming toward them. They pressed themselves to the ground to avoid being seen, and watched as one of the Germans climbed a tree with one end of a telephone wire. The other end was attached to a spool that the second German unwound as he slowly backed away. From time to time, he pressed the wire into the ground with his boots to hide it in the grass.

Motele realized that the German in the tree was a "cuckoo," which was what the Soviets called the snipers that the Germans hid in the trees to look out for partisans and tell the artillery where to concentrate their fire.

When the boys reported what they had seen, the partisans quickly jumped to their feet. They had known that the Germans were concentrating in the surrounding villages, but their informants had thought that the Germans were only there to requisition grain and livestock. The presence of cuckoos in the forest suggested that the Germans were preparing to attack the partisan camp and hunt down any partisans who escaped.

Uncle Misha took three immediate actions: He ordered the sick and wounded partisans to be moved to a secure location; he sent a squad of six partisans to go with Motele to kill the cuckoo;

and he dispatched a scout to spy on the Germans. When the scout returned with a report on the size of the German unit and which road they were taking, Uncle Misha ordered two heavily armed squads to outflank the Germans and attack them from the rear. Other partisans crossed the brook that bordered the camp and hid behind tall reeds in the adjacent swamp. Fifty partisans stayed in the camp, camouflaged and hidden in trenches.

Popov had been working to set up a defensive perimeter of land mines. Every day, he had taken partisans who were training to be saboteurs to the roads leading to the camp and had shown them how to lay mines. With the Germans on their way, he also created one of his special presents for them.

The German punitive expedition slowly and cautiously approached the partisan camp. They were led by search dogs and local peasants whom the Germans had forced to serve as guides. The Germans were still far away when they started launching mortars and firing their heavy machine guns. They grew emboldened when there was no responding fire from the camp, but paused when they approached the narrow bridge that led over the brook and into the camp. The other side of the bridge was completely blocked by the body of a dead horse lying in front of a pile of old wagon wheels, pieces of iron rails, and blocks of lumber. It would have taken hours to remove the heavy clutter from the bridge.

The Germans had grown familiar with partisan tricks. As the bulk of their unit observed from a distance, two soldiers walked to within twenty-five yards of the bridge. They threw a rope with a grappling hook that lodged between the horse's ribs. As soon as they pulled on the rope, there was a large explosion that echoed through the woods. The horse, the bridge, and all of the debris went flying into the air, wounding and killing several of the Germans standing nearby.

The rest of the Germans took off in a panic toward the forest, where they were met by the bullets of the two partisan squads that had taken up positions behind them. When the Germans turned around and ran back toward the bridge, the partisans who had been hiding in the swamp and in the camp sprang up and attacked them. Many of the Germans were killed or severely wounded. The small number who managed to survive were chased away by the partisans.

IT WAS WELL past midnight in the partisan camp. A full moon shone through the thick tree branches. The soft wind from a nearby lake carried the strong scent of pine resin through the air, mixing it with the lingering smell of smoke from the extinguished campfire. From time to time, the nightingales would start singing, first one, then more, until the forest quickly filled with a chorus of chirping, before being silenced by the hoot of an owl or the howl of a faraway wolf.

An older Soviet partisan named Ivan Timofeevich was in charge of the watch duty. He patrolled the camp with deliberate steps and a vigilant gaze, listening attentively to every sound. Suddenly he heard the voices of two women singing quietly. A soft, lyrical soprano and a low alto blended together in a harmonious duet. The women were singing "At the Edge of the Forest," a partisan song about a mother who lost her husband and seven sons to war, and decides to avenge their deaths by joining the partisans as a doctor. When she returns home in victory, her seven grandsons rush out to greet her. "At the Edge of the Forest" was popular among the Soviet partisans. The Jewish partisan Shmerke Kaczerginski would later create an abridged version in Yiddish.

Ivan climbed the hill to find a Soviet cook named Nadia and a Jewish nurse named Tsirele sitting together, hugging each other and singing.

"It's way past bedtime," he told the girls. "A partisan has to sleep when they can, because you never know when you'll have another opportunity."

"We can't sleep, dear Uncle," Nadia replied. "When you were young, did you sleep through such beautiful nights?"

"That would have been well and good, back in your village," the watchman replied. "But you can't sing here, behind enemy lines."

"It's not we who sing," Tsirele chimed in. "It's our souls singing out from inside us. Please, dear Ivan Timofeevich, don't deny us of this pleasure."

"Young people," he commented, sighing and walking away. "They should be sitting somewhere in a cherry orchard or a riverbank, enjoying life and being in love. Not here in the forest, uncertain of what tomorrow might bring. I did spend my years of youth better." He leaned against a tree and stood there for a long time, deep in his thoughts and listening to the girls sweetly singing the ballad.

Nadia was the daughter of Belarusian peasants, but had run away to a kolkhoz when she was fifteen. When the Germans had burned down their village, Nadia and several other kolkhoz workers had escaped to the forest to join the partisans. Nadia had quickly become popular among the partisans for her unwavering cheerfulness, her diligent work ethic, and her good looks. Many of the partisan men were attracted to Nadia's shapely figure, blue eyes, and long blond hair, but she was still in love with Petro, a blacksmith from the kolkhoz who had been conscripted into the Red Army.

Tsirele was the only child of a merchant from a Jewish village in Volhynia. She had grown up speaking several languages and playing the piano, but that life had come to an end when the Germans had occupied the village and sent all of its Jewish residents to a ghetto. Tsirele had lost her parents and her boyfriend, Simcha, during an *Aktion*. She had hidden in a cellar before escaping to the forest.

Tsirele had been rescued by Nadia and her unit of Soviet partisans, initiating a close friendship. The two "little sisters," as the partisans called them, spent hours sitting with each other in a distant corner of the camp, singing and talking about their pasts. Nadia talked a great deal about her love for Petro, and Tsirele would tell Nadia about Simcha.

"If we survive the war, you can come home with me," Nadia promised Tsirele. "You're well-educated. You can get a position in our kolkhoz and marry the most handsome man, and we can be together forever."

As with Nadia, the partisans respected Tsirele for her dedication. During marches, she walked at the end of the column, holding a green tarpaulin bag adorned with a red cross. She kept the bag filled with ointments, wool, and tourniquets made of parachute fabric, ready to provide first aid. During every battle, she would dig a foxhole with the small shovel she kept strapped to her belt. From her hiding place, she could monitor the fighting and immediately run to anyone who got wounded. On more than one occasion, she hoisted a wounded partisan onto her shoulders, ran through a hail of bullets to a safe location, and bandaged the wound before returning to her foxhole. The partisans swore that any pain disappeared the instant that Tsirele touched the wound with her thin, tender fingers.

With her curly black hair and petite figure, Tsirele also had to keep potential suitors at arm's length. When one of the partisans would profess his love for her, she would answer with a smile, stating, "It's wartime. For us Jews, the only task is revenge, and we have to forget about pleasure. When the war is over and every wound is healed, I'll allow the King of Love, 'Comrade Amour,' to breathe new life into my heart."

ONE DAY IN early August, the Stalin Partisan Federation learned that a well-armed punitive expedition of 320 Germans had arrived in Luben, two miles south of their base camp. Every partisan was given arms, even the cooks, the cartmen, and the wounded. Ushakov dispatched his deputy commander, Lieutenant Petr Sergeevich Podiachev, and a joint partisan detachment to outflank the Germans and attack them from behind.

At the front of the detachment, Srolke the Machine Gunner carried a Degtyaryov DP-27. The light machine gun was popular among the Soviets, who called it a "record player" because of its disk-shaped magazines. Nadia walked behind Srolke, carrying two heavy bags on her shoulders. One was full of bullets, and the other was filled with spare magazines for the DP-27. As always, Tsirele was at the tail end of the squad, holding her first aid kit.

The partisans attacked Luben while the Germans were eating lunch. The Germans ran to the trenches they had dug in the sandy earth and started returning fire. The partisans quickly took cover behind some felled trees, but a few were wounded. Tsirele crawled back and forth between them, bandaging their wounds. But she never lost sight of Nadia, who was quickly feeding bullets into the forty-seven-round magazines and handing them to Srolke.

Suddenly, though, Srolke jolted upright, dropped the DP-27, and fell to the ground. As Tsirele watched, Nadia grabbed Srolke's head with both hands and shook it, trying to wake him. Then she reverently straightened out his body and covered his face with his coat. She grabbed the DP-27, rested it on Srolke's body, and began to shoot in short bursts, as the commander had ordered.

As a warm tear slid down her face, Tsirele realized: "The always happy Srolke the Machine Gunner is dead."

There was a commotion on the German side. A tracer bullet fired by the partisans had set fire to the roof of a house next to the trenches. Podiachev used the panic to issue an order: "Attack!"

The partisans leaped from behind the felled trees with a wild "Oo-rah!" and started running toward the burning houses. The Germans once again returned fire, and Nadia wobbled and fell down.

Tsirele ran over immediately. Nadia was lying on the ground, pale and moaning. Bullets had passed through her left leg in several places, and the red stain on the gray sand under her wounded knee was growing wider with every second.

"My dear Nadia, you're wounded!" Tsirele shrieked. "Grab my neck. We'll crawl away from here, not far, to the raspberry bushes. I'll bandage your wound."

They crawled toward the bushes. Nadia was growing weaker and weaker, and heavier and heavier. It took every ounce of Tsirele's strength to keep dragging her friend forward. An unending barrage of bullets whistled over their heads.

Just before they reached the bushes, Tsirele was shot in her right arm and lost consciousness.

After a three-hour battle, the Germans fled from the village, leaving behind thirty-six dead and sixty-three wounded soldiers, along with thirty horses, thirty cows, and ten carts. They also left behind ammunition and supplies, as well as loot they had stolen from local villagers. Podiachev gathered the partisans on a square in the middle of the village to establish how many of their comrades had been killed or wounded.

"The little sisters are missing!" one of the partisans reported. They started searching for the girls everywhere.

The partisans found Nadia and Tsirele lying unconscious under the raspberry bushes, hugging each other. A red stream of blood was flowing from Tsirele's arm, which was wrapped tightly around Nadia's neck, seeping blood into her blond ponytail.

Three partisans had died in the battle. The others brought the nine wounded partisans back to the camp and laid them on overcoats and torn sacks in the large, dimly lit tent of the Sanitary Battalion. Nadia and Tsirele lay in one corner, holding each other tightly. Their eyes filled with joy and devotion as they discussed the recent battle.

"I can't wait to tell my Petro," Nadia said weakly, "that you, little Tsirele, risked her own life to save his golden Nadia."

ON AUGUST 4, a middle-aged man with a long beard walked down a dirt road leading to Radomyshl, a town less than twenty miles south of Malyn. He looked like any ordinary peasant. He was wearing a long linen shirt cinched with a flax rope, white linen trousers, and a pair of shoes woven from tree bark. A knotted stick balanced over his shoulder held a heavy linen sack. A barefoot peasant boy of about twelve years of age walked by his side. It was Uncle Misha and Motele.

In a dirty handkerchief, Uncle Misha carried a masterfully forged document showing him to be Ivan Grib, from Selezivka, a tiny village near Velidnyky in the Ovruch region. With the permission of the village council, Ivan and his young son, Mitka, were traveling to Radomyshl to find Ivan's older son, Petro, who was being held in a prisoner-of-war camp.

Uncle Misha and Motele were actually heading to Radomyshl to deliver a detonator. The partisans had decided to blow up a profitable brewery that had been commandeered by the Germans. With the help of an informant in the District Administrator's office, the partisans had recruited a night watchman at the brewery to sneak explosives into a factory cellar. All that the watchman needed to complete the mission was a detonator.

Uncle Misha had dispatched a squad to ambush a stone quarry that Organisation Todt was operating in a nearby district. They had returned a few days later with enough explosives and detonators to blow up the entire city. Although he had known that delivering the detonator to the watchman was a risky mission, Uncle Misha's many successes had instilled in him a confidence that was verging on carelessness, and he had decided that he and Motele would go.

After walking a dozen miles in the blazing sun, they arrived at a sprawling oak tree at the intersection of two roads, where the factory watchman was supposed to be waiting. They sat down, calmly took a bottle of milk and a couple of pierogies out of Uncle Misha's sack, and enjoyed a snack. They could see Radomyshl on a small hill, just over a mile away.

After waiting for an hour, Uncle Misha started to get worried. He dug a hole with his hands and buried the detonator.

"We can't sit here much longer," he said to Motele. "It seems our contact has been delayed."

"It's possible that he's betrayed us," Motele suggested. "If so, we should leave for the time being."

"We're not in any danger. Our contact is reliable, and our papers are fully in order. It's just a shame that we covered all those miles in this heat for nothing. Should we take a stroll through Radomyshl, since we're already so close? It might come in handy someday. It's possible that we'll be able to liberate Radomyshl before the Red Army gets here."

"We can try," Motele replied happily. "I'd actually enjoy the walk."

The city was quiet, as was typical for Ukrainian towns when all of the peasants were in the field for the harvest. Every now and then, Uncle Misha and Motele would see peasants hiding in the shade to avoid the heat. Wagons occasionally passed by, loaded with grain and pulled by pairs of well-fed, sleepy oxen with long, crooked horns. As they meandered through town, Uncle Misha and Motele walked right past a few Germans strolling confidently down the street. The Germans glanced at the Ukrainian strangers with contempt, but were not bothered by their presence. Uncle Misha and Motele progressed from one street to the next, reading the signs and committing everything to their memories.

As they walked onto one of the main streets, Uncle Misha suddenly felt a strong hand on his shoulder. He turned around to see a Ukrainian auxiliary policeman.

"Who are you?" the gravel-voiced policeman asked.

"A man," Uncle Misha answered calmly.

"I can see that you're not a horse," the auxiliary policeman said angrily. "Where are you from?"

"Selezivka."

"The devil knows where your Selezivka is. What are you doing in Radomyshl?"

"My son Petro is here, in your prisoner-of-war camp. I brought him some pierogies and underwear."

"I doubt that," the auxiliary policeman said, looking at Uncle Misha suspiciously. He reached out, grabbed Uncle Misha's beard, and tugged on it.

Uncle Misha slapped his hand away. "You rascal," he scolded the auxiliary policeman. "I'm old enough to be a grandfather, and you pull my beard?"

"I thought it might be glued on. But, all the same, you still look suspicious. Are you a partisan?"

"I'm a kolkhoz worker, not a partisan," Uncle Misha answered simply. He started to walk away.

"Don't be in such a hurry," the auxiliary policeman said, grabbing Uncle Misha by the hand. "I don't like you. Come to the military police headquarters."

"I don't have time for your military police headquarters. I'm heading back home today. Here's my identification. You can see who I am."

"They'll look at it there. They're more literate than me. They'll clear up the matter."

The auxiliary policeman pointed his rifle at Uncle Misha and ordered him forward. Uncle Misha gave Motele a wink to signal that he should follow them. "If anything happens to me, he'll be able to tell the detachment," Uncle Misha said to himself.

THEY WALKED DOWN several streets until they reached a large courtyard. A sign on the gate indicated that this was the head-quarters of the German military police. They entered the station to find a large, dimly lit waiting room lined with narrow wooden benches where peasants sat, anxiously waiting to be received by the commandant. The auxiliary policeman brought Uncle Misha directly to a large office furnished with heavy oak furniture. A young German officer with small, glittering eyes, a long face, and curly black hair sat behind a desk. Underneath a Hitler-style mustache, the officer's lips were curled into a smirk. A young Ukrainian translator in a white embroidered shirt was seated at a second desk.

Uncle Misha stood at the threshold and gave a low bow in accordance with Ukrainian custom. He leaned on his walking stick and waited indifferently.

"Ask him what he's doing in Radomyshl," the commandant instructed the Ukrainian, who translated it for Uncle Misha.

"My neighbor Makar was just in Radomyshl," Uncle Misha began, speaking slowly and calmly. "And he told me that there's a prisoner-of-war camp here, where my son Petro may be held. So I said to my youngest son, Mitka, 'Let's go to Radomyshl to find out if this is true.' Anyway, we packed some cornmeal pierogies with poppyseed filling—my Petro really loves them—and some underwear, and—"

"What's he carrying on about for so long?" the commandant interrupted. The Ukrainian translated the narrative.

The commandant's beady little eyes stared at Uncle Misha. "He looks suspicious," he said. "Try pulling on his beard to see whether it's natural or glued on."

The Ukrainian walked over to Uncle Misha and yanked on his beard a few times.

"What a strange custom you have here in Radomyshl," Uncle Misha said indignantly. "A decent man with a beard isn't allowed to show his face on the street. Shame on you! You should show more respect to your elders."

When the Ukrainian translated the admonishment, the officer burst out in laughter.

"Write down his general information and let him go," the commandant ordered, returning to the paperwork on his desk.

The Ukrainian demanded Uncle Misha's identification and started recording the details in a thick notebook.

"You're Ivan Grib?"

"Ivan, son of Daniel Grib," Uncle Misha answered confidently.

"Born in 1898?"

"Yes."

"In the village of Sele... Selez... It's not clearly written."

"From the village of Selezivka, near Velidnyky," Uncle Misha explained.

"Selezivka?" the commandant shouted, jumping from his chair. With one leap, he was standing in front of Uncle Misha. "You're a partisan!" he yelled, foaming at the mouth and shaking his pistol in Uncle Misha's face. "Admit it, you Ukrainian dog!"

Uncle Misha immediately realized that he had made a mistake, but could not imagine what it was. "I'm a kolkhoz worker," he replied calmly. "I don't even know what partisans look like."

"That's not true! All of the Ukrainians living in the forest region are partisans."

"Personally, I'm afraid of the partisans, Herr Commandant. I've never seen them with my own eyes."

"When did you leave Selezivka?" the commandant demanded, still pointing his pistol at Uncle Misha.

"Yesterday at dawn."

As the Ukrainian translated Uncle Misha's answer, the commandant grew even more irate. "You left Selezivka yesterday, and didn't see any partisans?" he screamed.

The commandant hit Uncle Misha in the face with his pistol, as hard as he could. Uncle Misha heard something crack in his mouth and felt excruciating pain. He quickly grew dizzy and started to lose consciousness. He fell to the floor covered in his own blood. The last thing he heard was the commandant bellowing, "Tomorrow you'll be hanged on the apothecary square!"

––––––––––––––

WHEN UNCLE MISHA woke up, he found himself lying on the concrete floor of a cellar. A ray of sunlight was shining through a small barred window high on the wall, just under the ceiling. His entire head throbbed with pain, but his mouth hurt the most. The jawbone on the left side of his face was broken, and he was missing five teeth.

Motele was there. He was kneeling over Uncle Misha, caressing his head and crying quietly.

Uncle Misha groaned.

"Uncle Misha, you're alive!" Motele called out joyfully. He held Uncle Misha closely and started sobbing loudly. He kept repeating, "Uncle Misha, they're going to hang us."

"They'll probably set you free," Uncle Misha tried to console him. "And I'm not afraid of death. It's much easier for me to die now than it would have been if they'd shot me along with the 2,200 other Jews from our town during the *Aktion*. Since then, I've killed enough Germans. I've taken revenge, and I can rest in peace, with the conviction that I've fulfilled my duty as a Jew and as a man." It was difficult for him to talk. His tongue was swollen, and his mouth ached every time he moved it.

Motele lay down next to him and went back to crying quietly.

"It's all over. By this time tomorrow, my stiff body will be hanging in a prominent location in the center of town, eliciting triumphant and mocking glances from the German and Ukrainian murderers," Uncle Misha said to himself. "I just wish I could have lived long enough to see Hitler's defeat, which, by all accounts, won't be much longer."

Then his thoughts turned to those he would be leaving behind. "I wonder what's happening right now in our detachment," he asked himself. "They'll figure out that I've been captured when we don't return at midnight, as we'd planned....This will be a terrible blow to my son....I wish I could live, if only for his sake.... Now he'll be completely alone. I wish I could have lived long enough to teach him to be a productive man and a proud Jew."

"Motele," he said aloud. "I need you to tell my Lionka that I was thinking of him before my death. Tell him that my last wish was that he carries on the struggle that we've been going through together, and that he finds solace in revenge."

Motele pressed his head against Uncle Misha's chest and continued to weep.

"They'll torture me before they kill me," Uncle Misha's internal monologue continued. "They'll want to extract information from me about the partisans... but they won't succeed.... I'll spit in their faces and show them how to die like a Jew."

He tore a sleeve from his linen shirt. With Motele's help, he wrapped the makeshift bandage around his head to stabilize his jaw. His pain eased, and he drifted back to sleep.

Through his slumber, he heard Motele exclaim, "Uncle Misha! There's shooting!"

He thought he was dreaming, but then he heard Motele's voice again. "Uncle Misha, our unit is coming!"

He opened his eyes and heard gunfire in the distance.

"That's our unit! That's our unit!" Motele shouted in joy.

"How could that be our unit?" Uncle Misha was skeptical.

"Of course, that's our unit," Motele said decisively. "Why would the Germans be shooting at each other?"

With each passing moment, the gunfire grew closer and closer.

Suddenly they heard grenades exploding, followed by the sound of several fighters shouting "Oo-rah!" as they burst into the courtyard of the military police headquarters. Rapid gunfire mixed with the cries of wounded military policemen. Desperate to let the fighters know where he and Uncle Misha were, Motele kept trying to scale the wall to reach the small window.

"How will they know that we're here?" Motele cried in desperation. He yelled, "Comrades, save us!" over and over, but his voice was drowned out by loud bursts from the heavy machine guns that the Germans had placed next to the window. As the military policemen retreated into the station, the noise from the courtyard grew softer and was replaced by a clamor above the cellar.

"They're not going to find us," Motele said nervously. "Move closer to the wall, Uncle Misha. I'll stand on your shoulders and reach the little window."

Uncle Misha pressed himself against the wall and Motele climbed on top of him. He pushed the shutter open with his fist and, as loudly as he could, yelled, "Save us!" There was no response.

"I hear Lionka's voice!" Motele declared. "I'll let him know we're here." He put two fingers in his mouth and gave their signal: a long whistle, two short whistles, and then another long whistle. They heard the same signal being whistled outside.

A few minutes later, there was an urgent banging on the cellar door. The door broke down with a loud crack and Lionka ran into the cellar with several partisans.

The partisans laid Uncle Misha in a well-padded German wagon heading down the same road that he had taken into town. The partisan doctor Nina Titova sat beside him, gently holding his head in her lap to protect him from feeling every bump as the wagon bounced down the road.

As they headed back into the forest, the partisans proudly sang "Through Valleys and Over Hills," a popular Red Army song from the Russian Civil War that is commonly known as the "Partisan's Song":

> *The glory of these years will never fade,*
> *They will never be forgotten—*
> *The partisan detachments*
> *Are occupying the cities.*

Lionka walked alongside Uncle Misha's cart, holding it with one hand while filling his father in on what had happened.

LIONKA HAD GOTTEN nervous about the mission as soon as Uncle Misha and Motele left for Radomyshl. His anxiety increased a few hours later, when a Ukrainian auxiliary policeman who was a partisan informant arrived. The policeman told the partisans that the watchman at the brewery had been arrested, and that the auxiliary police had been ordered to detain every suspicious person who came to Radomyshl and deliver them to the military police. Lionka was suspicious of the auxiliary policeman, and did not tell him that Uncle Misha had gone into the city.

That evening, a messenger from the partisans' informant in the District Administrator's office came running. He brought news that a partisan and a little boy were being held by the military police, and that they were going to be hanged the next day. The District Administrator had been ordered to gather the entire Ukrainian population at the apothecary square to watch the execution.

Lionka immediately convened the other partisan commanders whose units were encamped with Uncle Misha's Jewish Group, but they determined that a rescue operation would be impossible. With only four hundred partisans, their force was too small to mount a successful attack on such a well-fortified city. As a District Center, Radomyshl was protected by a strong garrison consisting of around 350 Germans, Ukrainians, and Hungarians armed with rifles, submachine guns, machine guns, and mortars.

Lionka left to consult with Ivan Khitrichenko, the commander of the Khrushchev Kyiv Partisan Federation. A joint detachment of seven hundred partisans from Khitrichenko's federation was encamped near the village of Khomivka, ten miles northeast of Radomyshl, and a little over a mile from where the units from the Stalin Partisan Federation were encamped. Khitrichenko's chief of staff, Dmitrii Burkov, had visited the Stalin federation earlier that day to exchange intelligence. He had shared the exciting news of Sydir Kovpak's successes during the Carpathian Raid, during which the partisans had killed thousands of Nazis and destroyed several trains, bridges, and warehouses.

What Burkov had not revealed was that Khitrichenko's federation was in the area specifically to launch an attack on Radomyshl. Their mission was to destroy the garrison, the German Army warehouses, the communication lines, and the power station. They had dispatched spies to Radomyshl the night before, and had learned where the sentries were and what types of weapons were used to guard the garrison.

"How many armed partisans do you have?" Khitrichenko asked Lionka.

"Four hundred!"

Khitrichenko invited Lionka and the units from the Stalin Partisan Federation to join the raid. "We can gain control of the city within an hour and free our Uncle Misha," Khitrichenko promised.

An hour later, the partisans were on their way to Radomyshl. By eleven that night, they had taken up positions just outside of the city. Precisely at midnight, they stormed Radomyshl from six directions, quickly taking out the soldiers guarding their primary targets. They met the most resistance in the center of the city, where two partisan detachments fought with the Ukrainian auxiliary police and the German military police for two hours.

During the attack, the partisans freed Uncle Misha, Motele, and sixty-eight other prisoners from the police station cellar. They destroyed the police station, the communication lines, the water supply, and the power station. They burned down the bridges over the Teteriv and Myka Rivers and dismantled the town's industrial infrastructure, destroying a tractor workshop, a factory for agricultural machinery, and 150 tons of fuel. They burned down a cooking oil plant and blew up the equipment in a textile mill, as well as the equipment in the brewery, which had been Uncle Misha's original target.

In addition to burning down a German farm and distributing 250 cows among the local population, the partisans reduced several warehouses to ashes, but not before plundering sugar, butter, honey, flour, and textiles, which they also gave to the peasants.

The partisans kept over eight hundred yards of fabric, three tons of sugar, one ton of butter, and twenty sacks of flour for themselves. They had killed sixty Ukrainians and fifteen Germans, while only two partisans had lost their lives.

"Oh, they'll remember our attack for a long time!" Lionka bragged.

ON SEPTEMBER 18, the Stalin Partisan Federation was ordered to rally in full strength to the forest near the Teteriv River, forty miles northwest of Kyiv, by September 25. As the Red Army was advancing, the Germans were retreating to the Dnieper River, which runs through Kyiv. The Stalin federation was to reunite with Saburov's federation and assist the Red Army with the liberation of the Ukrainian capital.

Every day, the radio broadcast the exciting news of hundreds of towns and villages being liberated by the Red Army, and of thousands of German soldiers being taken prisoner. Every night, weapons, ammunition, and medical supplies parachuted down from Soviet planes. The partisans were in high spirits, anticipating that their stressful and difficult lives in the forest would soon come to an end. The long-awaited time when they would meet up with the Red Army was quickly approaching.

The first signs of the impending German defeat were the newly recruited partisans. Some were Ukrainian officials, including entire police units, who had collaborated with the Germans, but who now wanted to defect to the partisans. Others were Russians and Belarusians who had managed to escape from prisoner-of-war camps, but who had settled into peaceful lives in Ukraine, while their compatriots were shedding their blood in the Red Army and in partisan detachments. The ground was shifting, and now they wanted to redeem themselves for their treason. They were all subjected to an accounting of their activities during the previous two years of war. The reckonings cost the worst offenders their lives, but others were accepted into the partisan ranks.

When the Central Staff of the Partisan Movement learned about the injuries Uncle Misha had sustained during his arrest in Radomyshl several weeks earlier, they offered to send an airplane to transfer him to a hospital in Moscow. Uncle Misha refused. He had confidence in the care he was receiving from Nina Titova. She had healed many partisans in rudimentary field hospitals, and assured him that he would make a full recovery. More importantly, he did not want to leave his detachment, especially when they were about to join up with the Red Army. He could not imagine missing that momentous occasion.

THE STALIN PARTISAN Federation received a new order on September 23. They were to join Colonel Georgy Pokrovsky's partisan federation in liberating Novoshepelychi, a village on the western bank of the Pripyat River, around fifteen miles from where the Pripyat flows into the Dnieper River. Germans were rallying there, as part of a larger strategy to fortify the western bank of the Dnieper—the third largest river in Europe—as an "Eastern Wall." But if the partisans could secure the area to the west of the Dnieper, the Red Army would be able to cross the river before the Germans could construct an impenetrable defensive line, and keep pushing westward.

The battle for Novoshepelychi started before dawn on September 25 and lasted for several hours, with neither side willing to back down. The partisans relentlessly attacked the two rows of trenches that surrounded the village, but the Germans put up a strong resistance. The western side of the village was stubbornly defended by German military policemen and Ukrainian auxiliary policemen—many of whom had been evacuated from villages and towns that had already been liberated by the Red Army. They knew the fate that awaited them if they were captured alive by the partisans, and were willing to fight to the last bullet.

By noon, the partisans had overpowered them and taken control of the village. Up to one hundred Germans and their collaborators had been killed or wounded, and the partisans had destroyed the military police headquarters, the commandant's headquarters, and the mayor's office. They had captured three food warehouses, two shops, two dairy factories, and the radio station. Most importantly, they had seized a crossing point on the western bank of the Pripyat for the Red Army.

Only a few Germans who had barricaded themselves in a two-story schoolhouse remained. The partisans were able to breach the schoolhouse, but only succeeded in forcing the Germans from the ground floor to the upper story, and then into the attic. The partisans could not follow the Germans into the attic, because the only entrance was a small access hatch. If a partisan dared to stick his head into the attic, he would be shot.

Uncle Misha arrived at the schoolhouse just as the partisans were preparing to set the building on fire. He insisted that they abandon those plans, arguing that it was the only schoolhouse in town and that it would be a shame to burn down a public institution that had survived the occupation just as Novoshepely-chi was being liberated. Instead, Uncle Misha suggested that the partisans go into the attic of the neighboring house and throw grenades onto the school's roof.

As soon as the first few grenades exploded, the partisans started hearing screams from wounded Germans inside the school attic. A moment later, one of the Germans started waving a white handkerchief through the damaged roof. They were surrendering.

Within a few minutes, the partisans emerged from the schoolhouse with ten frightened Germans: six officers and four soldiers. Uncle Misha ordered that they be marched beyond the town limits and shot.

Motele was standing in front of the schoolhouse when the ten Germans were led down the stairs. As he watched them go by, one of the prisoners caught his eye.

"Uncle Misha!" he exclaimed. "One of the Germans is an old acquaintance of ours—the military police commandant from Radomyshl!"

Uncle Misha had not recognized the frightened officer with the unshaven face as the elegant commander who had broken his jaw, knocked out five of his teeth, and sentenced him to death. He ordered the officer to step out of the line and placed him in the custody of Lionka and David of Yarevysche.

"Guard him closely," he instructed Lionka. "We'll interrogate him tonight."

"Don't worry, Uncle Misha," Motele called out. "We managed to escape from this murderer, but he won't get out of here alive."

THAT EVENING, AS Uncle Misha strolled through Novoshepely-chi, it seemed impossible that a fierce battle had been fought there just hours earlier. The liberated townspeople were walking the streets, making friends with the partisans. On a square in the middle of the town, a partisan from Uncle Misha's Jewish Group named Notke Zinman was playing a looted accordion while Ukrainian children danced. After inspecting the patrolmen on every corner, Uncle Misha returned to the nicest building in town, which the partisans had set up as their staff headquarters. He ordered that the commandant from Radomyshl be brought to him.

Ever since that encounter in the military police headquarters in Radomyshl, two questions had haunted Uncle Misha, and he hoped they would finally be answered: Why had the commandant become so enraged at the mention of Selezivka? And who had betrayed the night watchman at the brewery?

Worried that the German might refuse to answer his questions if he started too aggressively, Uncle Misha decided to tread lightly. He invited the commandant to sit down and asked him in a friendly voice, "Do you remember the time when a bearded partisan and a little boy were brought to you, and that night there was an attack on Radomyshl during which they were freed?"

"Yes, I remember," the German answered resignedly, not recognizing his clean-shaven interrogator.

"Can you explain to me why you became so upset when he said that he was from the village of Selezivka?"

"Because he said that he'd never seen any partisans, and there was no way that was true. Three days earlier, there had been a battle in Selezivka between Germans and partisans. Thirty-five Germans were killed in the fight, and the village was burned down as a punishment for helping the partisans. If he'd left the village the previous morning, as he claimed, he would have had to have known about it."

"Now, tell me, why did they arrest the watchman at the brewery?"

"Because he was planning to bomb the brewery at the instruction of the partisan leader Uncle Misha."

"How did you know that?"

"A Ukrainian auxiliary policeman who was working with the partisans told us."

That explained everything. The interrogation was over.

Uncle Misha ordered the German to stand. He walked up to him and looked straight into his frightened eyes. "That partisan, the one with the beard, that was me," he said loudly. "The Jewish partisan commander, Uncle Misha!"

As Uncle Misha stared at the commandant with contempt, the German's entire body started to tremble. He turned red and then to a chalky paleness as the blood drained from his face. His tiny eyes grew so big and round that they looked like they might pop out of his head at any second. Not a hint of his German arrogance remained.

"What kind of death does he deserve?" Uncle Misha asked the partisans who were watching the interrogation.

David of Yarevysche reached into the hunter's satchel that he used as an ammunition bag. He pulled out a pair of cobbler pliers and laid them on the table. Quoting the Book of Exodus, he replied calmly in Hebrew, "A tooth for a tooth."

When they threw the commandant's body into the Pripyat River the next day, his mouth was missing far more teeth than Uncle Misha had lost when the German had pistol-whipped him several weeks earlier.

CHAPTER 14

"A Young Soldier
Quietly Sings a Song"

The night is so dark that you can't see the moon.
The war sleeps, like a tired soldier.
Somewhere, just beyond the river,
A young soldier quietly sings a song.

—BORIS TUROVSKY, "GIRL, REMEMBER ME"
(FROM SIMCHA GILDENMAN'S SONGBOOK)

O N SEPTEMBER 27, 1943, THE partisans watched jubilantly as Colonel Porfiry Martynovich Gudz and his staff crossed the pontoon bridge that the partisans had built over the Pripyat River. Using the bridge, along with two large boats the partisans had prepared, Red Army soldiers crossed the river and established a bridgehead on its western bank. The partisans greeted the exhausted soldiers with kisses on the cheek and gave them food and supplies that they had captured from the Germans. Each partisan searched for soldiers from their hometown, asking for news about what was happening there and telling them about their lives in the forest.

In accordance with an order from the Central Staff of the Partisan Movement, the Stalin federation was disbanded on October 6. Uncle Misha's days as a partisan were over. The Soviet Union awarded him with a "To a Partisan of the Patriotic War," 2nd Class medal, for having distinguished himself in combat.

While some of the partisans were directed to continue guerrilla activities in western Ukraine, others were absorbed into the Red Army and assigned to various military units commensurate with their qualifications and weapons training. As a multilingual engineer, Uncle Misha was conscripted as a staff interpreter for a detachment of sappers—combat engineers—in the 151st Rifle Regiment of the 13th Army's 8th Rifle Division. Lionka joined the same sappers detachment as a submachine gunner.

The 151st Rifle Regiment gained ninety-four partisans from the Borovik Partisan Detachment. A total of 366 additional partisans from the Stalin federation were assigned to other regiments and staffs. The women and children were transferred to the eastern side of the Pripyat, where they were to be transported to the Soviet rear.

When Motele learned that he was being sent away, he begged to stay with Uncle Misha and Lionka. "I'm not a child anymore," he pleaded, with tears in his eyes, to the regiment staff. "I'm already more than twelve years old. I would be just as useful as a small scout on the front as I was in the forest. I'm an orphan, and I don't have anyone other than Uncle Misha and Lionka. I don't want to be separated from them." After Uncle Misha joined in the appeal, the staff agreed that the boy could stay with the regiment.

NEWLY AUGMENTED WITH the former partisans, the 8th Rifle Division joined the 148th Rifle Division in defending the area around the village of Nagortsy. Located ten miles northwest of the city of Chernobyl, in the area where the Chernobyl Nuclear Power Plant would later stand, Nagortsy was, at least for a little while, one of just a few locations where the Red Army held both sides of the Pripyat River.

The Soviets waged a bitter campaign against the Germans, but their ability to repel the frequent attacks grew weaker with every passing day. Only part of the Soviet Air Force had been able to establish bases close to the new front, and those were more than fifty miles east of the fighting. Ammunition was also lagging behind, leaving the Red Army without shells for the anti-aircraft guns. With the Soviets unable to defend themselves against air attacks, German airplanes battered the Nagortsy bridgehead.

The fighting went on for several days. At four in the morning on October 13, the 8th and 148th Rifle Divisions were defending the highway north of Karpilovka, a village southwest of Nagortsy, when the Germans launched an assault from the south. The Soviets were able to repel the Germans, but the Germans spent the next several hours concentrating heavy artillery and mortar fire on their location.

At three in the afternoon, two battalions from the 148th Rifle Division launched an attack to take Karpilovka. They were able to breach the northwestern outskirts of the village within forty minutes, but were forced to retreat back to their original position when the Germans opened fire with heavy machine guns, intensive artillery, and tanks.

That night, Uncle Misha and a squad of eighteen sappers were dispatched to lay mines on the roads leading from Karpilovka. Lionka and Motele went with them. There was a full moon, which made their clandestine mission even more difficult. The slightest mistake could have resulted in them being seen by the Germans who were a mere three hundred yards away. Crawling on the ground, Lionka and Motele brought the land mines to Uncle Misha and the other sappers, one by one. Uncle Misha and the sappers buried the mines in the sandy ground and covered them back up.

They completed their work just after midnight, and were preparing to return to camp, when the all-too-familiar whistle of an artillery shell interrupted the night's silence. A few seconds later, a shell exploded very close to them, followed immediately by another, and then another. The frightening blasts of exploding artillery shells echoed all around them.

They leaped into the trenches that had been dug throughout the entire area and waited for the shelling to end. An hour later, with the Germans not showing any signs of ending the barrage, the sappers started to realize just how precarious their situation was. They could not return to their camp without crossing an exposed area that was over half a mile wide, and they could not stay where they were, because they would be easily spotted once the sun came out.

There was only one way out: They would have to crawl eastward, toward the river, even though that was the opposite direction of where they needed to go. Once they got there, they would be able to hide behind the hills that stretched along the riverbank. They crawled on their hands and knees to the hills, where they dug foxholes with their shovels.

When dawn began to break, the Germans' artillery started shelling the entire embankment even more intensely. The riverbank was littered with the bodies of dead soldiers and horses. Leaflets calling on the Red Army to surrender flew through the air.

By ten in the morning on October 14, Uncle Misha, Lionka, and Motele were hungry and exhausted. Hundreds of artillery shells continued to fall around them. Suddenly a shell exploded right next to them, creating a deep crater and covering them with a thin layer of sand. When the smoke cleared, they realized that the four sappers who had been in the neighboring foxhole had been buried alive. They furiously tried to dig their comrades out, but it was too late. All four were dead. They returned to their foxhole and sat in silence for a long time, mourning the loss of their comrades.

ABOUT THREE HUNDRED yards away from their foxhole, to their left, Uncle Misha, Lionka, and Motele could see a patch of green bushes that looked like an oasis in the gray sand. To the right of the shrubs, in a trench closer to the river, there was a group of Soviet officers who had jumped out of a truck when it was hit by an artillery shell. Every time the officers moved, their golden epaulets sparkled in the sun.

Motele pointed toward the bushes and said, "Look, Uncle Misha, there's something slithering on the ground like a blue snake."

Uncle Misha saw a group of Germans, dressed in their blue-gray uniforms, crawling on the ground. They had spotted the Soviet officers, and were sneaking toward them, using the bushes as cover.

Uncle Misha, Lionka, and Motele shouted at the officers to warn them, but their voices were drowned out by the bursts of artillery fire and the whistles of flying shells. There was no point in trying to shoot the Germans, because the maximum range of their submachine guns was two hundred yards. They could see how much danger the officers were in, but there seemed to be nothing they could do to help.

"I'll run over there to warn them," Motele volunteered.

"Don't be foolish," Uncle Misha warned him. "The Germans will spot you before you're halfway to the officers."

"They won't see me. I'm small. I'll run crouched over and I'll hide behind the dead soldiers and horses." Before Uncle Misha could respond, Motele cried out, "Look! The Germans are getting close. I'm going."

Motele sprang from the foxhole and sprinted toward the officers' trench. To evade being targeted, he zigged and zagged back and forth as he ran. Every twenty-five yards, he dropped to the ground, lay there for a few seconds, and then popped back up and continued to run.

Uncle Misha and Lionka followed his every move with bated breath. They finally exhaled when the officers grabbed Motele and pulled him into their trench.

The officers immediately laid down heavy fire on the bushes. Realizing that they had been discovered, the Germans stood up and started running away. The officers were good shots. With each volley of gunfire, one fleeing Nazi after the other would throw his hands out and fall to the ground, never to get up again.

The German artillery changed their tactics and started shooting in short bursts. They would fire off a few dozen artillery shells, pause for a while, and then open fire again. During a lull around ten minutes after the Soviet officers had driven away the Germans, Uncle Misha and Lionka caught sight of Motele climbing out of the trench and running back, zigzagging and occasionally dropping to the ground. When he was around thirty yards from the foxhole, there was a sharp burst of fire from a heavy machine gun.

Motele pressed himself to the sand and glanced around in terror. After a few seconds, he lifted himself up to continue running, but before he could take one step, there was another burst of fire from the machine gun. Motele fell back to the ground with a heartrending cry.

Uncle Misha and Lionka quickly ran over, grabbed Motele by the hands, and dragged him into a trench. They ripped off his blood-soaked shirt and pants and saw that the entire right side of his body had been riddled with bullets. They took off their own shirts, shredded the fabric into pieces, and tried to bandage the wounds in an attempt to staunch the blood that was flowing freely.

"I wanted to be with the two of you," Motele murmured. He bit his lower lip and moaned quietly, trying to hide how much pain he was in.

Uncle Misha held Motele in his arms. Crying silently, Lionka held Motele's left hand and stroked his curly black hair. They were so consumed with grief that they barely noticed the German airplanes circling overhead, dropping dozens of bombs all around them.

Motele stopped moaning. His face grew pale and his breathing became labored. He was getting weaker by the minute. Suddenly he opened his eyes and, looking groggily at Uncle Misha, asked weakly, "Uncle Misha, when I die, will I see my parents again?"

"You're not going to die," Uncle Misha replied, trying to comfort him. "Once things calm down a bit, we'll carry you over to Nagortsy. We'll take you on the ferry to the field hospital on the other side of the river. They'll fix you back up, and you'll return to our regiment."

Motele looked at him with teary eyes. Uncle Misha knew that the boy understood the severity of his injuries, and did not believe his words.

Motele asked again, in a halting voice, "But when I die... will I see... my parents again?"

Uncle Misha could not answer. Tears started streaming down his face, the first tears he had shed since leaving the ghetto over a year earlier. They were tears of both grief and anger over being robbed of the brave boy whom he had grown to love as a son, and who was like a little brother to Lionka.

"Why?" Uncle Misha asked himself angrily. "Why now, when we've just met up with the Red Army? When our difficult and stressful lives as partisans in the forest have come to an end? When we're full of hope for a better tomorrow?"

Seeing Uncle Misha's tears, Motele stopped waiting for an answer.

The artillery suddenly fell silent. A deathly stillness permeated the air.

Motele sighed heavily and quietly groaned. "I will tell... my parents... and my little sister, Batyale... how I avenged them."

His entire body shivered. With a proud smile on his lips, Motele gave up his brave soul.

AT TWO-FORTY THAT afternoon, sixty German airplanes bombed the area where the 8th and 148th Rifle Divisions were fighting. Twenty minutes later, the Germans launched a ground offensive with a mechanized division of three thousand men and a tank division with as many as forty tanks, supported by artillery shelling. Their mission was clear: They intended to outflank the Soviets and encircle them by cutting them off from the river. After a second air raid at four-thirty, the German infantry recaptured Nagortsy and the bridgehead the Soviets had established there.

At one point in the battle, the sapper detachment received a report that a group of German submachine gunners had broken through the Soviet defenses and were fighting their way toward the command staff headquarters. Everyone who could hold a weapon was dispatched to repel the Germans.

"I'll go first," Lionka told Uncle Misha.

Lionka pressed forward, but the Soviet soldiers hesitated. "Go!" Uncle Misha ordered, threatening to shoot them unless they joined the attack. Then, yelling "Oo-rah!" he threw himself into the battle, bringing the entire sapper detachment with him and overrunning the Germans.

As Lionka was sprinting toward the Germans, he saw one aiming a submachine gun right at him. Lionka managed to fire his weapon first, and the German fell to the ground. Lionka grabbed the German's submachine gun and started beating him with it.

At that point, a German noncommissioned officer raised his hands in surrender.

"Papa, let's grab him and take him to the command staff, so they can find out what the Germans are up to," Lionka suggested. Just as Lionka started running toward the staff headquarters, a barrage of heavy mortar fire rained down. Looking for shelter, he leaped into a crater where a shell had already exploded. Instinctively he jumped back out, just as another shell landed inches away.

When Lionka reached the staff headquarters, he was welcomed as a hero. Thanks to his bravery, the counterattack had been a success, and the staff headquarters had been saved. One of the officers walked up to Lionka and remarked, "You know what, Lionka? We've had several Jews in our division, but none of them have been heroic like you!"

Lionka was outraged. He was still wearing the torn clothes he had worn as a partisan, and did not even hold a military rank. And here was this officer, spewing the antisemitic trope that Jews were cowardly by nature. In the presence of Colonel Georgy Tomilovskii, who was the commander of the 151st Rifle Regiment, and Tomilovskii's staff, Lionka slapped the officer in the face.

The officer stood there, completely thunderstruck by the audacity of the insubordination. "Why did he slap me?" the officer asked Uncle Misha. "What did I say?"

Uncle Misha, who had not heard the conversation, responded, "You tell me. What did you say to him?"

When the officer repeated his comment, Uncle Misha was equally offended. "You deserve what you got," he said. "Lionka is a proud Jew. It's insulting to him to suggest that all Jews are cowards and that his heroism is an exception. He certainly doesn't agree."

UNABLE TO HOLD their position against an onslaught of attacking Germans, the 151st Rifle Regiment withdrew to the forest northwest of Nagortsy at five-forty in the evening on October 14. Other regiments joined them later that evening. They attempted to retake Nagortsy, but were unsuccessful and were forced to retreat. Almost completely encircled in the small forest, their situation was dire.

Uncle Misha and Lionka started working on a plan. The German officer they had apprehended had given up valuable intelligence regarding the location, movements, and plans of the troops the Germans had assigned to defend the area. The Germans were concentrating their forces to the southeast, anticipating that the Soviets would try to fight their way back to the Pripyat in an attempt to cross the river and reunite with the rest of the Red Army. The Germans had not established much of a perimeter to the west.

There was a forest due west of where the Soviet soldiers were holed up. If they could cross that forest, they would be less than eight miles from the very same forest where Uncle Misha's Jewish Group had spent so much time with the 1st Stalin Partisan Detachment.

As Uncle Misha and Lionka were talking, a Soviet major who was a battalion commander walked over to them. "Well, partisans, what do you think?" he asked.

"My son has an idea," Uncle Misha responded. "He knows this area. He was the head of reconnaissance, and would often go on missions nearby."

"What do you know?" the major asked. "Let's go see Colonel Tomilovskii. I'm on my way there now. You can come as well."

At the staff headquarters, Tomilovskii took out a map of the area. There was no forest on the map.

"I know for sure that there's a forest," Lionka told him, pointing at the map. "Right here. The forest is here."

"What?" the colonel asked, raising his voice. "Can't you see that there's a field there?"

"There's a forest there," Lionka insisted.

"You're driving me crazy. Why are you making this up?"

"When was this map made?" The map, as it turned out, was almost twenty years old.

"It's possible that it's not a real forest," Lionka considered. "But it's at least an orchard. That would still give us enough cover to cross."

"You could be right," Tomilovskii conceded. He dispatched two officers to reconnoiter the area. Lionka volunteered to lead them.

"See?" he asked when they reached the trees. "There's a forest here."

Tomilovskii was still hesitant. Entering the forest would mean leaving their heavy artillery behind. But when the Germans started launching incendiary shells and the forest started burning, he turned to Uncle Misha and Lionka and asked them to save his men.

At nine that night, with Uncle Misha and Lionka leading the way, Tomilovskii and his men headed west. Before leaving, they buried all of their heavy equipment, taking with them only what they could carry.

They were met with some resistance from the German perimeter, but were able to continue after eliminating forty German soldiers. At two in the morning, they engaged some more Germans at the far rear of the German defense. They broke through an hour later, having suffered no casualties throughout the entire escape. By six in the morning, they were near the village of Nova Krasnytsia, fifteen miles southeast of Mukhoedy. They stopped there for the day because Lionka knew there would be German soldiers defending the nearby railway. That night, they continued on until they met up with partisans from Saburov's partisan federation.

"We've been waiting for you," the partisans welcomed them. The Central Staff of the Partisan Movement had informed Saburov that they were coming, and he had sent couriers to meet them. The partisans slaughtered a few cows and gave Tomilovskii and his men as much food and drink as they wanted. While they were in the area, Uncle Misha organized a group of three hundred men with whom he carried out several successful attacks on nearby garrisons. They "bombed" the farms of Nazi collaborators, confiscating the cattle and sheep before burning the property to the ground. They derailed a German train, annihilating its escort and confiscating several tons of flour that had been on the way to the front.

On November 22, 1943, Tomilovskii's men reunited with the Soviet front, which had liberated Chernobyl just a few days earlier. Uncle Misha was summoned to Moscow, where Kliment Voroshilov, the commander in chief of the Central Staff of the Partisan Movement, gave him a medal for having defended the command staff headquarters, for having brought the German officer to the command staff, and for having led the troops to safety. Tomilovskii had originally recommended a "For Battle Merit" medal, but Lieutenant General Nikolai Pukhov, the commander of the 13th Army, upgraded it to the Order of the Red Star. Lionka received the medal "For Courage." Voroshilov offered Uncle Misha a job working in the Moscow district as a civil engineer, but he refused. The Nazis had not been vanquished, so his mission was not yet complete.

"I want to continue on until victory!" Uncle Misha told Voroshilov. "I want to be on the front line. I want to be among the first to hang the banner of victory over the bandits' nest in Berlin."

CHAPTER 15

"Song of the Front-Line Driver"

Oh, the road and path of the front!
We're not afraid of the bombing.
We still have things to do at home,
And we're not ready to die.
—NAUM LABKOVSKY AND BORIS LASKIN,
"SONG OF THE FRONT-LINE DRIVER"
(FROM SIMCHA GILDENMAN'S SONGBOOK)

SINCE UNCLE MISHA HAD NEVER served in the army, he did not hold a military rank. To remedy this, he was sent to an officer-training course in Pavlovsky Posad, forty miles east of Moscow. After completing the course in four-and-a-half months, he was granted his request to be sent to the front. He was assigned as an engineer at the rank of junior lieutenant with the 13th Army's 150th Separate Construction Battalion.

The road construction battalions were special formations of engineers and construction workers who built and rebuilt highways and bridges for the Red Army. As the Germans retreated, they blew up bridges to slow down the Red Army's advance.

Uncle Misha and his battalion of sappers were sent in—ahead of
the rest of the troops, and often under fire—to restore the transportation infrastructure so the front line could march on. As a
sapper, Uncle Misha was wounded in combat three times and was
shell-shocked once. But he returned to the front after each injury.

In July 1944, Uncle Misha's sapper battalion played a significant role in the Lviv–Sandomierz Offensive, an operation that
liberated western Ukraine and eastern Poland. The sapper battalion built bridges over the San River and the Wisłok River, allowing the Red Army's 1st Ukrainian Front to liberate the large cities
of Lviv and Rzeszów. The crowning achievement of the offensive
was the establishment of a bridgehead on the western side of the
Vistula River. As Poland's longest river, the Vistula formed a geographical barrier not unlike the Dnieper River in Ukraine.

Uncle Misha led the construction of a bridge across the Vistula at the village of Siedleszczany, south of Sandomierz. The
battle to control the bridgehead was fierce. It lasted from July
29 through August 16, during which the bridge was destroyed
four times by German airplanes. Each time, it was rebuilt by
Uncle Misha and his battalion of sappers, who sometimes
worked through aerial bombardment and artillery shelling. Ultimately, the bridge allowed the 1st Ukrainian Front's tanks and
heavy artillery to cross the river and reinforce the Sandomierz
bridgehead. Shortly after the bridge was completed, Uncle
Misha was awarded the Order of the Patriotic War, 2nd Class
medal, "for his skillful leadership of the work and for demonstrating courage."

OVER THE NEXT few months, the Germans and the Soviets remained entrenched at the Sandomierz bridgehead, while larger
battles raged in the Eastern Front's northern and southern
flanks. Regular soldiers would use the downtime between skirmishes to catch up on sleep, write letters, do their laundry, or
tidy their tents, but the sappers' work was never done. Among

their tasks was collecting and defusing the countless artillery shells being lobbed at the Red Army by the Germans, repairing the roads and bridges that had been destroyed by German and Soviet airplanes, and preparing plans for the bridges they would build during the next offensive.

Uncle Misha would also map out routes to coordinate troop movements around the Sandomierz bridgehead. At regular intervals along every road leading toward the next target, he would place signs indicating the route's number, along with the name of the nearest village and the distance to that village. Every unit would receive the route number prior to embarking on the mission. If the routes were not well marked or not attentively followed, multiple units could find themselves in a bottleneck that would make them sitting ducks for a German attack. Worse yet, different squads could end up on separate routes, dividing the unit or isolating the artillery equipment from the mine shells.

While entrenched at the Sandomierz bridgehead, the Red Army built up its strength through the addition of 100,000 men, 550 tanks and self-propelled guns, and 14,600 guns and mortars. By late October, the Soviets started drawing up plans for the Vistula–Oder Offensive. The operation would advance past the Vistula River, through central Poland, and to the Oder River—just over forty miles from Berlin. The Soviets originally planned to begin the offensive on January 20, 1945, but it was moved up to January 12 at the last minute to accommodate a request from the American and British forces to put more pressure on the Eastern Front during the Battle of the Bulge on the Western Front.

On January 11, Uncle Misha received an order to map out a route in Iwaniska, a Polish town twenty miles northwest of Sandomierz and two-and-a-half miles from where the sappers battalion was encamped. To avoid any errors, Uncle Misha usually put up the signs by himself. But since the order dictated that the route be mapped overnight, he set out at ten o'clock with three sappers and a Russian engineer named Ishchenko.

In addition to being a fellow engineer, Ishchenko shared an intellectual curiosity and a love for music with Uncle Misha. They often organized informal concerts, in which Ishchenko would sing Russian folk songs in his pure, lyrical tenor, while Uncle Misha accompanied him on guitar or violin. Making music together forged a strong bond, and Ishchenko became Uncle Misha's first choice when he needed help carrying out particularly complicated or dangerous missions.

The Red Army had liberated Iwaniska, but it acted as something of a buffer zone between the Germans and the Soviets. The German trenches began on the other side of town, and were bombarded incessantly by Soviet artillery. The peasants had fled in the earliest days of the Lviv–Sandomierz Offensive. Most of their houses had since burned down, leaving only crumbling stone ovens and chimneys. Except for the fires that occasionally broke out in the smoldering ruins and the bloated horse corpses scattered on the streets, the town looked completely abandoned.

The sappers moved quickly and quietly from street to street, screwing the route signs in place. They finished their work in two hours and were preparing to leave when the wind drove away the clouds. The snow stopped falling and the moon came out, revealing the silhouette of the Saint Catherine of Alexandria Church. The church towered over the town ruins. Its neo-Gothic spire proudly soared into the sky.

"It's high time for a smoke," one of the sappers remarked as they walked over to the church. Once they were behind a brick wall that would obscure the flames of their lighters from the German snipers, they lit their cigarettes.

"See how this church is still intact?" Ishchenko asked Uncle Misha. "If I were a religious man, I'd believe that God has protected His own house. It's strange that while the entire town has been destroyed by shells, this church, of all places—the tallest building in town—hasn't been touched by one shell."

Uncle Misha did not respond. He was thinking about the attack the next day. He knew that the Soviets were prepared for the mission, and that the blow to the Germans would be a decisive one. If everything went as planned, they would break through the German line and continue on into Germany. He imagined marching through burning German towns and reducing German houses to rubble, just as the Jewish homes in Korets had been destroyed. The thought brought him great satisfaction.

Then his thoughts turned to Lionka. He had not seen his son since shortly after they had been absorbed into the Red Army over thirteen months earlier. While Uncle Misha had gone to officer-training school near Moscow, Lionka had been sent to Chernihiv for his officer course. Uncle Misha had not heard from him since, but had learned that Lionka was an officer in one of the many infantry divisions in the 1st Ukrainian Front. Uncle Misha wondered if Lionka would be leading his division into battle the next day, and, if so, whether they would reunite somewhere on the front line.

"COMRADE ENGINEER, DO you think the church organ still works?" Ishchenko interrupted Uncle Misha's reverie.

"If the church is still undamaged, then surely the organ's also in good shape," he responded.

"I can see that you're in a bad mood," Ishchenko continued. "Let's go into the church. I can sing something very quietly, and you can accompany me on the organ. It would brighten your mood in no time."

Their heavy boots echoed as they walked into the large, empty sanctuary and shuffled up the narrow staircase to the organ gallery. A thick layer of dust on the organ confirmed that it had not been touched for quite some time.

Uncle Misha played a chord in the bass register. Without taking his left hand off the keys, he ran his right hand downward from the highest pitches to the middle register. Ishchenko started singing a Russian folk song. At first, he sang softly and tenderly, but as he warmed up, he started singing with great emotion. He and Uncle Misha got so lost in the music that they forgot all about the outside world. They lost sight of the fact that it was past midnight on an evening when they would need their rest for a battle the next day. They even forgot that there were Germans sitting in trenches less than two hundred yards away, within earshot.

Suddenly the silence outside was broken by the dry bang of a mine launcher being loaded, followed by the whistle of a shell flying through the air. Within seconds, there was a loud explosion. The church walls shook, and the windows shattered onto the stone floor.

"They heard us!" Uncle Misha exclaimed. "Let's get out of here!"

They leaped up and ran down three flights of stairs, sprinting toward the exit. Explosions could soon be heard from all sides as artillery shells rained down. One shell came through a broken window and exploded just a few feet from them, kicking up a cloud of dust and bits of brick and glass. They had almost reached the door when a shell hit a nearby pillar and exploded. Uncle Misha felt a blunt blow to his stomach.

"I'm hit!" he exclaimed to himself. He put his hand to his stomach. He felt no blood, and realized that he also did not feel the familiar pain of shrapnel piercing the body. He assumed that he had been hit by a piece of brick.

The two engineers ran out of the church and hid behind tombstones in the church graveyard. Artillery shells continued to hit the church. The last one struck the heavy iron cross on top of the spire and blew it away. After that, the bombardment finally stopped. Uncle Misha and Ishchenko were back with their battalion within half an hour.

When they entered their tent, Ishchenko lit a small tin oven and started boiling tea. Uncle Misha had to write a report on the mapped-out routes for the command staff. When he picked up his leather satchel to remove his inkwell, he discovered that the glass had broken and ink had spilled out. At the same time, he noticed a hole in the front of the satchel. He quickly spread out his papers, his diary, and his copy of *Freedom's Songs* on his desk. Many of the papers were damaged and stained with ink.

At the bottom of the satchel, he found a piece of iron that weighed about a pound. It was shrapnel from the artillery shell that had exploded when they were exiting the church. It had punctured the satchel, broken the inkwell, and stopped when it had hit his documents.

"Do you see what kind of present the Germans sent me, Ishchenko?" he joked, holding up the shrapnel. "Had this piece of iron hit my stomach instead of my satchel, you'd be writing up the route report, as well as a report on my death."

"You can imagine how much I'd be sweating when I presented the second report," Ishchenko retorted. It would not have been easy to explain why they were in a church singing and playing an organ so close to the enemy.

The next morning, as Uncle Misha was packing his documents into a new satchel, he remembered the piece of iron shrapnel. After thinking about it for a few seconds, he decided to take it with him. "If I survive the war, I'll keep this shrapnel on my desk as a souvenir."

The battle began at five in the morning and lasted all day. Thousands of cannons, howitzers, and rocket launchers bombarded the Germans, along with 466 aircraft missions. The ground trembled from the incessant shelling and bombing. The howl of engines, the bangs of artillery being loaded, the whistles of flying mine shells, and the explosions of bombs blended together in a cacophony. By the end of the day, the German positions had been annihilated and the 1st Ukrainian Front had pushed the Germans backward twelve miles. Uncle Misha was back to building new bridges that would allow the tanks and heavy artillery to keep driving forward.

BY FEBRUARY 18, 1945, the 1st Ukrainian Front had occupied the town of Żagań, in western Poland. Uncle Misha's sapper battalion was tasked with constructing a bridge across the Bóbr River, which runs through the middle of town, so that Lieutenant General Dmitry Lelyushenko's 4th Tank Army could continue rolling toward Berlin. The sappers located all the supplies they needed in the city's forest warehouses, and decided that they could build a low-water crossing with a sixty-ton capacity in two days. It would go right next to where the Kaiser Wilhelm Bridge had stood just days earlier, before the Germans had blown it up during their retreat.

By that afternoon, they had erected scaffolding in the middle of the river for the piers. They set up pile drivers on the scaffolding and started working on the banks. At five in the evening, they noticed that the river was rising at a rapid rate. If the water level continued to rise, the scaffolding and all the equipment would be underwater by the morning. From a local villager, Uncle Misha learned that the river was rising because there were locks five miles downstream that were closed.

That night, after being informed that the east bank of the Bóbr had been cleared of Germans for more than a dozen miles downstream, Uncle Misha and Fedorenko, a captain in the sapper battalion, climbed into a boat carrying automatic rifles and two grenades. Uncle Misha operated the rudder, while Fedorenko, a burly Ukrainian, rowed. A few miles down the river, the water started moving so fast that they could no longer control the boat. They tried to steer the boat to the shore, but the current was too strong.

Suddenly the boat hit something hard in the water. Uncle Misha and Fedorenko were tossed overboard, and the boat quickly floated away. They spotted a couple of thick logs drifting on the river's surface and climbed on. As they caught their breaths, they realized that the logs were spinning in place. They also heard the loud rush of a waterfall coming from downstream and to the right. They deduced that the sound was from a dam that the Germans had built to generate hydroelectric power. The dam must have burst, allowing the water to rush into the river at a right angle and create the vortex in which they were whirling around.

"Did you dream last night that we were going to take a ride on a carousel?" Uncle Misha joked.

Fedorenko laughed and replied, "We're lucky that it's a carousel on the Bóbr River rather than some river in the netherworld, which is where we could've easily gone when our boat collided with these logs."

"Apparently, you've forgotten, Fedorenko, that only two kinds of death await the sapper: from one's own mine, or by drowning. So we'd have died a typical sapper death if we'd choked on the Bóbr's water. But we're getting philosophical here, when the day after tomorrow General Lelyushenko and his tanks need to be able to cross the river using our bridge. That's the first thing. The second thing is that it's a bad idea to keep one's feet in the water for long periods of time in February. My mother always told me: Don't get your feet wet, or you'll catch a cold. So here's what I think we should do: The rifles that survived so miraculously on our backs will have to be thrown into the water. Our overcoats are too bulky, so they'll have to go as well. We'll keep only our grenades. We may need them, if not against the Germans, then for ourselves to make sure we don't fall into their hands alive. Now, let's cinch our belts and swim to the locks."

At first, it was easy to swim with the current. But as they grew closer to the locks, the strong current once again made it increasingly difficult for them to control their direction. The water lifted Uncle Misha and tossed him over a lock gate. He dropped six feet onto a concrete surface, tumbling several times before finally coming to a stop. He spat out water from his mouth and breathed deeply a few times. He stood up and called

out for Fedorenko. The Ukrainian was lying a few feet away, trying unsuccessfully to rise. When Fedorenko finally got back on
his feet, he started cursing and rubbing his right knee.

"There's no reason to swear," Uncle Misha remarked. "You
bruised your right knee, and I bruised my left, so at least we're
symmetrical."

They were on a landing on the other side of a lock, where the
water was only ankle deep. The gate they had just gone over was
behind them. They could not see what was in front of them. To
each side was a slippery six-foot concrete wall.

"Stand next to the wall," Fedorenko suggested. "I'll climb on
your shoulders and then pull you up."

A few minutes later, they were on the riverbank. A narrow
bridge, just two planks wide, crossed over the lock. Every
three or four yards, there was a post with a handwheel. Each
wheel was attached to a chain that opened a sluice. They tried
to turn the first crank, but the water pressure held the sluice
closed. After a great deal of effort, the wheel started spinning
and the first sluice opened. They progressed along the bridge,
opening the sluices, one by one. The water burst through,
quickly filling the lock chamber in which they had been standing minutes earlier.

ON THEIR WAY back to the camp, Uncle Misha and Fedorenko
saw an abandoned factory next to a waterfall, which confirmed
their theory about a tributary causing the vortex. Later, they
came upon a large forest warehouse. There were large piles of
timber on the riverbank, waiting to be floated down the river.
Further inland were logs, boards, and woodworking equipment.
They heard muffled conversations in German, the steady pound-
ing of hammers hitting wood, and the clamor of boards being
dropped to the ground. Uncle Misha and Fedorenko stopped,
hid behind a pile of timber, and listened. They heard the sound
of an approaching car.

"We've stumbled upon some Germans," Uncle Misha whispered.

"Yes, even though the division headquarters promised us that this side of the river has been cleared of Germans for ten to twelve miles," Fedorenko whispered back, clearly displeased. "So much for that."

"The riverbank is cleared, but this is either some stragglers or a group that was deliberately left behind to cover the retreating troops. We'll have to find a good hiding place, because there's no telling how long we'll need to stay here."

They quietly assembled a simple structure out of a few logs, adding more on the Germans' side to make it look like an overturned lumber pile. They climbed into their hideout and huddled close to each other for warmth. They were wet, tired, and hungry, and desperately wanted to smoke.

When dawn broke, they were able to see a group of about thirty Germans next to a car. An officer was quietly giving orders, while the soldiers were silently carrying boards to two boats that were sitting on the riverbank. The soldiers laid the boards across the boats and nailed them down to create a crude raft. They took a length of rope from the car and tied one end to a tree about twenty paces away from Uncle Misha and Fedorenko. Three soldiers took the other end of the rope and swam to the other side of the river, where they tied it to another tree.

The Germans stretched the rope across the river. Back on the eastern shore, the Germans dragged the makeshift raft into the water. A few of the Germans held on to pieces of rope that they had thrown over the line that stretched across the river to stop the raft from floating away with the strong current. Others pushed the raft across the river with long rods. They returned after a few minutes, apparently deeming the test run to have been a success.

The soldiers loaded the car onto the center of the raft. "That's it!" the officer shouted in German. "Let's go!"

Uncle Misha and Fedorenko were so absorbed with watching the German soldiers get the officer's car across the river that they forgot that they were cold and hungry. As the Germans left for the other side, Uncle Misha started thinking like a partisan again.

"The Germans are all gone from our side of the river. Let's throw a grenade against the tree with the rope tied to it. The rope will be severed, and the Germans will flow down the river to the carousel, and then to the locks."

"Good idea," Fedorenko responded.

They stood up, unpinned their grenades, and threw them toward the tree at the same time. There were two explosions, followed by the desperate shouts of Germans. The sappers peered from behind their hideout to see the raft with a few of the German soldiers, their officer, and his car being carried swiftly down the river.

IN THE VILLAGE of Trzebiel, near the German border, the Red Army captured a detachment of German engineers. They sent the officers and most of the soldiers to the rear, but retained some of the craftsmen and put them to work as blacksmiths, carpenters, and locksmiths. One of their prisoners was a sixty-year-old blacksmith named Karol, who had a knack for being able to fabricate precise parts for construction machinery—even though he was using the most primitive of tools. One day, Uncle Misha showed him the shrapnel that had almost killed him in Iwaniska.

"This piece of iron should have been my Angel of Death, but it failed," he explained. "I'd like to make it into some kind of useful object, as a souvenir. But I still want it to be obvious that it's shrapnel."

Karol took several minutes to examine the piece of iron. "I can make this into a small knife or a letter opener," he finally said. "Tell me which you'd prefer, and I'll get it done in no time."

"I don't care what shape it is. You can even make it into a swastika," Uncle Misha joked.

"I am a God-fearing German from the older generation," Karol said modestly. "Were it not for that damned swastika, I wouldn't have become a soldier at my age, much less a prisoner of war. I'll think of something that will make you happy, Herr Engineer."

A few days later, Karol brought Uncle Misha a knife he had made out of the shrapnel. Karol had left the handle untouched, but had forged the rest of the shrapnel into a miniature version of an ancient Teutonic sword. From that point on, Uncle Misha proudly carried his custom knife in his satchel.

ON APRIL 25, 1945, Soviet troops from the 1st Ukrainian Front met up with members of the United States Army on a bridge over the Elbe River, near Torgau, Germany. Their unit commanders convened in Torgau the following day for an official handshake. The convergence of the armies from the Western and Eastern Fronts marked an important milestone in the war against Germany.

Uncle Misha was among those who liberated a labor camp for "Eastern workers" in Torgau. A satellite camp of the Buchenwald concentration camp, the Torgau labor camp was where 250 Polish and Czech women had been imprisoned and forced to work at a German munitions factory. It was one of more than 44,000 prisoner-of-war camps, ghettos, transit camps, labor camps, concentration camps, and killing centers of various sizes that Nazi Germany and its allies had established since 1933.

Throughout his march through Poland and into Germany, Uncle Misha had participated in the liberation of a number of camps like the one in Torgau. He would never forget the filthy yet radiant faces of the former prisoners as they realized they were being set free. As they were separated into groups according to their nationalities, they would start singing their national anthems, coming together into a single, strong, unified song of liberation. As they filed out of the camps, through the wide-open gates or the torn-down barbed wire, the liberated prisoners would wave makeshift flags from their home countries.

It brought Uncle Misha immense joy to watch the former prisoners take their first steps as free people. It was worth having gone through all of the suffering, starvation, cold, and fear as a partisan, and then being in constant danger on the front line, in order to see the day when he would stroll down Polish and German streets as an officer in the Red Army, tearing down statues and portraits of Hitler and trampling German flags with his feet. The proudest moments of his life were when he, a son of the "inferior Jewish race," opened the gates of German camps and brought liberation to thousands of people.

WHILE HE WAS in Torgau, Uncle Misha took advantage of some downtime to sew fresh shirts and underwear for his sappers. There was a bountiful supply of white fabric in the German shops, and sewing machines could be requisitioned from the local population. The battalion doctor, a Mrs. Kuznetsov, took over the tailoring and identified a few seamstresses among the liberated women prisoners whom the Soviets were keeping in the camp until the front was a little farther away.

One day, Mrs. Kuznetsov asked Uncle Misha, "Comrade Engineer, did you know that one of my seamstresses is a Jewish girl from Łódź? When I told her that our battalion engineer is also Jewish, and is from Poland of all places, she was overjoyed and asked to meet you." Uncle Misha identified more as Polish than Ukrainian. "Join me for dinner. She'll be there. She's a very nice girl."

That evening, Uncle Misha visited the lavishly furnished former home of a Gestapo officer where Mrs. Kuznetsov was now residing. He found her sitting at a table with a young woman of about twenty-two or twenty-three years of age.

"I'm Eva," she introduced herself with a friendly smile. "I'm happy to meet a Polish Jew fighting in the ranks of the Red Army, who has participated in our liberation."

After a delicious meal, they adjourned to an ornate sitting room.

"So, we, the Jews of Volhynia, chose not to set out on the path that Hitler had chosen for us," Uncle Misha said, continuing the story he had been telling in the dining room. "Because we knew that path would lead to death through humiliation and pain. We chose a second, albeit equally difficult path, which led through terrible experiences, hunger, and deprivation. But this path also led to victory and vengeance. And even when it led to death, it was a noble death with a weapon in hand."

Noticing that Eva was crying, he decided to end on a happier note. "And I have lived to this glorious moment when I, as an officer in the victorious Red Army, sit in a magnificent home that was carefully decorated for me by a Gestapo officer, in a German town that my army has occupied, in the company of a nice Jewish girl whom my battalion liberated from forced labor. Now, I'd be interested in learning how you found yourself in a camp for gentile women."

In early 1940, Eva, her elderly parents, and her little sister, Sorele, had been confined to the Łódź ghetto, where Eva had worked as a seamstress in a factory that made German Army uniforms. In January 1942, the Germans deported Eva and her family to the Chełmno killing center, along with a large group of other Jews from the ghetto. When the train broke down on the second day of the voyage, the Jews were ordered to walk the rest of the way in snow up to their knees. As they marched, anyone who walked too slowly was beaten or shot. The captain of the guards, a blond German with freckles and sunken, watery eyes, rode his horse from one end of the column to the other, pummeling the Jews and cheering on the Ukrainian and Lithuanian guards when they did the same.

That night, while the prisoners were locked in a stable, the blond captain dragged the thirteen-year-old Sorele to a nearby peasant hut, where he raped her before turning her over to the other guards. The next day, Sorele was so weakened and injured from her trauma that she could barely stand. When she was unable to keep up with the march, the blond captain shot her and her mother with his pistol. Eva's father also disappeared during the march. He may have been shot, too, or may have fallen down and gotten trampled by the thousands of feet.

Eva managed to escape from the death march that night. Just as she was stepping into a wide, snow-filled ditch, a Jewish woman walking behind her was shot and fell on top of her. Eva was buried under the woman's body and was covered with her blood. Eva was unconscious, but the guards took her for dead. By the time she woke up, everybody was long gone. She crawled out from underneath the woman's body and made her way to a hut, where two elderly peasants who had lost three sons and a daughter-in-law took her in. After two weeks, they gave her their dead daughter-in-law's paperwork identifying her as an Aryan and got her a job as a maid in a faraway village. A few months later, young men and women from the village were deported to Germany as "Eastern workers," which is how she ended up at the Torgau labor camp.

A FEW DAYS after Uncle Misha met Eva, the Soviet military commander agreed to allow the women prisoners to leave Torgau. Since the railway lines were still congested with military transports, he suggested that they go on foot. The spring breezes were blowing, and the former prisoners were not intimidated by the prospect of walking hundreds of miles to get home. The women started to leave in groups, according to their nationalities. The Polish women organized themselves and decided to leave within the next few days. Uncle Misha gave his new friend, Eva, a handcart into which she loaded her belongings, along with canned food and bread he had given her.

As a final parting gift, Uncle Misha decided to make Eva a pair of durable shoes for the long journey ahead of her. There was plenty of leather in the battalion's warehouse, and there was a well-equipped shoemakers workshop in nearby Fort Zinna, a former military prison and prisoner-of-war camp that the Soviets had converted into a prison for German soldiers.

Eva accompanied Uncle Misha to Fort Zinna. As they approached the prison, they could see Germans walking around. Eva gripped Uncle Misha's hand.

"You know, Comrade Engineer, even now, when I see those murderers, they scare me," she said. "Even though I know that they're completely harmless and can't hurt me anymore."

Just as Uncle Misha and Eva were approaching the camp office, a group of Germans emerged from nearby barracks. "That's him!" Eva cried out. "I recognize him!" She fainted before Uncle Misha could even react.

He carried Eva to the infirmary, where the camp medic brought her back to consciousness.

"I saw the blond German who raped my little sister, Sorele, and then shot her and my mother," she explained with tears in her eyes.

Uncle Misha shared Eva's story with Captain Kalinin, the camp commander. Kalinin was sympathetic to her ordeal, but doubted that the man she had seen was the same German.

"The men in my camp are all soldiers from the front," he told Uncle Misha. "Whoever killed your friend's sister and mother was a Gestapo or SS man."

"You're very naive, Captain," Uncle Misha responded. "Now, with their defeat imminent, more than one ranking officer is hiding in the camps, donning the innocent uniform of a regular front soldier."

"It's him, it's him!" Eva insisted. "I recognized him. I've been thinking about his blond hair and his watery eyes for three years."

"If it's him, we'll find him," Captain Kalinin promised. "But among my two thousand German prisoners of war, there are many blond men with watery eyes. Come back tomorrow after work. I'll have all of the prisoners stand in groups. Forty men in each group, three per row, and they'll march by the window of

the office. From the office, you'll be able to see every German.
You'll recognize the murderer if he is indeed in my camp."

Uncle Misha and Eva returned the next day and watched as
the German prisoners of war paraded by. Eva spotted the blond
German in the sixth row of the twelfth group. It was all Eva
could do not to faint again.

THE BLOND GERMAN'S name was Robert Litke. As he stood
at attention in front of Uncle Misha, his eyes staring off into
the distance, Uncle Misha flipped through Litke's military service book.

"Why are two pages torn out?" Uncle Misha asked.

"The book got damaged when I was wounded," Litke answered calmly.

"Where were you wounded?"

"Near Bryansk, on the Eastern Front."

"In your book, there's a round stamp from Field Hospital
Number 2210. Where was this located?"

"In Litzmannstadt," Litke responded, using the German name
for Łódź.

"Tell us where you were after you left the hospital. There
aren't any records in your book about that period."

Litke did not respond immediately. A look of confusion
flashed across his face.

"Here we go," Uncle Misha said to himself.

Litke recovered quickly and reported, "In the 135th Infantry
Regiment."

Uncle Misha turned to Captain Kalinin and said, "As you can
see, we're dealing with a dangerous degenerate. The crime that
my friend described was undoubtedly not his first, or his last. I
ask you to place him into my custody. I'll investigate further and
mete out the appropriate punishment."

"I wonder, Comrade Engineer, how you can make such a
request. You know full well that I'm responsible for each and

every German in my camp. More importantly, you're not a judicial body, and have no authority to punish him."

"Comrade Captain, what would happen if this Robert Litke was building a bridge alongside other prisoners of war and fell from the scaffolding into the river and drowned? Or if, while logging in the forest, a hundred-year-old pine tree fell on him and crushed him? Would you be responsible then?"

"In either case, I'd prepare a document that would be signed by the captain of the guard and the technical supervisor of that work detail. Then I'd be all set."

"I can provide you with the second signature. Write up the document, and don't worry about the first signature."

"No," Kalinin said flatly. "I can't do that. I'd be committing a crime, and abusing my power."

Uncle Misha changed tactics. "I'm sure, Comrade Captain, and you no doubt also believe, that after the war every Nazi, Gestapo officer, and German criminal will be apprehended and sentenced," he said. "It will be an enormous task to incarcerate all these Germans and put them on trial. If I were to take care of this murderer, we'd save all those expenses and thereby benefit the state treasury. Moreover, you'll have the great moral satisfaction of helping an unfortunate woman take revenge on the murderer of her parents and the rapist of her underage sister."

"You should've been a lawyer rather than an engineer," Kalinin joked. "You've convinced me. Come back here tomorrow morning at ten. When I send the prisoners off to work, I'll keep Litke here and hand him over to you."

UNCLE MISHA RETURNED the next morning with Eva and his driver, Krugliakov. In the fall of 1942, a German punitive expedition had come to Krugliakov's village in the occupied Sumy region. They had herded all of the families of Red Army soldiers into a stable and set it on fire. Krugliakov's entire family—his mother, younger sisters, sisters-in-law, and young wife, with their three children—had been burned alive. Uncle Misha knew that Krugliakov shared his thirst for revenge, and had teamed up with him on other personal missions.

They drove Robert Litke to the derelict hangars of a former German airfield less than a mile away. Uncle Misha, Eva, and Krugliakov sat in a burned-out plane, while Litke stood in front of them, his hands still bound. The interrogation started, with Uncle Misha translating his questions and Litke's answers into Russian for Krugliakov.

"We are continuing our hearing from yesterday," Uncle Misha said solemnly. "Do you know, Robert Litke, that I have proof that you spent a long time in Łódź after you left the hospital? Do you admit to this?"

Litke did not respond.

Uncle Misha thought back to the German military police commandant who had interrogated him in Radomyshl. He remembered how terrifying it had been when the commandant had kept a gun pointed in his face the entire time. He pulled out his pistol and did the same.

"Why are you so silent? Answer me." Paraphrasing the German military police commandant who had interrogated Boris Goldfarb after the bombing in Naroulia, he added, "I have other ways of making you talk."

"Jawohl, Herr Officer," Litke mumbled. "While I was recovering, I spent six months with the local command in Łódź."

"What did you do there?"

"I was in a special squad for internal affairs."

"Did the special squad also escort Jewish transports from the ghetto to Chełmno?"

"No!"

Uncle Misha stepped close to Litke and stared into his eyes. "This woman is one of the Jews you marched to Chełmno," he said slowly.

Litke shivered and turned pale, but soon regained control of himself. "Jawohl, Herr Officer, I remember that there was indeed one such time."

Krugliakov was losing his patience. "Why are you wasting so much time with this questioning?" he demanded. "It's all clear, and he's admitted to almost everything."

"I'm doing this for a reason. I've been in his shoes. I know what kind of pleasure a prolonged interrogation brings to the one asking the questions, and how much stress it causes the one being questioned." Then he continued. "On a winter night, while you were escorting a transport of Jews to be slaughtered, you grabbed from their ranks a thirteen-year-old Jewish girl and raped her. The next day, you shot her and her mother. They were the sister and mother of this woman."

Litke lowered his head and started trembling. He fell to his knees and wailed, "Forgive me, dear people! I confess my sin! Some evil spirit came over me and forced me to commit this crime."

Uncle Misha had heard enough. He was cocking his pistol when Krugliakov grabbed his hand.

"What are you going to do, Comrade Engineer?" Krugliakov shouted. "Are you going to shoot him? Would that be the appropriate sentence for the horrible crime this murderer committed? No, that's too easy of a death. I'm sure that Eva's thirteen-year-old sister was neither the first nor the last innocent child he raped. We have to come up with a manner of death that will remind him of all the crimes he has committed."

Krugliakov thought for a moment, and then pronounced his sentence. "We should castrate him. Before he dies, let him feel the most horrible pain in the same spot where he used to seek degenerate, bestial pleasure."

Anyone who had known Uncle Misha before the Holocaust would have been shocked that the peaceful civil engineer and community leader would even consider such a thought. But at that moment, as with so many other moments over the previous three years, he was consumed by his thirst for vengeance. All he could think about was that sunny day in May 1942. Next to two pits, sixty-five feet long, sixty-five feet wide, and ten feet deep stood a table with snacks and a bottle of cognac. At that table sat a *different* Robert Litke, with a submachine gun in his hand. Six battered, naked, and frightened Jews were marched to the pit. That Robert Litke ordered them to lie down with their faces on the ground, and casually ordered their deaths between sips of cognac.

Uncle Misha thought about his wife, Golda, and their daughter, Feigela, who had been murdered at the same age as Eva's sister, Sorele. He envisioned how Feigela must have begged for her life with terror in her sky-blue eyes. He imagined the smirk on that Robert Litke's face, and the sound of the gunfire that struck down Golda and Feigela. That Robert Litke had shown no mercy to them. It was only just that this Robert Litke should feel at least some of their fear and pain.

He took his knife out of his satchel and ordered Litke to stand. "This knife with the Teutonic cross was forged by a German blacksmith out of shrapnel from a German artillery shell that should have killed me," he told him. "But as fate would have it, this German knife will mete out justice to a German murderer."

An hour later, Uncle Misha, Eva, and Krugliakov returned to Torgau. Deep in their own thoughts and memories, nobody spoke. But from the glances they exchanged with each other, nobody doubted that they had done the right thing.

ON APRIL 30, with Soviet troops just blocks away, Hitler committed suicide in a bunker under the garden of the Reich Chancellery in Berlin. He was succeeded as Germany's chancellor by Joseph Goebbels, who killed himself in the chancellery garden on May 1. The next day, while what was left of the German government fled to the Danish border, General Helmuth Weidling unconditionally surrendered Berlin to the Red Army.

On that same day, May 2, 1945, Uncle Misha became one of the first conquering heroes to walk the streets of Berlin. Almost three years after the *Aktion* in Korets, he had fulfilled the promise he had made to himself on that day to avenge the murders of his wife and daughter.

He went to the Reich Chancellery. In Goebbels's office, on the wall above the desk from which Goebbels had briefly led Germany, he wrote in large letters in Russian, German, and Yiddish: *Hitler and Goebbels! I, Moshe, son of Asher ha-Levi of Korets, have outlived you and your ridiculous racial theory.* He signed his note with his legal name as well as his partisan name: *Moshe Gildenman—Uncle Misha.*

With the defeat of Nazi Germany, his mission as the guerrilla fighter Uncle Misha was finally complete. He was ready to lay down his arms and return to the peaceful life of Moshe Gildenman.

Epilogue

F|ROM BERLIN, MOSHE WAS DISPATCHED to Czechoslovakia, where German troops continued to fight. On May 9—the day after the Allies accepted Germany's unconditional surrender—he was among the Red Army soldiers who liberated Prague. While demining a road to prepare the way for Pavel Rybalko's tank army to participate in a parade celebrating the end of the war, Moshe was severely wounded when a mine exploded. He was in the hospital for three months. After being discharged from the Red Army in November 1945, Moshe returned to Korets, where he was reunited with his son, Simcha, for the first time in two years.

As the commander of an infantry company, Simcha had been among the Red Army soldiers who had liberated Korets on January 13, 1944. He had been given a two-day leave, but had ended up staying for several weeks to bring order to his hometown and to assist a small number of Jews who had returned after the liberation. While Simcha was in Korets, he had run into a Ukrainian who had been a schoolmate and friend before participating in the *Aktion* on May 21, 1942. The Ukrainian had denied ever knowing Simcha, despite the fact that he was wearing clothes that he had stolen from the Gildenman home. Simcha had pulled out his pistol and had shot him on the spot.

Simcha had been confined to his quarters for one day for conduct unbecoming an officer. He had then been transferred to a disciplinary battalion for six weeks for having been so late in reporting back to the front. After returning to combat, he had suffered a serious wound to his hand on May 19, 1944, and had spent the next several months in a military hospital.

It was around that time that Simcha had started compiling a songbook that he would keep with him for the rest of his life. Most of the lyrics are to Soviet war songs, but the songbook also includes one text in Polish and two in Yiddish—one of which is a postwar copy of his father's song "Come to the Forest." The handwriting is different for each song, and a few include personalized inscriptions. This suggests that Simcha collected the lyrics as mementos of people he met during and after the war.

After being declared unfit for combat, Simcha had returned to Korets on January 18, 1945, as the military inspector of a Polish school. He also worked with the NKVD to apprehend Ukrainian nationalists who were still in the area.

UPON MOSHE'S RETURN to Korets in November 1945, he was offered various high-profile positions, all of which he turned down. The town had ceased to be his home. His wife and daughter were dead, his property had been plundered, and the Jewish community was gone.

Moshe and Simcha moved to Szczecin, Poland, where Moshe became a leader in a new community of 27,500 resettled Jewish refugees. Given how closely he had treasured his copy of *Freedom's Songs*, it is surprising that he did not join the small Bund chapter in Szczecin. Instead, he organized a branch of Ihud ("Unity"), a Zionist movement that advocated for a peaceful end to the Jewish–Arab conflict in Palestine through the creation of a single, shared state. He would serve as the chairman of the Szczecin Ihud chapter for a year and a half. In 1946, he attended Ihud's first national conference in Wrocław, where he was welcomed with a warm ovation and elected to the organization's national council.

In the years following the war, Moshe became a popular figure in the Jewish community, with photographs of him wearing his combat medals appearing in the Jewish and general press. In addition to his "To a Partisan of the Patriotic War," 2nd Class medal; Order of the Red Star; and Order of the Patriotic War, 2nd Class medal, after the war, Moshe received a "For the Victory over Germany in the Great Patriotic War 1941–1945" medal from the Soviet Union. Poland awarded him a Grunwald Berlin Badge, a Medal of Victory and Freedom 1945, the Partisan Cross, the Order of the Cross of Grunwald, and a Wound Decoration with two stars.

At the urging of others, Moshe started chronicling his activities as a partisan and soldier. He published essays in Yiddish and Polish about his life during the war and gave lectures throughout Poland. On May 17, 1947, he delivered a speech in front of a packed hall for the Łódź chapter of Ihud in which he spent over an hour recounting his path from Korets to the forest and then the Red Army.

In his writings and lectures, his main goal was to share what he had expressed to Eva in the final days of the war: There had indeed been a path for Jews during the Holocaust that had led to being murdered, but there had also been a path of armed resistance that had led to victory. And even if one was killed in battle, Moshe would say, then at least they died a noble death, with a weapon in their hand.

Moshe immigrated to Israel in 1951, settling in Ness Ziona, south of Tel Aviv and northwest of Jerusalem. In 1955, he was struck with a terminal illness that left him paralyzed. After struggling with the disease for two years, he died on August 9, 1957.

Author's Note

I HAVE BEEN WANTING TO write this book ever since completing my last book, *Violins of Hope*, which tells the stories of six violins from the Holocaust that were restored by violinmaker Amnon Weinstein. *Violins of Hope* includes a chapter on Motele Schlein, a young violinist who became something of a second son to the subject of this book, Moshe "Uncle Misha" Gildenman. After Motele died in combat, Gildenman held on to Motele's violin, passing it down to his son, Simcha, who, in turn, passed it down to Seffi Hanegbi, Simcha's son and Moshe's grandson. It was Seffi who brought Motele's violin to Amnon for repairs and who ultimately donated it to Yad Vashem—the World Holocaust Remembrance Center—where it is on permanent display in the Holocaust History Museum.

Long after finishing *Violins of Hope*, I could not stop thinking about Gildenman, a civil engineer, community leader, musician, and man of peace who had never even held a weapon before the Holocaust. But after the Nazis killed 2,200 Jews from his hometown, including his wife and their thirteen-year-old daughter, he vowed revenge. He escaped to the forest with his son, and formed one of the most successful partisan units in the war to liberate Ukraine from Nazi occupation.

I spent the next several years collecting Gildenman's writings, along with those of his son and other partisans in his brigade. Gildenman wrote four books in which he mentioned musical activities among the partisans, without offering many clues about what they were actually singing and playing. Gildenman was an avid musician and songwriter, and I knew that it would be impossible to truly understand him and his fellow partisans without also understanding the music that they made together.

In May 2022, while perusing a reprint of Motele's story on the website of *The Mendele Review: Yiddish Literature and Language* from 2008, I noticed a cryptic reference to a "Songbook of Misha." The link to a page on Yad Vashem's website was broken, but thanks to the Internet Archive's Wayback Machine, I found myself looking at the image of a tattered copy of what the old webpage described as "a songbook belonging to the partisans of Misha (Diadia) Gindelman" [*sic*] (*Diadia* is Russian for "Uncle").

When I reached out to Yad Vashem, Noa Or in the museum's artifacts collection confirmed that this was "a songbook with lyrics and melodies of songs that were sung by the partisans under the command of Moshe 'Diadia Misha' Gindelman [*sic*]. The book was folded and carried in the pocket of Diadia Misha's shirt." The book's cover was faded and broken in half, but Bret Werb, the music curator at the United States Holocaust Memorial Museum, helped me identify it as a copy of Joseph Gladstein's Yiddish songbook *Freedom's Songs*. Noa also pointed me toward a number of other artifacts in Yad Vashem's collection, including "a songbook that belonged to the partisan Simcha Gildenman." The texts in the songbook are in Russian, Yiddish, and Polish, and are in different handwriting, suggesting that Simcha collected them as mementos of people he met during and after the war. Between Gildenman's personal copy of *Freedom's Songs*, and the songs that his son collected, I finally understood the music that they not only made, but also carried with them throughout the war as treasured memories of their lives before and during the Holocaust. At last, I was ready to tell Gildenman's story.

GILDENMAN'S HEROISM HAS been well documented in the literature about Jewish partisans during World War II. In 1956, former partisan Moshe Kahanovich included several vignettes about Gildenman in his two-volume work *The War of the Jewish Partisans in Eastern Europe*. Kahanovich also provided an obituary of Gildenman for the *Yad Vashem Bulletin* in 1958, as well as an article on Gildenman's partisan unit for the Yizkor book about Zviahel (Novohrad-Volynskyi) in 1962. Noted Holocaust historian Shmuel Spector recorded some of Gildenman's partisan activities in a 1983 article in *Yad Vashem Studies* and in his 1990 book, *The Holocaust of Volhynian Jews 1941–1944*, writing the entry on Gildenman for the *Encyclopedia of the Holocaust* that same year. Yehuda Bauer and Yitzhak Arad also wrote about Gildenman in their books, *The Death of the Shtetl* and *In the Shadow of the Red Banner: Soviet Jews in the War against Nazi Germany*, respectively.

Much of what is known about Gildenman comes from the books and essays that Gildenman himself wrote. Kahanovich included several excerpts from Gildenman's writings in *The War of the Jewish Partisans in Eastern Europe*. Also in 1956, Yitzhak Zuckerman and Moshe Basak published a different essay in *Book of the Ghetto Wars: Between the Walls, in the Camps, and in the Forests*. Yuri Suhl translated three of Gildenman's writings into English for his 1967 anthology, *They Fought Back: The Story of the Jewish Resistance in Nazi Europe*, and later dramatized the story of Motele Schlein in *Uncle Misha's Partisans*—as did Gertrude Samuels in her 1976 novel, *Mottele: A Partisan Odyssey*. Gildenman's writings are also quoted in Leni Yahil's 1987 book, *The Holocaust: The Fate of European Jewry*.

Gildenman's motivation for documenting his stories was not just to bear witness. He wanted to inspire a post-Holocaust Jewish audience that was in desperate need of heroic tales. In the preface to his fourth book, *Motele, the Young Partisan*, Gildenman noted that the countries that had been victorious in World War II were memorializing numerous military heroes in books, films, and monuments, while tales of Jewish heroism were largely missing. This realization inspired him to chronicle not only the struggles, but also the victories of those who—like him—took up arms and fought back against the Nazis.

As early as December 1946, Gildenman told the Polish newspaper *Opinion* that he was writing a book about his experiences. "It is not my intention to describe Jewish martyrdom under German rule. There are already plenty of works of that nature, and there will be more," he explained. "I just want the next generation of Jews to know that in times of great misery, there were Jews who fought uncompromisingly against the human beast, even when the outcome was uncertain. And they won. They won with honor."

In his first book, *On the Way to Victory* (1949), Gildenman chronicled the story of young Motele blowing up a German canteen, along with the heroic tales of partisans Fridek the Magyar, Reizele Osterman, and David of Yarevysche. His next book, *The Destruction of Korets* (1949), was a chronicle of his life in Korets during the Nazi occupation. Gildenman dedicated *On the Way to Victory* to: "My unforgettable campmates who died for the honor of the Jewish nation and whose graves are spread throughout the forests of Ukraine and Belarus." He wrote *The Destruction of Korets* as a memorial to all of "the unmarked graves scattered in the fields and forests of Ukraine."

Gildenman's third book, *Jewish Daughters* (1950), focuses specifically on five women partisans, including Sarah-Liba "Luba" Zigman and Reizele Osterman. "I consider it my duty to talk about our heroes in general, and in particular about the enormous contributions that Jewish daughters made to the fight against the horrors of Nazism. I want Jewish youth to be proud of the brave warriors and warrioresses who fought for the honor of the Jewish people—who, in the darkest days of the destruction of Jews, wrote the brightest pages in the history of Jewish heroism," he wrote in the book's preface. "Moreover, Jewish women should know that the golden chain of heroic Jewish daughters, which began in the days of the prophets, continued in the partisan forests." Gildenman reprinted that preface in *The Jewish Partisans* (1955), which is itself a reprint of Luba's story. Just as Gildenman wrote *Jewish Daughters* as a tribute to women partisans, *Motele, the Young Partisan* (1950) is dedicated to the heroism of Jewish children during the Holocaust. Gildenman once mentioned writing a book about his experiences with the Red Army, but he apparently never did so.

In conducting the research for *Partisan Song*, it was my goal to assemble the first complete chronicle of Gildenman's activities during the Holocaust. This proved to be no easy task, as his writings are spread over several places. There are unpublished writings in Yad Vashem and the Ghetto Fighters' House in Israel, as well as essays in various publications, such as Yizkor books, *Opinion*, and the Yiddish newspaper *The New Life*. His four books present a number of vignettes in no particular order, making it difficult to establish a chronology. Several of the stories are undated, and almost every date that Gildenman did provide proved to be incorrect. This misremembering of specific dates is not surprising when one considers the immense trauma to which Gildenman was subjected during the Nazi occupation of his hometown, the slaughters of his wife and daughter during a mass murder, and the years he spent fighting as a fugitive, a partisan, and a soldier in the Red Army.

The locations of various events were equally difficult to pin down, as Gildenman was sometimes writing about tiny villages that no longer exist, using Polish or Russian names that he then transliterated into the Hebrew alphabet for Yiddish publications. On at least one occasion, he conflated the name of a town with that of a neighboring city. As with all witness accounts, especially those recorded years after the fact, it is possible that other details may have been mistaken as well.

WHILE GILDENMAN IS often the sole source for many of the specifics about his life during the Holocaust, there are several documents that corroborate various aspects of his accounts. In *The Destruction of Korets*, Gildenman himself authenticated his memories by publishing documentation from that period that is consistent with files from Korets in the Ghetto Fighters' House. A number of details about Korets are also confirmed in the published memoirs of Nyuma Anapolsky, Yafa Dembski, and Anna Podgajecki, as well as essays by other survivors in the Korets Yizkor book. Similarly, the testimonies of fellow partisans Aleksander Kuc, Zvi Pe'er, Issachar Trosman, Haya Volkon, and Tadeusz Weinberg verify several details of Gildenman's earliest months in the forest. Not surprisingly, the testimony and writings of Simcha Gildenman also align with his father's memories.

To assist with the chronology and other details of some of Gildenman's experiences with the Soviet partisans, I turned to archival documents in the Central State Archives of Public Organizations and Ukrainians [TsDAHOU]. Several entries in the 1st Stalin Partisan Detachment's combat reports and combat logs between January and March 1943 correlate with accounts in Gildenman's writings. This includes the German attack on the partisan camp in Khilchikha in January, the shoot-out at Iakovets and the assault on Rozvazhiv in February, and the battles in Antonovka and Aleksandrovka in March. Yet Gildenman is never mentioned. In fact, his name only comes up in personnel records and in the bylines of the articles he wrote for the partisan magazine *Stalinets*.

After March 1943, when Vasilii Ushakov replaced Evgenii Mirkovsky as the commander of the Stalin Partisan Federation, the victories of Gildenman and his "Jewish Group" were completely omitted from the Soviet records. With the exception of a battle in Luben in August in which Jewish partisans played only a minor role, there are no references in Stalin Partisan Federation records to any of the events about which Moshe and Simcha Gildenman would later write, until the well-documented battle at Novoshepelychi in late September 1943. Details of the partisan attack on the city of Radomyshl in early August are corroborated by the records of the Khrushchev Kyiv Partisan Federation, as well as by the memoirs of its commander, Ivan Khitrichenko—although neither mentions the participation of Jewish partisans.

In my search for contemporaneous sources that can verify Gildenman's chronicles, it became obvious that his fellow Jewish survivors corroborated his acts of heroism, while the Soviets all but ignored them. This erasure can only be attributed to antisemitism. Just as Gildenman noted that tales of Jewish heroism were conspicuously absent after the war, during the war itself the Soviets neglected tales of Jewish valor in favor of narratives that bolstered their distinctly Russocentric worldview. In the Red Army, for example, Jewish soldiers were neither promoted nor awarded medals as often as their ethnic Russian counterparts. It was also Soviet practice to exclude Jews from media reports on soldiers who distinguished themselves in combat.

Despite an official limit on Jewish soldiers receiving medals, Gildenman received the Order of the Red Star and an Order of the Patriotic War, 2nd Class medal, during his time with the Red Army, in addition to his "To a Partisan of the Patriotic War," 2nd Class medal. The document decorating him with the Order of the Red Star, now in the Central Archives of the Russian Ministry of Defense [TsAMO], corroborates Moshe and Simcha Gildenman's reports that they led a counterattack on German submachine gunners, apprehended a German officer, and guided their regiment to safety on October 14, 1943. Similarly, the document decorating Gildenman with the Order of the Patriotic War, 2nd Class medal, confirms his account of supervising the construction of a bridge over the Vistula River in early August

1944, while under attack from German artillery and airplanes. There is no question that Gildenman exhibited extraordinary heroism throughout his mission to avenge the murders of his loved ones by defeating the Nazis.

Acknowledgments

O NE OF THE GREAT PLEASURES of researching and writing books is not only the work itself, but the supportive people you invariably meet along the way. This book has benefited immensely from the input of Dr. Timothy Collins, who, after learning of Motele's story through the Violins of Hope project, uncovered many fascinating details about the boy's biography in his book *Finding Motele: A Family's Odyssey Searching for a Young Jewish Partisan.* From the very beginning, Tim was extremely helpful in pointing me toward valuable sources, particularly the partisan files at the now defunct Ukraine Memory Book website and the Red Army files at the Memory of the People website (pamyat-naroda.ru). As the project unfolded, he spent a great deal of time helping me untangle the chronology, geography, and at times even topography of Gildenman's odyssey and offering feedback on several drafts.

I was also exceedingly fortunate to receive a great deal of assistance from Dr. Mihály Kálmán. Mihály's fluency in Hebrew, Yiddish, Russian, and Ukrainian proved to be indispensable in translating Gildenman's writings, which were mostly in Yiddish, but would often use terms borrowed from Hebrew, Russian, and Ukrainian. As a scholar of modern East European Jewish history, with a specialty in Jewish paramilitaries and self-defense units in the pogroms of the Russian Civil War, Mihály's expertise was essential in every stage of this project.

I would like to thank a number of individuals at museums and archives who graciously furnished copies of various documents and images: Greta Barak, Shoshi Nerson Norman, and Zvi Oren at the Ghetto Fighters' House; Volodymyr Forsiuk at the Korets Historical Museum; and David Cahn, Dan Dwek, Noa Or, and Dodi Tolchin at Yad Vashem. Oleksandra Bezkorovaina provided invaluable service as a research assistant in Kyiv. Aneta Dmochowska at the Muzeum Historii Żydów Polskich POLIN and Beata Hebzda-Sołogub at the Fundacja Forum Dialogu Między Kulturami were also accommodating in supplying images. The photos from the Fundacja Forum Dialogu Między Kulturami originate from the collections of the Cyfrowe Archiwum Ziemi Dzierzoniowskiej (www.dzierzoniowskiearchiwum.pl).

I am honored to enjoy the continued support of the administration at the University of North Carolina at Charlotte, its College of Arts and Architecture, and the Department of Music. Most of all, I must thank my wife, Elizabeth, and our children, Helen and William, for their love, patience, and encouragement. Large projects such as this one would simply not be possible without them by my side.

I will forever be indebted to Amnon Weinstein (1939–2024), the patriarch of the Violins of Hope project, and his wife, Assaela—the daughter of the famous Jewish partisan Asael Bielski—who welcomed me into their home and into their hearts. It is no exaggeration to say that Amnon's eagerness to share so many stories, including that of Motele Schlein and by extension Moshe Gildenman, changed my life. I am also grateful to their son, Avshalom, who encouraged me to write this book. Finally I thank Seffi Hanegbi, the grandson of Moshe Gildenman and the son of Simcha Gildenman, for his support of this project.

Source Notes

CHAPTER 1: "IN THE SALTY SEA OF HUMAN TEARS"

Moshe Gildenman wrote about his postwar return to Korets in *The Destruction of Korets* (Paris, 1949). Additional information about Gildenman's life in Korets is from Moshe Gildenman, Testimony, Yad Vashem Archives, Testimonies, Diaries, and Memoirs Collection, O.33/521; Simcha Gildenman, Transcript of Testimony, Yad Vashem Archives, Testimonies Department, O.3/6863; S[imcha] G[ildenman], "Uncle Misha," in *Korets (Volyn): In Memory of Our Community That Is No More*, ed. Eliezer Leoni (Tel Aviv: Former Residents of Korets in Israel, 1959), 503–5; "Uncle Misha," *Opinion* 9 (December 20, 1946): 14; and Allan Levine, *Fugitives of the Forest: The Heroic Story of Jewish Resistance and Survival During the Second World War* (Guilford, CT: Lyons Press, 2009). Many thanks to Dr. Timothy Collins for sharing Feiga Zelda Gildenman's nickname, which he learned from Feigela's childhood friend Fania Wedro.

Additional information about the Jewish community in Korets prior to the German occupation is from Leoni, ed., *Korets;* and Shmuel Spector, *The Holocaust of Volhynian Jews 1941–1944,* trans. Jerzy Michalowicz (Jerusalem: Yad Vashem—The Federation of Volhynian Jews, 1990). For information about Cooperative Banks, see Tzvi Goldberg, "The Cooperative Bank," in *The Staszów Book,* ed. Elhanan Erlich (Tel Aviv: Former Residents of Staszów in Israel and in the Diaspora, 1962), 71–72, trans. Kutzi Weill in *Staszów Memorial Book,* ed. Jean-Pierre Stroweis, Leonard Levin, and Dobrochna Fire (New York: JewishGen, 2020), 49–50.

For more on "In the Salty Sea," see Eliahu Adelman, "In Zaltsikn Yam—A Yiddish Workers' Song," Jewish Music Research Center, June 2014, https://jewish-music.huji.ac.il/content/zaltsikn-yam-yiddish-workers -song.

For data on Jewish deaths during the Holocaust, see United States Holocaust Memorial Museum, "How Many People Did the Nazis Murder?" Holocaust Encyclopedia, https://encyclopedia.ushmm.org/content/en/article/documenting-numbers-of-victims-of-the-holocaust-and-nazi-persecution.

Moshe Gildenman wrote about the arrival of the Soviets in *The Destruction of Korets*, as well as in his Report on the Town of Korets, Ukraine, Ghetto Fighters' House Archives, Collections Section, 2277; in his Testimony; and in "Zviahel in the Years 1920 to 1941," in *Zviahel (Novohrad-Volynskyi)*, ed. Azriel Uri and Mordekhai Boneh (Tel Aviv: Association of Former Residents of Zviahel and Surroundings, 1962), 200–10, trans. Tina Lunson at https://www.jewishgen.org/yizkor/zvhil/zvhy200.html. See also Simcha Gildenman, Transcript of Testimony.

Additional information on the Soviet occupation of Ukraine, Volhynia, and Korets is from Alexander Gogun, *Stalin's Commandos: Ukrainian Partisan Forces on the Eastern Front* (London: I.B. Tauris, 2016); Leoni, ed., *Korets*; Anna Podgajecki, *Anna: A Teenager on the Run*, trans. Sandy Bloom (Amberly Publishing—Yad Vashem, 2016); and Spector, *The Holocaust of Volhynian Jews*.

5   **"Where are you..."**: Moshe Gildenman, *The Destruction of Korets*, 12.

12   **"How much effort..."**: Ibid., 19.

13   **"Who are you..."**: Ibid., 21.

13   *What are you doing...*: Ibid., 22.

16   *The King of the Schnorrers:* Aizik Chimenes, who sang the title role, later shared Gildenman's lyrics for the "Song of the Schnorrers" with Simcha Baraz (Baraz, "The Korets Jewish Drama Lovers' Circle," in Leoni, ed., *Korets*, 147–48).

16   **"A friend and a companion..."**: Yosef Wachbroit, "The Art Life in Korets," in Leoni, ed., *Korets*, 141–42, trans. Sara Mages at https://www.jewishgen.org/yizkor/korets/kor133.html.

17   *Freedom's Songs:* The collection of Yiddish songs is sometimes misattributed to the poet and literary critic Jacob Glatstein. It was actually compiled by his cousin Joseph [Józef] Gladstein [Gladsztejn/Glatstein] (1891–1942), a music educator, conductor, and music critic who died in the Warsaw Ghetto.

19   **"To our aid!"**: Aizik Chimenes, "When the Soviets Came," in Leoni, ed., *Korets*, 336, trans. Mages at https://www.jewishgen.org/yizkor/korets/kor331.html.

21   **Paragraph 11:** Ironically, in some cases being exiled eastward proved to be a blessing in disguise, as the Jews who were deported were

spared from the Nazi invasion (Simcha Gildenman, Transcript of Testimony, 2).

CHAPTER 2: "DO YOU KNOW THE PEOPLE?"

Moshe Gildenman wrote about the German occupation of Korets in "The Attitude of the Non-Jewish Population Toward the Jews," in *Rivne: A Memorial Book*, ed. Aryeh Avitahi (Tel Aviv: Former Residents of Rivne in Israel, 1956), 518–20, trans. Naomi Gal in *Rovno: Memorial Book*, ed. Ann Glickman Goldberg (New York: JewishGen, 2020), 738–40; *The Destruction of Korets;* and "The Yellow Patch," *Opinion* 10 (January 15, 1947): 13. He wrote about the 1919 pogroms in "The Bloody Days of Petliura," in *Rivne*, ed. Avitahi, 40–43, trans. Gal in *Rovno*, ed. Glickman Goldberg, 41–45; and "The End of Hataman Askilko," in *Rivne*, ed. Avitahi, 49–51, trans. Gal in *Rovno*, ed. Glickman Goldberg, 55–57.

Additional survivor testimony is from Nyuma Anapolsky, "Thanks to Kind People—Ukrainians and Poles," in *In Life in the Shadow of Death—Recent Memories about the Holocaust in Ukraine: Testimonies and Documents*, ed. Boris Zabarko, trans. Marina Guba and Vladimir Matveyev, Vol. 1 (Melitopol, Ukraine: Publishing House of Melitopol City Printing House, 2019), 123–39; Yafa Dembski, *I Must Stay Alive: The Story of Shaindel* (Ra'anana, Israel: Docostory, 2019); Yehudit Kersch (Shapira), Testimony, Yad Vashem Archives, Testimonies Department, O.3/2796; Aleksander Kuc, Testimony, Yad Vashem Archives, Testimonies Department, O.3/3268; Leoni, ed., *Korets;* and Podgajecki, *Anna.*

Additional information is from I. A. Altman and A. I. Kruglov, "Korets," in *Holocaust in the Territory of the USSR*, ed. I. A. Altman (Moscow: Rosspen, 2009), 463–64; Alexander Kruglov and Andrew Koss, "Korzec," trans. Ester-Basya Vaisman, in *The United States Holocaust Memorial Museum Encyclopedia of Camps and Ghettos, 1933–1945*, vol. 2, *Ghettos in German-Occupied Eastern Europe*, ed. Martin Dean and Mel Hecker (Bloomington: Indiana University Press, 2012), 1385–86; Spector, *The Holocaust of Volhynian Jews;* Isaiah Trunk, *Judenrat: The Jewish Councils in Eastern Europe under Nazi Occupation* (New York: Macmillan, 1972); and Leni Yahil, *The Holocaust: The Fate of European Jewry, 1932–1945*, trans. Ina Friedman and Haya Galai (New York: Oxford University Press, 1990). See also Leonid D. Grenkevich, *The Soviet Partisan Movement, 1941–1944: A Critical Historiographical Analysis*, ed. David M. Glantz (London: Frank Cass, 1999).

23   **"Out of the confinement..."**: Ian Klinke and Mark Bassin, "Introduction: Lebensraum and Its Discontents," *Journal of Historical Geography* 61 (2018): 57.

26   **"Open the door..."**: Moshe Gildenman, *The Destruction of Korets*, 29.

27   **"Children, don't leave me..."**: Dembski, *I Must Stay Alive*, 31.

27   **"Why are you hitting my father?"**: Ibid., 34.

28   **"That's it! This is the end!"**: Ibid.

28   **"All weapons owned by Jews..."**: Moshe Gildenman, *The Destruction of Korets*, 30–31.

29   **"Jew!" and "Swine!"**: Anapolsky, "Thanks to Kind People," 124.

30   **"The element that settled our cities..."**: Spector, "The Jews of Volhynia and Their Reaction to Extermination," *Yad Vashem Studies* 15 (1983): 160.

31   **"The Germans are strangers..."**: Podgajecki, *Anna*, 105.

31   **"Doesn't the Ukrainian police commandant deserve to be rich?"**: Ibid.

33   **"Locally undertaken attempts..."**: Spector, *The Holocaust of Volhynian Jews*, 69.

34   **"Fine. Take it all..."**: Kersch, Testimony, 11.

35   **"Only the best..."**: Gildenman published a copy of Hanzelman's handwritten and stamped document in *The Destruction of Korets*, 37; reprinted in Leoni, ed., *Korets*, 374. A typed copy of the document can be found in the Ghetto Fighters' House Archives, Catalog Number 1971.

36   **"Don't worry..."**: Podgajecki, *Anna*, 47.

37   **"Our fingers shriveled and contracted..."**: Dora Rabinowitz (Strassberg), "A Drop from the Sea of Blood and Tears," in Leoni, ed., *Korets*, 431.

41   **"Clean this dirt off the street."**: Moshe Gildenman, *The Destruction of Korets*, 67.

CHAPTER 3: "MAY SONG"

Moshe Gildenman wrote about the *Aktion* in Korets in *The Destruction of Korets; Jewish Daughters* (Paris, 1950); and in his Testimony. See also Simcha Gildenman, Transcript of Testimony; and Ariel Uri, "As Told by the Partisan Simcha Gildenman," in *Zviahel*, ed. Uri and Boneh, 304–6. For additional survivor testimony, see Anapolsky, "Thanks to Kind People"; Dembski, *I Must Stay Alive*; Leoni, ed., *Korets*; Museum of Jewish Heritage, "Meir [Krasnostavski]'s Story," https://education.mjhnyc.org/survivor

-stories/meirs-story; Podgajecki, *Anna;* and Yad Vashem. "Murder Story of Korzec Jews in the Kozak Forest," Untold Stories—Murder Sites of Jews in Occupied Territories of the USSR, https://collections.yadvashem.org/en/untold-stories/killing-site/14627900. Additionally, see Kruglov and Koss, "Korzec"; and Spector, "The Jews of Volhynia."

43   **"It is true that here and there..."**: Yitzhak Feiner, "The Last Path of our Martyrs," in Leoni, ed., *Korets,* 357, trans. Yocheved Klausner at https://www.jewishgen.org/yizkor/korets/kor331.html. Emphasis mine.

43   **"All we need is patience..."**: Podgajecki, *Anna,* 78.

43   **"Yids! Kikes! Out!..."**: Ibid., 72.

44   **"Where are you going?..."**: Simcha Gildenman, Transcript of Testimony, 4.

44   **"All Jews must go to a special registration!..."**: Moshe Gildenman, *The Destruction of Korets,* 46.

45   **"Hear, O Israel"**: Anapolsky, "Thanks to Kind People," 128.

46   **"I'm still young..."**: Simcha Gildenman, Transcript of Testimony, 5.

46   **Robert:** See Zelig Charif, "How I Escaped from the Claws of Death," in Leoni, ed., *Korets,* 414; Moshe Gildenman, *The Destruction of Korets,* 40; and Simcha Gildenman, Transcript of Testimony, 4.

47   **"He works for me at the barracks..."**: Simcha Gildenman, Transcript of Testimony, 5.

47   **Robert:** Later that day, Robert would save the lives of blacksmith Zelig Charif and his son by convincing the German officer at Korets that they, too, were indispensable (Charif, "How I Escaped from the Claws of Death," 414).

49   **"Heil, Hitler! Heil, Hitler!"**: Moshe Gildenman, *The Destruction of Korets,* 50.

51   **"The *Aktion* is over!..."**: Ibid., 53.

53   **"This is the Eve of Shavuot..."**: Ibid., 55–56.

54   **"What? You're still here?..."**: Simcha Gildenman, Transcript of Testimony, 5–6.

55   **"We're not going anywhere..."**: Ibid., 6.

CHAPTER 4: "COME TO THE FOREST"

Moshe Gildenman wrote about living in and escaping from the Korets ghetto in *The Destruction of Korets;* "Fighting and Struggle in the Forest

(From My Memories as a Partisan)," in *Korets*, ed. Leoni, 443–50, trans. Klausner at https://www.jewishgen.org/yizkor/korets/kor443.html; in his Testimony; and in "The Yellow Patch." See also Simcha Gildenman, Transcript of Testimony; Simcha Gildenman, "Vengeance is Mine, and Recompense (Deuteronomy 32:35)," in *Korets*, ed. Leoni, 490–93; and Uri, "As Told by the Partisan Simcha Gildenman." For the recollections of other survivors, see Leoni, ed., *Korets*; and Podgajecki, *Anna*. See also Kruglov and Koss, "Korzec"; and Spector, *The Holocaust of Volhynian Jews*.

57   **Hanzelman:** Moshe Gildenman published a copy of Hanzelman's certificate certifying, "The Jew Moshe Gildenman has been commissioned to demolish old buildings and to bring the building materials to Holovnytsya" in *The Destruction of Korets*, 59; reprinted in Leoni, ed., *Korets*, 392.

57   **"Why are you demolishing a house…":** Moshe Gildenman, *The Destruction of Korets*, 58–60.

58   **"Tonight, one of the guards…":** Ibid., 61.

59   **"These aren't ordinary blocks…":** Ibid., 62.

61   **"Jewish Skilled Worker":** Gildenman published copies of his identity card and registration card in *The Destruction of Korets*, 64 and 65; reprinted in Leoni, ed., *Korets*, 398 and 400.

62   **"Get to know the dog…":** Simcha Gildenman, Transcript of Testimony, 6.

62   **"You'll ruin us all!…":** Moshe Gildenman, *The Destruction of Korets*, 70.

62   ***Days of anguish and suffering…:*** Moshe Gildenman, *The Destruction of Korets*, 68–69; reprinted in Leoni, ed., *Korets*, 400–401. The text, including the song's title, can also be found in Moshe Gildenman's Testimony, 2–3, as well as in Simcha Gildenman, "A Notebook Containing Handwritten Poems/Songs in Yiddish, Russian, and Polish," Yad Vashem Artifacts Collection, 6622/2. Courtesy of Yousef (Seffi) Hanegbi.

64   **"Moshe, I thought you were smarter than that…":** Moshe Gildenman, *The Destruction of Korets*, 70.

64   **"The head of the printing house…":** Ibid., 69.

64   **"Can you imagine…":** Ibid., 70–71.

66   **"Do you think the Germans…":** Ibid., 72.

66   **Wulach:** Dr. Wulach fled to the forest prior to the liquidation of the Korets ghetto and joined partisans who were operating nearby. He spent the rest of the war tending to wounded partisans, and returned to Korets after the war to assist Holocaust survivors. After serving as

a doctor at the Displaced Persons camp in Steyr, Austria, he emigrated
to Israel.

68 **Survivors:** One of the few survivors of the final liquidation of the Korets ghetto was eleven-year-old Shmuel Vidro. As Shmuel and other
children were being pulled to the Kozak forest on a cart, they loudly
sang *"Hatikvah"* ["The Hope"], the Zionist hymn that would later become the Israeli national anthem. Shmuel was the last to descend into
the pit. As Shmuel sat on the bodies of women and other children,
Mitka Zavirukha walked over to him and shot him twice in the ribs.
Shmuel lost consciousness, but miraculously survived the wounds. He
awoke after the *Aktion* had ended, and was able to escape to the forest
(Shmuel Vidro, "How I Escaped from the Pit of Death," in *Korets*, ed.
Leoni, 433–39).

69 **"Whoever can come, should come!":** Simcha Gildenman, Transcript
of Testimony, 7.

70 **"If they kill us...":** Moshe Gildenman, "The Yellow Patch," 13. See also
Moshe Gildenman, "Fighting and Struggle in the Forest," 443, trans.
Klausner at https://www.jewishgen.org/yizkor/korets/kor443.html.

70 **Escapees:** The group included Moshe, Simcha, and Siomke, along
with Lazar Gershfeld, Zvi Pe'er, Avigdor Zayka, and Dvora and Faige
Kaftan, as well as Mottel Borzyk, Moshe Milrod, Noah Reisenberg,
and a man whom Gildenman later remembered only as "Shternshus
(son-in-law of the merchant Malye)" (Moshe Gildenman, *The Destruction of Korets*, 73). Simcha also mentioned "someone from Mezhyrichi
whose name I do not recall" (Simcha Gildenman, "Vengeance is Mine,"
490), but they did not meet up with that man until a few days later. In
his testimony, Simcha recalled fleeing Korets with Lazar Gershfeld
rather than with Moshe and Siomke (Simcha Gildenman, Transcript
of Testimony, 7 and 8).

70 **Other Jews who escaped the liquidation:** See Leoni, ed., *Korets*,
especially Batya Zaluska (Fuchs), "In the Korets Ghetto and in the
Woods," 451–69; Dov Bergel, "The Road to the Partisans and to Liberation," 470–79; Chaim Bergel, "In the Storm of Battle," 494–97; and
Yitzhak Kleiner, "From the Nightmares of Those Days," 500–502.

70 **Yaakov Pe'er:** When Yaakov had returned to Korets after confirming
that new pits were being dug near Kozak, he had seen what was happening in the ghetto and had hidden in the New Town. He fled Korets
that night with a few other Jews and survived the Holocaust (Yaakov
Pe'er, "Wandering," in Leoni, ed., *Korets*, 486–89).

70 **"Do you have bread?..."**: Simcha Gildenman, Transcript of Testimony, 9.

71 **"We were no master strategists."**: Ibid., 10.

72 **Lazar and Avigdor:** Lazar and Avigdor returned to Vasil's house, where they hid through the winter. They headed back into the forests in the spring, when the snow began to melt and after partisans had started operating nearby. Lazar would be killed in combat, but Avigdor would survive the Holocaust (Zayka, "The Massacre in the 'New Town,'" in Leoni, ed., *Korets*, 408–12).

CHAPTER 5: "IN STRUGGLE"

Moshe Gildenman wrote about his earliest days in the forest in "And Since Then I Have Been 'Uncle Misha,'" Yad Vashem Archives, Testimonies, Diaries, and Memoirs Collection, O.33/522; and in his Testimony. See also Simcha Gildenman, Transcript of Testimony; S[imcha] G[ildenman], "Uncle Misha"; and Simcha Gildenman, "Vengeance is Mine, and Recompense." See also Spector, *The Holocaust of Volhynian Jews*.

For the testimonies of other partisans, see Aleksander Kuc, Testimony; Zvi Pe'er, "This Is How I Took Revenge on the Murderers," in Leoni, ed., *Korets*, 480–85; Issachar Trosman, Testimony, Yad Vashem Archives, Testimonies Department, O.3/3477; and Haya Volkon (Pinchuk), "Wanderings and Hardships during the Holocaust," in *Rokytne (Volyn) and the Surrounding Area: A Book of Testimony and Memory*, ed. Eliezer Leoni (Tel Aviv: Former Residents of Rokytne in Israel, 1967), 301–8, trans. Ala Gamulka in *Rokitno-Wolyn and Surroundings: Memorial Book and Testimony (Ukraine)* (New York: JewishGen, 2015), 313–21.

Information on the partisan movement is from Reuben Ainsztein, *Jewish Resistance in Nazi-Occupied Eastern Europe* (New York: Barnes and Noble, 1974); Yitzhak Arad, *In the Shadow of the Red Banner: Soviet Jews in the War against Nazi Germany* (Jerusalem: Yad Vashem, 2010); John A. Armstrong, ed., *Soviet Partisans in World War II* (Madison: University of Wisconsin Press, 1964); Matthew Cooper, *The Phantom War: The German Struggle against Soviet Partisans 1941–1944* (London: Macdonald and Jane's, 1979); Gogun, *Stalin's Commandos*; Grenkevich, *The Soviet Partisan Movement*; Dmitry Medvedev, *Stout Hearts: This Happened Near Rovno* (Honolulu: University Press of the Pacific, 2002); and Kenneth Slepyan, *Stalin's Guerrillas: Soviet Partisans in World War II* (Lawrence, KS: University Press of Kansas, 2006).

73   **Unfurl the large banners:** In his copy of *Freedom's Songs*, Gildenman crossed out the Yiddish word *"royte"* and replaced it with *"groyse,"* changing the line from "Unfurl the red banners" to "Unfurl the large banners."

73   **"Halt! Halt! Who goes there?":** Zvi Pe'er, "This Is How I Took Revenge on the Murderers," 482.

76   **"My group consists of ten men and two women...":** Moshe Gildenman, "And Since Then I Have Been 'Uncle Misha,'" 1.

77   **"I'm the only one left from my family...":** Kuc, Testimony, 29.

78   **"All around we are encountering groups of Jews...":** Gogun, *Stalin's Commandos*, 173. See also Arad, *In the Shadow of the Red Banner*, 320.

80   **"Take the child...":** Volkon, "Wanderings and Hardships during the Holocaust," 304, trans. Gamulka in *Rokitno-Wolyn and Surroundings*, 317.

80   **"If I'm just going to ride out the war...":** Kuc, Testimony, 30.

81   **"Halt! Halt!":** Volkon, "Wanderings and Hardships during the Holocaust," 305.

82   **"Ladies, we can't continue like this...":** Simcha Gildenman, Transcript of Testimony, 13.

83   **"It's not going to be easy to find partisans...":** Moshe Gildenman, "And Since Then I Have Been 'Uncle Misha,'" 1–4.

CHAPTER 6: "DEATH TO THE GERMAN ROBBERS!"

Moshe Gildenman wrote about his first experiences as a partisan in "Expedition to Rybałki," *Opinion* 14 (March 20, 1947): 6; "The First Ambush," *The New Life* 22 (March 1947): 5; and in his Testimony. Simcha's memories of this period can be found in Simcha Gildenman, Transcript of Testimony; and Simcha Gildenman, "Vengeance is Mine, and Recompense." See also Armstrong, ed., *Soviet Partisans in World War II* and Spector, *The Holocaust of Volhynian Jews*.

For the memories of other partisans, see Kuc, Testimony; Chanan Weinberg, "A Doctor in the Forest," in *Memorial Book of the Community of Sarny*, ed. Yosef Kariv (Tel Aviv: Former Residents of Sarny and Vicinity in Israel, 1961), 366–68, trans. Jacob Solomon Berger and ed. Karen Leon at https://www.jewishgen.org/yizkor/sarny/sar350.html; Tadeusz Weinberg (Gadi T. Carmon), "Poland Is Not Yet Lost," in *Jewish Fate: Testimonies of the Living*, Vol. 2, ed. Marian Turski (Warsaw: Association of Jewish Veterans and Victims of World War II, 1999), 5–13, available online at https://zapis

pamieci.pl/tadeusz-weinberg; and Tadeusz Weinberg (Gadi T. Carmon), *The Thirties and the Forties*, ed. Orna Parnes (Zikhron Ya'akov, Israel, 2010).

88   **"Uncle Misha!":** Moshe Gildenman, "The First Ambush," 5.
88   *The Red Army Is Fighting…:* Alexander Dallin, Ralph Mavrogordato, and Wilhelm Moll, "Partisan Psychological Warfare and Popular Attitudes," in *Soviet Partisans in World War II*, ed. Armstrong, 258.
89   *Hello, people of Polesia!!!!…:* Moshe Gildenman, "Death to the German Robbers!" Ghetto Fighters' House Archives, Holdings Registry, File No. 1235. Courtesy of Yousef (Seffi) Hanegbi.
90   **"We should imagine ourselves lying in the mass grave…":** Moshe Gildenman, "The First Ambush," 5.
91   **"Uncle Misha…I hear some voices…":** Ibid.
93   **"Papa, just look at how big the sky is!…":** Ibid.
97   **"Oh, I'm so happy to see real Russian partisans…":** Moshe Gildenman, "Expedition to Rybałki," 6.
98   **"There they are!…":** Ibid.
100 **"What do we do now?":** Simcha Gildenman, Transcript of Testimony, 16.
100 **"Uncle Misha, I'm wounded…":** Moshe Gildenman, "Expedition to Rybałki," 6.
102 **"I formulated a salve…":** Chanan Weinberg, "A Doctor in the Forest," 368, trans. Berger and ed. Leon at https://www.jewishgen.org/yizkor/sarny/sar350.html.

CHAPTER 7: "AWAKE!"

Moshe Gildenman wrote about his winter in the forest in "Fighting and Struggle in the Forest"; *Jewish Daughters;* in his Testimony; and in "The Yellow Patch." See also Simcha Gildenman, Transcript of Testimony. For the memories of other partisans, see Kuc, Testimony; Chanan Weinberg, "A Doctor in the Forest"; Tadeusz Weinberg, "Poland Is Not Yet Lost"; and Tadeusz Weinberg, *The Thirties and the Forties.*

Records of Saburov's partisan federation can be found in Presidium of the Supreme Soviet of the Ukrainian Soviet Socialist Republic, Commission for the Affairs of Former Partisans of the Great Patriotic War, 1941–1945, "Lists of Personnel in the Partisan Federation under the Command of A. N. Saburov," Central State Archives of Supreme Bodies of Power and Government of Ukraine [TsDAVO], f. 1, op. 26, s. 553. For more information on the partisans, see Armstrong, ed., *Soviet Partisans in World War II;* Cooper, *The Phantom War;* Gogun, *Stalin's Commandos;* Sydir Kovpak, *Our Partisan Course,* trans. Ernst and Mira Lesser (London: Hutchinson & Co., 1947); Slepyan, *Stalin's Guerrillas;* and Spector, *The Holocaust of Volhynian Jews.*

103 **"Friends, don't shoot!":** Tadeusz Weinberg, *The Thirties and the Forties,* 79.

106 **"What will become of us?...":** Simcha Gildenman, Transcript of Testimony, 16.

106 **Weinbergs:** The Weinbergs later treated Zofia Dróżdż-Satanowska, who was the head of press and propaganda for a partisan group led by her husband, Robert Satanowski. The Weinbergs joined Satanowski's partisan group, which called itself "Poland Is Not Yet Lost" after the Polish national anthem. The group is credited with killing four hundred German soldiers, derailing nine trains, and blowing up eight bridges. Tadeusz survived the Holocaust and received Poland's Partisan Cross medal for his courageous activities as a fifteen-year-old partisan with "Poland Is Not Yet Lost." Robert Satanowski earned a number of military and civilian decorations. He went on to become an orchestral conductor and, later in his life, a politician.

109 **"Father of the partisan movement in Ukraine":** Gogun, *Stalin's Commandos,* 161.

109 **"Come with us!...":** Simcha Gildenman, Transcript of Testimony, 16.

110 ***Thanks so much...:*** Kuc, Testimony, 35.

111 **"All these familial partisan detachments...":** Gogun, *Stalin's Commandos,* 11.

112 **"Why have you come here?...":** Kuc, Testimony, 34.

113 **"Enough! We're done!...":** Simcha Gildenman, Transcript of Testimony, 19.

113 **"Which commander?...":** Kuc, Testimony, 35.

114 **"Wherever Saburov has passed through...":** Gogun, *Stalin's Commandos,* 97.

114 **"The incubator of the partisan movement":** Ibid., 4.

114 **"General Saburov is sitting north of Ovruch...":** Ibid., 163.

115 **"The entire group under Uncle Misha's command...":** Kuc, Testimony, 35.

115 **"You've done well!...":** Ibid., 35–36.

115 **"I'll redistribute you...":** Ibid., 36.

116 **"Yes, I've heard about this..."**: Ibid., 37.
116 **"Whatever the future holds..."**: Simcha Gildenman, Transcript of Testimony, 21.
116 **Sasha Kuc:** Because of his training with Medvedev and his knowledge of Volhynia, Sasha was assigned as the liaison between Saburov's staff and one of Kovpak's detachments. Two months later, Sasha was transferred to a unit in Svarytsevychi, sixteen miles west of Vysotsk, where he worked with the underground Komsomol party in the nearby town of Sernyky to drum up support for the partisans. After a German attack on Svarytsevychi in late 1943, Sasha once again escaped to the forest, where he was named deputy commander and then commander of a partisan unit. Sasha received the Soviet Union's "To a Partisan of the Patriotic War," 1st Class medal, and the Order of the Red Banner, as well as a Gold Cross of Merit, from Poland.

CHAPTER 8: "FORWARD INTO THE RANKS OF COMBAT!"

Moshe Gildenman wrote about his first two months with the Soviet partisans in "Fighting and Struggle in the Forest"; "How I Captured a Pair of German Boots," *The New Life* 48 (July 1947): 4; "In the Forests of Zhytomyr," *The New Life* 30 (April 1947): 5 and 31 (April 1947): 5; *Jewish Daughters*; his Testimony; and "The Yellow Patch." For a translation of the passage from *Jewish Daughters* on the attack on Rozvazhiv, see Yuri Suhl, ed. and trans., *They Fought Back: The Story of the Jewish Resistance in Nazi Europe* (New York: Schocken Books, 1967), 268–70. See also Simcha Gildenman, Transcript of Testimony; and Uri, "As Told by the Partisan Simcha Gildenman."

The records of the 1st Stalin Partisan Detachment are in Borovik Partisan Federation, "Journal of the Federation's Combat Operations," Central State Archives of Public Organizations and Ukrainians [TsDAHOU], f. 1, op. 72, s. 4; Borovik Partisan Federation, "Resolution of the Ukrainian Staff of the Partisan Movement on the Federation's Combat Activities. Report (draft) on the Organization and Combat Activities of the Federation and Its Detachments. UShPD's Combat Characterization of the Federation's Commander," TsDAHOU, f. 1, op. 72, s. 1; Presidium of the Supreme Soviet of the Ukrainian Soviet Socialist Republic, Commission for the Affairs of Former Partisans of the Great Patriotic War, 1941–1945, "Lists of Personnel in the Partisan Federation Named after Stalin under the Command of V. S. Ushakov," Central State Archives of Supreme Bodies of Power and Government of Ukraine [TsDAVO], f. 1, op. 26, s. 561; and Zhytomyr Partisan Federation, J. V. Stalin Partisan Detachment, "Lists of Detachment Personnel," TsDAHOU, f. 1, op. 65, s. 121. See also Armstrong, ed., *Soviet Partisans in World War II;* Gogun, *Stalin's Commandos;* and Slepyan, *Stalin's Guerrillas.*

For information on German trains, see Wilhelm Keitel, *The Memoirs of Field-Marshal Keitel,* ed. Walter Gorlitz, trans. David Irving (New York: Stein and Day, 1966) and Hans Pottgiesser, *The German Reich Trains in the Eastern Campaign, 1939–1944* (Neckargemünd, Germany: Kurt Vowinckel Verlag, 1960).

119 **"We're going on a mission…":** Moshe Gildenman, "How I Captured a Pair of German Boots," 4.

121 **"Well…I made sure he gets a cross.":** Ibid.

122 **"Hang the *starostas*…":** Moshe Gildenman, "The Yellow Patch," 13. See also Moshe Gildenman, "Fighting and Struggle in the Forest," 444.

122 *For their homeland* **and** *their Jewish people:* Arkadi Zeltser, "How the Jewish Intelligentsia Created the Jewishness of the Jewish Hero," in *Soviet Jews in World War II: Fighting, Witnessing, Remembering,* ed. Harriet Murav and Gennady Estraikh (Boston: Academic Studies Press, 2014), 115. Emphasis mine.

124 **"Ready your weapons!":** Moshe Gildenman, "The Yellow Patch," 13. See also Moshe Gildenman, "Fighting and Struggle in the Forest," 446.

125 **"Lionka is coming!…":** Moshe Gildenman, "The Yellow Patch," 13.

126 **"There's an officer!…":** Ibid.

127 **"Do you know what these are?…":** Moshe Gildenman, "Fighting and Struggle in the Forest," 448–49, trans. Klausner at https://www.jewishgen.org/yizkor/korets/kor443.html. See also Moshe Gildenman, "The Yellow Patch," 13.

129 **"This is a Jew…":** Moshe Gildenman, "Fighting and Struggle in the Forest," 450, trans. Klausner at https://www.jewishgen.org/yizkor/korets/kor443.html.

129 **"The Army by itself…":** Keitel, *The Memoirs of Field-Marshal Keitel,* 177.

133 **Rozvazhiv:** In *Jewish Daughters,* Moshe Gildenman recalled the attack on Rozvazhiv taking place on New Year's Eve, but he did not join the 1st Stalin Partisan Detachment until January 11, 1943 (Zhytomyr Partisan Federation, J. V. Stalin Partisan Detachment, "Lists of Detachment Personnel," 68). The records of the 1st Stalin Partisan Detachment place the raid as occurring between February 11 and 17 (Borovik Partisan Federation, "Journal of the Federation's Combat Operations," 76zv–77zv).

135 **"It's about time you got here...":** Moshe Gildenman, *Jewish Daughters*, 120–21.

137 **"Tell us, how were you connected...":** Ibid., 123.

138 **"Good people, death is the lightest punishment I deserve...":** Ibid., 166.

139 **"I want to be a regular fighter...":** Ibid., 167.

140 **"I miss our Volhynian Jews...":** Ibid., 168.

140 **Sonya:** Six months after the attack on Rozvazhiv, the partisans learned that Sonya's husband, Vasya Zorin, was encamped with another partisan detachment nearby. Just before Vasya arrived to reunite with Sonya and Kostik, Sonya hanged herself. She left a note explaining to Vasya, "I could never forgive myself for my shameful deed" (Moshe Gildenman, *Jewish Daughters*, 180).

CHAPTER 9: "THE OATH"

Moshe Gildenman wrote about Uncle Misha's Jewish Group, Fridek the Magyar, and the battles in Antonovka and Aleksandrovka in "In the Forests of Zhytomyr"; *On the Way to Victory* (Paris: Organization for Polish Jews in France, 1949); his Testimony; and "We Were With You, Heroes of the Warsaw Ghetto! From the Diary of Engineer M. Gildenman, 'Uncle Misha,'" Yad Vashem Archives, Testimonies, Diaries, and Memoirs Collection, O.33/523, trans. in *Book of the Ghetto Wars: Between the Walls, in the Camps, and in the Forests*, ed. Yitzhak Zuckerman and Moshe Basak (Tel Aviv: Kibbutz Hameuchad, 1956), 664–66, reprinted in *Zviahel*, ed. Uri and Boneh, 299–302, trans. in *The Fighting Ghettos*, trans. and ed. Meyer Barkai (Philadelphia: J.B. Lippincott, 1962), 265–70.

Details regarding the 1st Stalin Partisan Detachment are from Borovik Partisan Federation, "Journal of the Federation's Combat Operations"; Presidium of the Supreme Soviet of the Ukrainian Soviet Socialist Republic, Commission for the Affairs of Former Partisans of the Great Patriotic War, 1941–1945, "Lists of Personnel in the Partisan Federation Named after Stalin under the Command of V. S. Ushakov"; and Zhytomyr Partisan Federation, J. V. Stalin Partisan Detachment, "Orders to the Federation, Orders and Excerpts of Orders to the Detachment, Report of the Detachment and of the Federation Staff on the Combat Operations Conducted in May 1943, and Intelligence Reports of the Detachment Staff Liaison," TsDAHOU, f. 1, op. 65, s. 119. See also Armstrong, ed., *Soviet Partisans in World War II*.

142 **"Little Jews":** Moshe Gildenman, "In the Forests of Zhytomyr" [Part I], 5; and Moshe Gildenman, Testimony, 5.

142 **"I am a Jew":** Moshe Gildenman, Testimony, 7.

143 **"Uncle Misha, there's a Hungarian...":** Moshe Gildenman, *On the Way to Victory,* 17–19.

144 **"The lightest head is a hothead...":** Ibid., 19.

146 **"I've been praying every day...":** Ibid., 21.

150 **"If we could divert the attention...":** Moshe Gildenman. "In the Forests of Zhytomyr" [Part I], 5.

151 **"I'm not letting you go by yourself...":** Moshe Gildenman. "In the Forests of Zhytomyr" [Part II], 5.

153 **"How many Germans are in the village...":** Ibid.

154 **"An attack by many partisans!...":** Ibid.

155 **"Who's there?...":** Ibid.

157 **"Why should I shoot at a partisan?...":** Zhytomyr Partisan Federation, J. V. Stalin Partisan Detachment, "Orders to the Federation, Orders and Excerpts of Orders to the Detachment, Report of the Detachment and of the Federation Staff on the Combat Operations Conducted in May 1943, and Intelligence Reports of the Detachment Staff Liaison," 32.

157 **"Keep driving, Ukrainian swine...":** Moshe Gildenman, "We Were With You, Heroes of the Warsaw Ghetto!" 4. Gildenman recalled the attack on Aleksandrovka occurring after the Warsaw Ghetto Uprising, which started on April 19, 1943, but the records of the 1st Stalin Partisan Detachment show that the attack occurred on March 19 (Borovik Partisan Federation, "Journal of the Federation's Combat Operations," 86zv).

159 **"I'll run out...":** Moshe Gildenman, "We Were With You, Heroes of the Warsaw Ghetto!" 6.

160 ***Baron von Hellman...:*** Ibid., 7.

CHAPTER 10: "THE 'YOUTH' OATH"

Moshe Gildenman wrote about Motele "Mitka" Schlein in *Motele, The Young Partisan* (Paris, 1950) and *On the Way to Victory.* See also Moshe Gildenman, *Jewish Daughters;* and his Testimony. For a translation of the passage from *Motele* in which Simcha meets Motele, see Timothy Collins, *Finding Motele: A Family's Odyssey Searching for a Young Jewish Partisan* (Columbia, SC:

Lulu Press, 2021), 62–65. For translations of the story of Motele blowing up the canteen, see Collins, *Finding Motele*, 8–17; and Suhl, ed., *They Fought Back*, 261–67.

There is, unfortunately, no documentary evidence of the canteen story in either German or Russian records. As Michael Tal, the Director of Yad Vashem's Artifacts Collection, has asserted, "There was a Motele Schlein, he played violin, he spied for the partisans, and he was killed. That is all we definitely know" (Renee Ghert-Zand, "Oscar-Qualifying Short Film Strikes Chord with Story of Heroic Young WWII Partisan," *Times of Israel*, December 20, 2022, https://www.timesofisrael.com/oscar-qualifying-short -film-strikes-chord). It is, however, quite possible that researchers have been looking for evidence of this story in the wrong places. The sabotage of the canteen occurred prior to May 1, 1943—not, as Gildenman wrote, in the autumn of 1943. Gildenman may have misremembered the location, as well, as he did in at least one other story in *Motele*.

Motele's violin is on permanent display in Yad Vashem's Holocaust History Museum. It is played on special occasions, including the opening ceremony of Yad Vashem's Moshal Shoah Legacy Campus in July 2024.

Details regarding the 1st Stalin Partisan Detachment are from Borovik Partisan Federation, "Journal of the Federation's Combat Operations."

162 **"There's someone there...":** Moshe Gildenman, *Motele*, 9–13.
165 **"What are you going to say...":** Ibid., 13–16.
167 **"Move!...Go!...":** Ibid., 18–20.
170 **Saint Basil's Convent:** Collins, *Finding Motele*, 104–5.
170 **"Come with me...":** Moshe Gildenman, *On the Way to Victory*, 8; and *Motele*, 129.
174 **"Fiddler, play 'Volga, Volga'...":** Ibid., 14–16; and Ibid., 135–37. For more on "Volga, Volga" and "Forest Joy," see Collins, *Finding Motele*, 113–16.

CHAPTER 11: "NEVER SAY THAT YOU HAVE REACHED THE END OF THE ROAD"

For information about the song "Never Say That You Have Reached the End of the Road," see Shmerke Kaczerginski, *I Was a Partisan: The Green Legend* (Buenos Aires, 1952) and *Songs of the Ghettos and Camps* (New York: Cyco Farlag, 1948). See also Ruth Rubin, *Voices of a People: The Story of Yiddish Folksong* (Urbana: University of Illinois Press, 2000); Bret Werb, Liner notes to *Rise Up and Fight! Songs of Jewish Partisans*, recorded 1995–1996, United States Holocaust Memorial Museum (USHMM-02, 1996, CD); and Bret Werb, "Yiddish Songs of the Shoah: A Source Study Based on the Collections of Shmerke Kaczerginski" (Ph.D. diss., University of California Los Angeles, 2014).

For the Warsaw Ghetto Uprising, see United States Holocaust Memorial Museum. "Warsaw Ghetto Uprising." Holocaust Encyclopedia. https://encyclopedia.ushmm.org/content/en/article/warsaw-ghetto-uprising.

For documentation of the partisan magazine *Stalinets*, see Borovik Partisan Federation, "Journal of the Federation's Combat Operations"; Borovik Partisan Federation, "Handwritten Journal Stalinets (No. 2)," TsDAHOU, f. 1, op. 72, s. 8; and Borovik Partisan Federation, "Memoirs of M. S. Bliner, the Editor of the Handwritten Journal of the Federation, *Stalinets*, about the Occupation Regime, Combat Activities of Partisans against Enemy Troops, and the Federation's Mass Propaganda and Publishing Activities," TsDAHOU, f. 1, op. 72, s. 10.

178 **"They'll find their nest soon…":** Moshe Gildenman, "We Were With You, Heroes of the Warsaw Ghetto!" 2–3.
180 **"Hello! Hello!…":** Kaczerginski, *I Was a Partisan*, 107–8.
181 **"In moments when it seemed…":** Kaczerginski, *Songs of the Ghettos and Camps*, xvi.
183 **"The circus is here!…":** Moshe Gildenman, *Motele*, 23–24.
184 **"You know what, Papa?…":** Ibid., 25–28.
187 **"Where am I?…":** Moshe Gildenman, *On The Way to Victory*, 30–34; and *Jewish Daughters*, 181–85.
190 **"Ask him how he's feeling…":** Ibid., 35–37; and Ibid., 187–89.
192 **"Here. Take this blanket…":** Ibid., 38–42; and Ibid., 191–96.

CHAPTER 12: "BRAVE IN THE FACE OF THE ENEMY!"

For the records of the Stalin Partisan Federation during this period, see Borovik Partisan Federation, "Journal of the Federation's Combat Operations"; Borovik Partisan Federation, "Orders (Copies) of the Ukrainian Staff of the Partisan Movement. Orders, Combat Orders, and Instructions to the Federation," TsDAHOU, f. 1, op. 72, s. 2; and Presidium of the Supreme Soviet of the Ukrainian Soviet Socialist Republic, Commission for the Affairs of Former Partisans of the Great Patriotic War, 1941–1945, "Lists of Personnel in the Partisan Federation Named after Stalin under the Command of V. S. Ushakov." See also Gogun, *Stalin's Commandos.*

195 **"Finally, I've met some real partisans..."**: Moshe Gildenman, *Jewish Daughters*, 21–24.
198 **"Any news?..."**: Ibid., 25–27.
201 **"What are you reading, Yossele?..."**: Ibid., 39.
202 **"They're fed up with all of my Russian dances..."**: Ibid., 40–46.
207 **"I'm hit!..."**: Ibid., 49–51.
209 **"There's something important..."**: Ibid., 52–55.
212 *The net has been cast...*: Ibid., 64–78.

CHAPTER 13: "AT THE EDGE OF THE FOREST"

Details regarding Gildenman's partisan activities during the summer of 1943 are from Borovik Partisan Federation, "Journal of the Federation's Combat Operations"; Borovik Partisan Federation, "Orders (Copies) of the Ukrainian Staff of the Partisan Movement. Orders, Combat Orders, and Instructions to the Federation"; Khrushchev Kyiv Partisan Federation, "Report of the Federation Command on the Combat and Party-Political Activities of the Federation," TsDAHOU, f. 77, op. 1, s. 1; Khrushchev Kyiv Partisan Federation, "Reports of the Federation Staff on the Combat, Intelligence, and Party-Political Activities of the Federation for the Period between April 13 and October 9, 1943. Information on the Disbanding of the Federation and the Transfer of Personnel, Weapons, Ammunition, and Property to the Disposal of the Military Units of the Red Army," TsDAHOU, f. 77, op. 1, s. 2; Presidium of the Supreme Soviet of the Ukrainian Soviet Socialist Republic, Commission for the Affairs of Former Partisans of the Great Patriotic War, 1941–1945, "Lists of Personnel in the N. S. Khrushchev Partisan Federation under the Command of I. A. Khitrichenko," TsDAVO, f. 1, op. 26, s. 564; and Presidium of the Supreme Soviet of the Ukrainian Soviet Socialist Republic, Commission for the Affairs of Former Partisans of the Great Patriotic War, 1941–1945, "Lists of Personnel in the Partisan Federation Named after Stalin under the Command of V. S. Ushakov." See also Armstrong, ed., *Soviet Partisans in World War II*; David M. Glantz, *The History of Soviet Airborne Forces* (Ilford, England: Frank Cass, 1994); Gogun, *Stalin's Commandos*; Grenkevich, *The Soviet Partisan Movement*; Ivan Khitrichenko, *The Path of the People's Wrath* (Kyiv: Political Literature of Ukraine Publishing House, 1990); and Sergey Smirnov, *Stories of Unsung Heroes* (Moscow: Soviet Writer, 1985).

215 **"Gangs organized partly in military style..."**: Gogun, *Stalin's Commandos*, 55.
218 **"It's way past bedtime..."**: Moshe Gildenman, *Jewish Daughters*, 198–99.
220 **"If we survive the war..."**: Ibid., 203–5.
221 **"The always happy Srolke the Machine Gunner..."**: Ibid., 207–8.
224 **"We can't sit here much longer..."**: Moshe Gildenman, *Motele*, 156–59.
226 **"Ask him what he's doing in Radomyshl..."**: Ibid., 159–61.
228 **"Uncle Misha, you're alive!..."**: Ibid., 162–65.
232 **"How many armed partisans do you have?..."**: Ibid., 166–67. Gildenman recalled being arrested in Malyn, but the records of the Khrushchev Kyiv Partisan Federation show that the city in question was Radomyshl—less than twenty miles south of Malyn (Khrushchev Kyiv Partisan Federation, "Report of the Federation Command on the Combat and Party-Political Activities of the Federation," 152–56; and Khrushchev Kyiv Partisan Federation, "Reports of the Federation Staff on the Combat, Intelligence, and Party-Political Activities of the Federation for the Period between April 13 and October 9, 1943. Information on the Disbanding of the Federation and the Transfer of Personnel, Weapons, Ammunition, and Property to the Disposal of the Military Units of the Red Army," 16).
234 **"Eastern Wall"**: Glantz, *The History of Soviet Airborne Forces*, 262.
236 **"Uncle Misha!..."**: Moshe Gildenman, *Motele*, 169–70.
237 **"Do you remember the time..."**: Ibid., 171–72.

CHAPTER 14: "A YOUNG SOLDIER QUIETLY SINGS A SONG"

The events surrounding Gildenman's transition into the Red Army are chronicled in Borovik Partisan Federation, "Lists of Command Staff and Personnel, Members and Candidates of VKP(b), VLKSM Members, and Partisans Who Fell in Combat against the Enemy. Information on the Transfer of Personnel, Weapons, Ammunition, and Property to Parts of the Red Army during the Disbandment of the Federation," TsDAHOU, f. 1, op. 72, s. 6; and Borovik Partisan Federation, "Orders (Copies) of the Ukrainian Staff of the Partisan Movement. Orders, Combat Orders, and Instructions to the Federation."

Information on Gildenman's service in the 8th Rifle Division is from Combat Log of the 654th Regiment, 148th Rifle Division, Central Archives of the Russian Ministry of Defense [TsAMO], f. 7310, op. 60123, d. 19, accessed at https://pamyat-naroda.ru/documents/view/?id=131026410; Viktor Nikolaevich Lupshev, *8th Rifle Division* (Alma-Ata, Kazakhstan: 1975); and Order to the Troops of the 13th Army and the 1st Ukrainian Front, November 28, 1943, No. 212/N, TsAMO, f. 33, op. 686044, d. 2987, accessed at https://pamyat-naroda.ru/heroes/podvig-chelovek_nagrazhdenie46294697. See also Soviet General Staff, *The Battle of the Dnepr: The Red Army's Forcing of the East Wall, September–December 1943*, ed. and trans. Richard W. Harrison (Solihull, England: Helion & Company, 2018).

240 **"I'm not a child anymore…":** Moshe Gildenman, *Motele*, 190.

243 **"Look, Uncle Misha…":** Ibid., 193–94.

244 **"I wanted to be with the two of you…":** Ibid., 195–97. For a translation of the passage on Motele's death, see Collins, *Finding Motele*, 128–31. See https://www.youtube.com/watch?v=ck_wlJWsRSc for a video about Motele's death produced by Yad Vashem.

246 **"I'll go first…":** Simcha Gildenman, Transcript of Testimony, 28. See also Uri, "As Told by the Partisan Simcha Gildenman," 305.

246 **"Oo-rah!":** Order to the Troops of the 13th Army and the 1st Ukrainian Front, November 28, 1943, 15.

246 **"Papa, let's grab him…":** Simcha Gildenman, Transcript of Testimony, 29. See also Uri, "As Told by the Partisan Simcha Gildenman," 305.

248 **"Well, partisans, what do you think?…":** Simcha Gildenman, Transcript of Testimony, 30–31.

250 **"I want to continue on until victory!…":** "Uncle Misha," *Opinion*, 14.

CHAPTER 15: "SONG OF THE FRONT-LINE DRIVER"

Information on Gildenman's service as a Red Army engineer is from Order to the Troops of the 13th Army and the 1st Ukrainian Front, September 1, 1944, No. 202/N, TsAMO, f. 33, op. 690155, d. 2447, p. 1, accessed at https://pamyat-naroda.ru/heroes/podvig-chelovek_nagrazhdenie31124256. See also David M. Glantz and Jonathan M. House, *When Titans Clashed: How the Red Army Stopped Hitler* (Lawrence, KS: University Press of Kansas, 1995).

For information about the Nazi camp system, see United States Holocaust Memorial Museum, "Nazi Camps." Holocaust Encyclopedia, https://encyclopedia.ushmm.org/content/en/article/nazi-camps.

252 **"For his skillful leadership…"**: Order to the Troops of the 13th Army and the 1st Ukrainian Front, September 1, 1944, 15.

254 **"It's high time for a smoke…"**: Moshe Gildenman, *Jewish Daughters*, 82.

255 **"Comrade Engineer, do you think the church organ still works?…"**: Ibid., 83–87.

259 **"Did you dream last night…"**: Moshe Gildenman, "By the Bóbr River," *Opinion* 17 (May 5, 1947): 7.

261 **"We've stumbled upon some Germans…"**: Ibid., 7–8.

262 **"This piece of iron…"**: Moshe Gildenman, *Jewish Daughters*, 89.

264 **"Inferior Jewish race"**: Ibid., 91.

264 **"Comrade Engineer…"**: Ibid., 92–94.

267 **"You know…"**: Ibid., 104–6.

268 **"Why are two pages torn out?…"**: Ibid., 106–8.

270 **"We are continuing our hearing…"**: Ibid., 110–15. Courtesy of Yousef (Seffi) Hanegbi.

273 ***Hitler and Goebbels!…***: Moshe Gildenman, Testimony, 10; "Uncle Misha," *Opinion*, 14; and "Comrade Engineer M. Gildenman ('Uncle Misha') visits 'Ihud' in Łódź," *Opinion* 19 (June 16, 1947): 11. See also S[imcha] G[ildenman], "Uncle Misha," 505.

EPILOGUE

Moshe Gildenman wrote about his postwar life in his Testimony. See also "Comrade Engineer M. Gildenman ('Uncle Misha') visits 'Ihud' in Łódź"; S[imcha] G[ildenman], "Uncle Misha"; "Uncle Misha," *Opinion*; and Moshe Kahanovich, "Moshe Gildenman—Partisan Commander of the 'Yevgruppa,'" *Yad Vashem Bulletin* 3 (1958): 13–14. For Simcha's return to Korets, see Simcha Gildenman, Transcript of Testimony; Simcha Gildenman, "Upon My Return to the Town," in *Korets*, ed. Leoni, 530–32; and Uri, "As Told by the Partisan Simcha Gildenman." For information on Szczecin, see Achim Wörn, "Jews in Szczecin, 1945–50: At the Crossroad between Emigration and Assimilation," *Region: Regional Studies of Russia, Eastern Europe, and Central Asia* 6:1 (2017): 55–85.

Bibliography

ARCHIVAL SOURCES

Borovik Partisan Federation. "Handwritten Journal *Stalinets* (No. 2)" [Russian]. Central State Archives of Public Organizations and Ukrainians [TsDAHOU], f. 1, op. 72, s. 8.

————. "Journal of the Federation's Combat Operations" [Russian]. Central State Archives of Public Organizations and Ukrainians [TsDAHOU], f. 1, op. 72, s. 4.

————. "Lists of Command Staff and Personnel, Members and Candidates of VKP(b), VLKSM Members, and Partisans Who Fell in Combat against the Enemy. Information on the Transfer of Personnel, Weapons, Ammunition, and Property to Parts of the Red Army during the Disbandment of the Federation" [Russian]. Central State Archives of Public Organizations and Ukrainians [TsDAHOU], f. 1, op. 72, s. 6.

————. "Memoirs of M. S. Bliner, the Editor of the Handwritten Journal of the Federation, *Stalinets*, about the Occupation Regime, Combat Activities of Partisans against Enemy Troops, and the Federation's Mass Propaganda and Publishing Activities" [Russian]. Central State Archives of Public Organizations and Ukrainians [TsDAHOU], f. 1, op. 72, s. 10.

————. "Orders (Copies) of the Ukrainian Staff of the Partisan Movement. Orders, Combat Orders, and Instructions to the Federation" [Russian]. Central State Archives of Public Organizations and Ukrainians [TsDAHOU], f. 1, op. 72, s. 2.

————. "Resolution of the Ukrainian Staff of the Partisan Movement on the Federation's Combat Activities. Report (draft) on the Organization and Combat Activities of the Federation and Its Detachments. UShPD's Combat Characterization of the Federation's Commander" [Russian]. Central State Archives of Public Organizations and Ukrainians [TsDAHOU], f. 1, op. 72, s. 1.

Combat Log of the 654th Regiment, 148th Rifle Division [Russian]. Central Archives of the Russian Ministry of Defense [TsAMO], f. 7310, op. 60123, d. 19. Accessed at https://pamyat-naroda.ru/documents/view/?id=131026410.

Gildenman, Moshe. "And Since Then I Have Been 'Uncle Misha'" [Polish]. Yad Vashem Archives, Testimonies, Diaries, and Memoirs Collection, O.33/522.

———. "Death to the German Robbers!" [Russian]. Ghetto Fighters' House Archives, Holdings Registry, File No. 1235.

———. Report on the Town of Korets, Ukraine [Yiddish]. Ghetto Fighters' House Archives, Collections Section, 2277.

———. Testimony [Yiddish]. Yad Vashem Archives, Testimonies, Diaries, and Memoirs Collection, O.33/521.

———. "We Were With You, Heroes of the Warsaw Ghetto! From the Diary of Engineer M. Gildenman, 'Uncle Misha'" [Yiddish]. Yad Vashem Archives, Testimonies, Diaries, and Memoirs Collection, O.33/523.

Gildenman, Simcha. "A Notebook Containing Handwritten Poems/Songs in Yiddish, Russian, and Polish." Yad Vashem Artifacts Collection, 6622/1–13.

———. Transcript of Testimony [Hebrew]. Yad Vashem Archives, Testimonies Department, O.3/6863.

Gladstein, Joseph. *Freedom's Songs: Popular Workers Songs and Workers Folksongs with Notation for Singing and Playing* [Yiddish]. Warsaw: Lire, 1919. Moshe Gildenman's Personal Copy. Yad Vashem Artifacts Collection, 4955/1.

Kersch (Shapira), Yehudit. Testimony [Polish]. Yad Vashem Archives, Testimonies Department, O.3/2796.

Khrushchev Kyiv Partisan Federation. "Report of the Federation Command on the Combat and Party-Political Activities of the Federation" [Russian]. Central State Archives of Public Organizations and Ukrainians [TsDAHOU], f. 77, op. 1, s. 1.

———. "Reports of the Federation Staff on the Combat, Intelligence, and Party-Political Activities of the Federation for the Period between April 13 and October 9, 1943. Information on the Disbanding of the Federation and the Transfer of Personnel, Weapons, Ammunition, and Property to the Disposal of the Military Units of the Red Army" [Russian]. Central State Archives of Public Organizations and Ukrainians [TsDAHOU], f. 77, op. 1, s. 2.

Kuc, Aleksander. Testimony [Hebrew and Polish]. Yad Vashem Archives, Testimonies Department, O.3/3268.

Order to the Troops of the 13th Army and the 1st Ukrainian Front, November 28, 1943, No. 212/N [Russian]. Central Archives of the Russian Ministry of Defense [TsAMO], f. 33, op. 686044, d. 2987. Accessed at https://pamyat-naroda.ru/heroes/podvig-chelovek _nagrazhdenie46294697.

Order to the Troops of the 13th Army and the 1st Ukrainian Front, September 1, 1944, No. 202/N [Russian]. Central Archives of the Russian Ministry of Defense [TsAMO], f. 33, op. 690155, d. 2447. Accessed at https://pamyat-naroda.ru/heroes/podvig-chelovek _nagrazhdenie31124256.

Presidium of the Supreme Soviet of the Ukrainian Soviet Socialist Republic, Commission for the Affairs of Former Partisans of the Great Patriotic War, 1941–1945. "Lists of Personnel in the N. S. Khrushchev Partisan Federation under the Command of I. A. Khitrichenko" [Russian]. Central State Archives of Supreme Bodies of Power and Government of Ukraine [TsDAVO], f. 1, op. 26, s. 564.

———. "Lists of Personnel in the Partisan Federation Named after Stalin under the Command of V. S. Ushakov" [Russian]. Central State Archives of Supreme Bodies of Power and Government of Ukraine [TsDAVO], f. 1, op. 26, s. 561.

———. "Lists of Personnel in the Partisan Federation under the Command of A. N. Saburov" [Russian]. Central State Archives of Supreme Bodies of Power and Government of Ukraine [TsDAVO], f. 1, op. 26, s. 553.

Trosman, Issachar. Testimony [Hebrew]. Yad Vashem Archives, Testimonies Department, O.3/3477.

Zhytomyr Partisan Federation, J. V. Stalin Partisan Detachment. "Lists of Detachment Personnel" [Russian]. Central State Archives of Public Organizations and Ukrainians [TsDAHOU], f. 1, op. 65, s. 121.

———. "Orders to the Federation, Orders and Excerpts of Orders to the Detachment, Report of the Detachment and of the Federation Staff on the Combat Operations Conducted in May 1943, and Intelligence Reports of the Detachment Staff Liaison" [Russian]. Central State Archives of Public Organizations and Ukrainians [TsDAHOU], f. 1, op. 65, s. 119.

BOOKS

Ainsztein, Reuben. *Jewish Resistance in Nazi-Occupied Eastern Europe*. New York: Barnes and Noble, 1974.

Arad, Yitzhak. *In the Shadow of the Red Banner: Soviet Jews in the War against Nazi Germany*. Jerusalem: Yad Vashem, 2010.

Armstrong, John A., ed. *Soviet Partisans in World War II*. Madison: University of Wisconsin Press, 1964.

Avitahi, Aryeh, ed. *Rivne: A Memorial Book* [Hebrew]. Tel Aviv: Former Residents of Rivne in Israel, 1956. Translated by Naomi Gal as *Rovno: Memorial Book*, edited by Ann Glickman Goldberg. New York: JewishGen, 2020.

Barkai, Meyer, ed. *The Fighting Ghettos*. Philadelphia: J.B. Lippincott, 1962.

Bauer, Yehuda. *The Death of the Shtetl*. New Haven: Yale University Press, 2009.

Collins, Timothy. *Finding Motele: A Family's Odyssey Searching for a Young Jewish Partisan*. Columbia, SC: Lulu Press, 2021.

Cooper, Matthew. *The Phantom War: The German Struggle against Soviet Partisans 1941–1944*. London: Macdonald and Jane's, 1979.

Dembski, Yafa (née Shaindel Chimenes). *I Must Stay Alive: The Story of Shaindel* [Hebrew]. Ra'anana, Israel: Docostory, 2019.

Erlich, Elhanan, ed. *The Staszów Book* [Hebrew, Yiddish, and English]. Tel Aviv: Former Residents of Staszów in Israel and in the Diaspora, 1962). Translated by Kutzi Weill as *Staszów Memorial Book*, edited by Jean-Pierre Stroweis, Leonard Levin, and Dobrochna Fire. New York: JewishGen, 2020.

Gildenman, Moshe. *The Destruction of Korets* [Yiddish]. Paris, 1949.

———. *Jewish Daughters* [Yiddish]. Paris, 1950.

———. *The Jewish Partisans* [Yiddish]. Tel Aviv: New Life, 1955.

———. *Motele, The Young Partisan* [Yiddish]. Paris, 1950.

———. *On the Way to Victory* [Yiddish]. Paris: Organization for Polish Jews in France, 1949.

Glantz, David M. *The History of Soviet Airborne Forces*. Ilford, England: Frank Cass, 1994.

——— and Jonathan M. House. *When Titans Clashed: How the Red Army Stopped Hitler*. Lawrence, KS: University Press of Kansas, 1995.

Gogun, Alexander. *Stalin's Commandos: Ukrainian Partisan Forces on the Eastern Front*. London: I.B. Tauris, 2016.

Grenkevich, Leonid D. *The Soviet Partisan Movement, 1941–1944: A Critical His-toriographical Analysis,* edited by David M. Glantz. London: Frank Cass, 1999.

Grymes, James A. *Violins of Hope: Violins of the Holocaust—Instruments of Hope and Liberation in Mankind's Darkest Hour.* New York, NY: Harper Perennial, 2014.

Kaczerginski, Shmerke. *I Was a Partisan: The Green Legend* [Yiddish]. Buenos Aires, 1952.

———. *Songs of the Ghettos and Camps* [Yiddish]. New York: Cyco Farlag, 1948.

Kahanovich, Moshe. *The War of the Jewish Partisans in Eastern Europe* [Yiddish]. 2 vols. Buenos Aires: Central Association of Polish Jews in Argentina, 1956.

Kariv, Yosef, ed. *Memorial Book of the Community of Sarny* [Hebrew and Yiddish]. Tel Aviv: Former Residents of Sarny and Vicinity in Israel, 1961.

Keitel, Wilhelm. *The Memoirs of Field-Marshal Keitel,* edited by Walter Gorlitz, translated by David Irving. New York: Stein and Day, 1966.

Khitrichenko, Ivan. *The Path of the People's Wrath* [Russian]. Kyiv: Political Literature of Ukraine Publishing House, 1990.

Kovpak, Sydir. *Our Partisan Course,* translated by Ernst and Mira Lesser. London: Hutchinson & Co., 1947.

Leoni, Eliezer, ed. *Korets (Volyn): In Memory of Our Community That Is No More* [Hebrew and Yiddish]. Tel Aviv: Former Residents of Korets in Israel, 1959.

———. *Rokytne (Volyn) and the Surrounding Area: A Book of Testimony and Memory* [Hebrew and Yiddish]. Tel Aviv: Former Residents of Ro-kytne in Israel, 1967. Translated by Ala Gamulka as *Rokitno-Wolyn and Surroundings: Memorial Book and Testimony (Ukraine).* New York: JewishGen, 2015.

Levine, Allan. *Fugitives of the Forest: The Heroic Story of Jewish Resistance and Survival During the Second World War.* Guilford, CT: Lyons Press, 2009.

Lupshev, Viktor Nikolaevich. *8th Rifle Division* [Russian]. Alma-Ata, Ka-zakhstan: 1975.

Medvedev, Dmitry. *Stout Hearts: This Happened Near Rovno,* translated by David Skvirsky. Honolulu: University Press of the Pacific, 2002.

Podgajecki, Anna. *Anna: A Teenager on the Run*, translated by Sandy Bloom. Amberly Publishing—Yad Vashem, 2016.

Pottgiesser, Hans. *The German Reich Trains in the Eastern Campaign, 1939–1944* [German]. Neckargemünd, Germany: Kurt Vowinckel Verlag, 1960.

Rubin, Ruth. *Voices of a People: The Story of Yiddish Folksong.* Urbana: University of Illinois Press, 2000.

Samuels, Gertrude. *Mottele: A Partisan Odyssey.* New York: Harper & Row, 1976.

Slepyan, Kenneth. *Stalin's Guerrillas: Soviet Partisans in World War II.* Lawrence, KS: University Press of Kansas, 2006.

Smirnov, Sergey. *Stories of Unsung Heroes* [Russian]. Moscow: Soviet Writer, 1985.

Soviet General Staff. *The Battle of the Dnepr: The Red Army's Forcing of the East Wall, September–December 1943*, edited and translated by Richard W. Harrison. Solihull, England: Helion & Company, 2018.

Spector, Shmuel. *The Holocaust of Volhynian Jews 1941–1944*, translated by Jerzy Michalowicz. Jerusalem: Yad Vashem—The Federation of Volhynian Jews, 1990.

Suhl, Yuri, ed. and trans. *They Fought Back: The Story of the Jewish Resistance in Nazi Europe.* New York: Schocken Books, 1967.

Suhl, Yuri. *Uncle Misha's Partisans.* New York: Four Winds Press, 1973.

Trunk, Isaiah. *Judenrat: The Jewish Councils in Eastern Europe under Nazi Occupation.* New York: Macmillan, 1972.

Uri, Azriel and Mordekhai Boneh, eds. *Zviahel (Novohrad-Volynskyi)* [Hebrew and Yiddish]. Tel Aviv: Association of Former Residents of Zviahel and Surroundings, 1962.

Weinberg, Tadeusz (Gadi T. Carmon). *The Thirties and the Forties* [Hebrew], edited by Orna Parnes. Zikhron Ya'akov, Israel, 2010.

Werb, Bret. "Yiddish Songs of the Shoah: A Source Study Based on the Collections of Shmerke Kaczerginski." Ph.D. diss., University of California Los Angeles, 2014.

Yahil, Leni. *The Holocaust: The Fate of European Jewry, 1932–1945*, translated by Ina Friedman and Haya Galai. New York: Oxford University Press, 1990.

Zuckerman, Yitzhak and Moshe Basak, eds. *Book of the Ghetto Wars: Between the Walls, in the Camps, and in the Forests* [Hebrew]. Tel Aviv: Kibbutz Hameuchad, 1956.

ARTICLES, CHAPTERS, AND ESSAYS

Adelman, Eliahu. "In Zaltsikn Yam–A Yiddish Workers' Song." Jewish Music Research Center. June 2014. https://jewish-music.huji.ac.il/content/zaltsikn-yam-yiddish-workers-song.

Altman, I. A. and A. I. Kruglov. "Korets." In *Holocaust in the Territory of the USSR* [Russian], edited by I. A. Altman, 463–64. Moscow: Rosspen, 2009.

Anapolsky, Nyuma. "Thanks to Kind People—Ukrainians and Poles." In *Life in the Shadow of Death—Recent Memories about the Holocaust in Ukraine: Testimonies and Documents*, edited by Boris Zabarko, translated by Marina Guba and Vladimir Matveyev, Vol. 1, 123–39. Melitopol, Ukraine: Publishing House of Melitopol City Printing House, 2019.

Armstrong, John A. and Kurt DeWitt. "Organization and Control of the Partisan Movement." In *Soviet Partisans in World War II*, edited by John A. Armstrong, 73–139. Madison: University of Wisconsin Press, 1964.

Avisar (Schwarzman), Pinchas. "The 'Tarbut' Library in Korets." In *Korets (Volyn): In Memory of Our Community That Is No More* [Hebrew and Yiddish], edited by Eliezer Leoni, 134–35. Tel Aviv: Former Residents of Korets in Israel, 1959. Translated by Sara Mages at https://www.jewishgen.org/yizkor/korets/kor133.html.

Baraz, Simcha. "The Korets Jewish Drama Lovers' Circle." In *Korets (Volyn): In Memory of Our Community That Is No More* [Hebrew and Yiddish], edited by Eliezer Leoni, 144–48. Tel Aviv: Former Residents of Korets in Israel, 1959.

Barber, Noach. "The 'Heder' and the 'Yeshiva' in Our City." In *Korets (Volyn): In Memory of Our Community That Is No More* [Hebrew and Yiddish], edited by Eliezer Leoni, 120–23. Tel Aviv: Former Residents of Korets in Israel, 1959. Translated by Sara Mages at https://www.jewishgen.org/yizkor/korets/kor111.html.

Basyuk, Eliezer. "Livelihoods in Korets." In *Korets (Volyn): In Memory of Our Community That Is No More* [Hebrew and Yiddish], edited by Eliezer Leoni, 162–63. Tel Aviv: Former Residents of Korets in Israel, 1959. Translated by Sara Mages at https://www.jewishgen.org/yizkor/korets/kor153.html.

Bergel, Chaim. "In the Storm of Battle." In *Korets (Volyn): In Memory of Our Community That Is No More* [Hebrew and Yiddish], edited by Eliezer Leoni, 494–97. Tel Aviv: Former Residents of Korets in Israel, 1959.

Bergel, Dov. "The Road to the Partisans and to Liberation." In *Korets (Volyn): In Memory of Our Community That Is No More* [Hebrew and Yiddish], edited by Eliezer Leoni, 470–79. Tel Aviv: Former Residents of Korets in Israel, 1959.

———. "This Is How the Town Was Ruined." In *Korets (Volyn): In Memory of Our Community That Is No More* [Hebrew and Yiddish], edited by Eliezer Leoni, 338–47. Tel Aviv: Former Residents of Korets in Israel, 1959.

Bernstein, Dov. "The Economic Life of the Korets Jews." In *Korets (Volyn): In Memory of Our Community That Is No More* [Hebrew and Yiddish], edited by Eliezer Leoni, 157–61. Tel Aviv: Former Residents of Korets in Israel, 1959. Translated by Sara Mages at https:// www.jewishgen.org/yizkor/korets/kor153.html.

———. "'TOZ' in Korets." In *Korets (Volyn): In Memory of Our Community That Is No More* [Hebrew and Yiddish], edited by Eliezer Leoni, 172–76. Tel Aviv: Former Residents of Korets in Israel, 1959. Translated by Sara Mages at https://www.jewishgen.org/yizkor/ko-rets/kor167.html.

Charif, Zelig. "How I Escaped from the Claws of Death." In *Korets (Volyn): In Memory of Our Community That Is No More* [Hebrew and Yiddish], edited by Eliezer Leoni, 413–14. Tel Aviv: Former Residents of Korets in Israel, 1959.

Chimenes, Aizik. "When the Soviets Came." In *Korets (Volyn): In Memory of Our Community That Is No More* [Hebrew and Yiddish], edited by Eliezer Leoni, 336–37. Tel Aviv: Former Residents of Korets in Israel, 1959. Translated by Sara Mages at https://www.jewishgen .org/yizkor/korets/kor331.html.

"Comrade Engineer M. Gildenman ('Uncle Misha') visits 'Ihud' in Łódź." *Opinion* [Polish] 19 (June 16, 1947): 11.

Dallin, Alexander, Ralph Mavrogordato, and Wilhelm Moll. "Partisan Psychological Warfare and Popular Attitudes." In *Soviet Partisans in World War II*, edited by John A. Armstrong, 197–337. Madison: University of Wisconsin Press, 1964.

Dembski, Yafa (née Shaindel Chimenes). "The Shadow of Death." In *Korets (Volyn): In Memory of Our Community That Is No More* [Hebrew and Yiddish], edited by Eliezer Leoni, 415–20. Tel Aviv: Former Residents of Korets in Israel, 1959.

Feiner, Yitzhak. "The Last Path of our Martyrs." In *Korets (Volyn): In Memory of Our Community That Is No More* [Hebrew and Yiddish], edited by Eliezer Leoni, 357–60. Tel Aviv: Former Residents of Korets in Israel, 1959. Translated by Yocheved Klausner at https://www.jewishgen.org/yizkor/korets/kor331.html.

Gelber, N. M. "The History of the Jews in Korets." In *Korets (Volyn): In Memory of Our Community That Is No More* [Hebrew and Yiddish], edited by Eliezer Leoni, 15–31. Tel Aviv: Former Residents of Korets in Israel, 1959.

Ghert-Zand, Renee. "Oscar-Qualifying Short Film Strikes Chord with Story of Heroic Young WWII Partisan." *Times of Israel*, December 20, 2022. https://www.timesofisrael.com/oscar-qualifying-short-film-strikes-chord.

Gildenman, Moshe. "The Attitude of the Non-Jewish Population Toward the Jews." In *Rivne: A Memorial Book* [Hebrew], edited by Aryeh Avitahi, 518–20. Tel Aviv: Former Residents of Rivne in Israel, 1956. Translated by Naomi Gal in *Rovno: Memorial Book*, edited by Ann Glickman Goldberg, 738–40. New York: JewishGen, 2020.

———. "The Bloody Days of Petliura." In *Rivne: A Memorial Book* [Hebrew], edited by Aryeh Avitahi, 40–43. Tel Aviv: Former Residents of Rivne in Israel, 1956. Translated by Naomi Gal in *Rovno: Memorial Book*, edited by Ann Glickman Goldberg, 41–45. New York: JewishGen, 2020.

———. "By the Bóbr River." *Opinion* [Polish] 17 (May 5, 1947): 7–8.

———. "The End of Hataman Askilko." In *Rivne: A Memorial Book* [Hebrew], edited by Aryeh Avitahi, 49–51. Tel Aviv: Former Residents of Rivne in Israel, 1956. Translated by Naomi Gal in *Rovno: Memorial Book*, edited by Ann Glickman Goldberg, 55–57. New York: JewishGen, 2020.

———. "Expedition to Rybałki." *Opinion* [Polish] 14 (March 20, 1947): 6.

———. "Fighting and Struggle in the Forest (From My Memories as a Partisan)." In *Korets (Volyn): In Memory of Our Community That Is No More* [Hebrew and Yiddish], edited by Eliezer Leoni, 443–50. Tel Aviv: Former Residents of Korets in Israel, 1959. Translated by Yocheved Klausner at https://www.jewishgen.org/yizkor/korets/kor443.html.

———. "The First Ambush." *The New Life* [Yiddish] 22 (March 1947): 5.

———. "How I Captured a Pair of German Boots." *The New Life* [Yiddish] 48 (July 1947): 4.

———. "In the Forests of Zhytomyr." *The New Life* [Yiddish] 30 (April 1947): 5 and 31 (April 1947): 5.

———. "Uncle Misha's Diary (An Excerpt)." *Opinion* [Polish] 9 (December 20, 1946): 14.

———. "The Yellow Patch." *Opinion* [Polish] 10 (January 15, 1947): 13.

———. "Zviahel in the Years 1920 to 1941." In *Zviahel (Novohrad-Volynskyi)* [Hebrew and Yiddish], edited by Azriel Uri and Mordekhai Boneh, 200–10. Tel Aviv: Association of Former Residents of Zviahel and Surroundings, 1962. Translated by Tina Lunson at https://www.jewishgen.org/yizkor/zvhil/zvhy200.html.

G[ildenman], S[imcha]. "Uncle Misha." In *Korets (Volyn): In Memory of Our Community That Is No More* [Hebrew and Yiddish], edited by Eliezer Leoni, 503–5. Tel Aviv: Former Residents of Korets in Israel, 1959.

Gildenman, Simcha. "Upon My Return to the Town." In *Korets (Volyn): In Memory of Our Community That Is No More* [Hebrew and Yiddish], edited by Eliezer Leoni, 530–32. Tel Aviv: Former Residents of Korets in Israel, 1959.

———. "Vengeance is Mine, and Recompense (Deuteronomy 32:35)." In *Korets (Volyn): In Memory of Our Community That Is No More* [Hebrew and Yiddish], edited by Eliezer Leoni, 490–93. Tel Aviv: Former Residents of Korets in Israel, 1959.

Goldberg, Tzvi. "The Cooperative Bank." In *The Staszów Book* [Hebrew, Yiddish, and English], edited by Elhanan Erlich, 71–72. Tel Aviv: Former Residents of Staszów in Israel and in the Diaspora, 1962. Translated by Kutzi Weill in *Staszów Memorial Book*, edited by Jean-Pierre Stroweis, Leonard Levin, and Dobrochna Fire, 49–50. New York: JewishGen, 2020.

Kahana, Meir. "At the Outbreak of the War." In *Korets (Volyn): In Memory of Our Community That Is No More* [Hebrew and Yiddish], edited by Eliezer Leoni, 333–35. Tel Aviv: Former Residents of Korets in Israel, 1959. Translated by Sara Mages at https://www.jewishgen.org/yizkor/korets/kor331.html.

Kahanovich, Moshe. "Moshe Gildenman—Partisan Commander of the 'Yevgruppa.'" *Yad Vashem Bulletin* 3 (1958): 13–14.

———. "The Partisan Detachment of 'Dyadye Misha." In *Zviahel (Novohrad-Volynskyi)* [Hebrew and Yiddish], edited by Azriel Uri and Mordekhai Boneh, 219–23. Tel Aviv: Association of Former Residents of Zviahel and Surroundings, 1962. Translated by Tina Lunson at https://www.jewishgen.org/yizkor/zvhil/zvhy200.html.

Kersch (Shapira), Yehudit. "'Write This for a Memorial in a Book' ... (Exodus 17:14)." In *Korets (Volyn): In Memory of Our Community That Is*

No More [Hebrew and Yiddish], edited by Eliezer Leoni, 349–56. Tel Aviv: Former Residents of Korets in Israel, 1959.

Kleiner, Yitzhak. "From the Nightmares of Those Days…" In *Korets (Volyn): In Memory of Our Community That Is No More* [Hebrew and Yiddish], edited by Eliezer Leoni, 500–502. Tel Aviv: Former Residents of Korets in Israel, 1959.

Kligerman, Hinda. "The Great Fire in Korets." In *Korets (Volyn): In Memory of Our Community That Is No More* [Hebrew and Yiddish], edited by Eliezer Leoni, 97–98. Tel Aviv: Former Residents of Korets in Israel, 1959. Translated by Sara Mages at https://www.jewishgen.org/yizkor/korets/kor065.html.

Kligerman, Yosef. "The 'Fair' in Town." In *Korets (Volyn): In Memory of Our Community That Is No More* [Hebrew and Yiddish], edited by Eliezer Leoni, 164–66. Tel Aviv: Former Residents of Korets in Israel, 1959. Translated by Sara Mages at https://www.jewishgen.org/yizkor/korets/kor153.html.

Klinke, Ian and Mark Bassin. "Introduction: Lebensraum and Its Discontents," *Journal of Historical Geography* 61 (2018): 53–58.

Kruglov, Alexander and Andrew Koss. "Korzec," translated by Ester-Basya Vaisman. In *The United States Holocaust Memorial Museum Encyclopedia of Camps and Ghettos, 1933–1945.* Vol. 2, *Ghettos in German-Occupied Eastern Europe*, edited by Martin Dean and Mel Hecker, 1385–86. Bloomington: Indiana University Press, 2012.

Leoni, Eliezer. "Publishing Houses and Printing Shops in Korets." In *Korets (Volyn): In Memory of Our Community That Is No More* [Hebrew and Yiddish], edited by Eliezer Leoni, 48–62. Tel Aviv: Former Residents of Korets in Israel, 1959.

———. "Rabbi Pinchas of Korets." In *Korets (Volyn): In Memory of Our Community That Is No More* [Hebrew and Yiddish], edited by Eliezer Leoni, 32–47. Tel Aviv: Former Residents of Korets in Israel, 1959. Translated by David Goldman at https://www.jewishgen.org/yizkor/korets/kor031.html.

Mendele Review: Yiddish Literature and Language. "Der oyfrays fun a soldatn-heym" (Part One) ("The Demolition of a Soldier's Home") [Moyshe Gildenman (Dyadya/Diadia Misha, pseud.)]" [English and Yiddish] https://yiddish.haifa.ac.il/tmr/tmr12/tmr12005.htm.

Museum of Jewish Heritage. "Meir [Kransnostawski]'s Story." https://education.mjhnyc.org/survivor-stories/meirs-story.

Pe'er, Yaakov. "Wandering." In *Korets (Volyn): In Memory of Our Community That Is No More* [Hebrew and Yiddish], edited by Eliezer Leoni, 486–89. Tel Aviv: Former Residents of Korets in Israel, 1959.

Pe'er, Zvi. "This Is How I Took Revenge on the Murderers." In *Korets (Volyn): In Memory of Our Community That Is No More* [Hebrew and Yiddish], edited by Eliezer Leoni, 480–85. Tel Aviv: Former Residents of Korets in Israel, 1959.

Rabinowitz (Shochen), Shoshana. "The Korchyk River." In *Korets (Volyn): In Memory of Our Community That Is No More* [Hebrew and Yiddish], edited by Eliezer Leoni, 72–74. Tel Aviv: Former Residents of Korets in Israel, 1959. Translated by Sara Mages at https://www.jewishgen.org/yizkor/korets/kor065.html.

Rabinowitz (Strassberg), Dora. "A Drop from the Sea of Blood and Tears." In *Korets (Volyn): In Memory of Our Community That Is No More* [Hebrew and Yiddish], edited by Eliezer Leoni, 431–32. Tel Aviv: Former Residents of Korets in Israel, 1959.

Riess (Goldman), Zahava. "This Was My Home." In *Korets (Volyn): In Memory of Our Community That Is No More* [Hebrew and Yiddish], edited by Eliezer Leoni, 75–76. Tel Aviv: Former Residents of Korets in Israel, 1959. Translated by Sara Mages at https://www.jewishgen.org/yizkor/korets/kor065.html.

Rutenberg, Z. "The Old Jewish Cemetery in Korets." In *Korets (Volyn): In Memory of Our Community That Is No More* [Hebrew and Yiddish], edited by Eliezer Leoni, 527–29. Tel Aviv: Former Residents of Korets in Israel, 1959.

Shostak, Eliezer. "The 'Heavenly Yeshiva' in Korets." In *Korets (Volyn): In Memory of Our Community That Is No More* [Hebrew and Yiddish], edited by Eliezer Leoni, 123–26. Tel Aviv: Former Residents of Korets in Israel, 1959. Translated by Sara Mages at https://www.jewishgen.org/yizkor/korets/kor111.html.

Smolier, Moshe. "The 'Tarbut' Library and the Man Asher Blovstein." In *Korets (Volyn): In Memory of Our Community That Is No More* [Hebrew and Yiddish], edited by Eliezer Leoni, 135–37. Tel Aviv: Former Residents of Korets in Israel, 1959. Translated by Sara Mages at https://www.jewishgen.org/yizkor/korets/kor133.html.

Spector, Shmuel. "Gildenman, Moshe." In *Encyclopedia of the Holocaust*, edited by Israel Gutman. New York: Macmillan Publishing Company, 1990.

———. "The Jews of Volhynia and Their Reaction to Extermination." *Yad Vashem Studies* 15 (1983): 159–86.

"Uncle Misha." *Opinion* [Polish] 9 (December 20, 1946): 14.

United States Holocaust Memorial Museum. "How Many People Did the Nazis Murder?" Holocaust Encyclopedia. https://encyclopedia .ushmm.org/content/en/article/documenting-numbers-of-victims -of-the-holocaust-and-nazi-persecution.

———. "Lodz." Holocaust Encyclopedia. https://encyclopedia.ushmm.org/ content/en/article/lodz.

———. "Nazi Camps." Holocaust Encyclopedia. https://encyclopedia .ushmm.org/content/en/article/nazi-camps.

———. "Warsaw." Holocaust Encyclopedia. https://encyclopedia.ushmm .org/content/en/article/warsaw.

———. "Warsaw Ghetto Uprising." Holocaust Encyclopedia. https://ency clopedia.ushmm.org/content/en/article/warsaw-ghetto-uprising.

Uri, Ariel. "As Told by the Partisan Simcha Gildenman." In *Zviahel (No-vohrad-Volynskyi)* [Hebrew and Yiddish], edited by Azriel Uri and Mordekhai Boneh, 304–6. Tel Aviv: Association of Former Residents of Zviahel and Surroundings, 1962.

Vidro, Shmuel. "How I Escaped from the Pit of Death." In *Korets (Volyn): In Memory of Our Community That Is No More* [Hebrew and Yiddish], edited by Eliezer Leoni, 433–39. Tel Aviv: Former Residents of Korets in Israel, 1959.

Volkon (Pinchuk), Haya. "Wanderings and Hardships during the Holocaust." In *Rokytne (Volyn) and the Surrounding Area: A Book of Testimony and Memory* [Hebrew and Yiddish], edited by Eliezer Leoni, 301–8. Tel Aviv: Former Residents of Rokytne in Israel, 1967. Translated by Ala Gamulka in *Rokitno-Wolyn and Surroundings: Memorial Book and Testimony (Ukraine)*, 313–21. New York: JewishGen, 2015.

Wachbroit, Yosef. "The Art Life in Korets." In *Korets (Volyn): In Memory of Our Community That Is No More* [Hebrew and Yiddish], edited by Eliezer Leoni, 140–43. Tel Aviv: Former Residents of Korets in Israel, 1959. Translated by Sara Mages at https://www.jewishgen .org/yizkor/korets/kor133.html.

Weinberg, Chanan. "A Doctor in the Forest." In *Memorial Book of the Community of Sarny* [Hebrew and Yiddish], edited by Yosef Kariv, 366–68. Tel Aviv: Former Residents of Sarny and Vicinity in Israel, 1961. Translated by Jacob Solomon Berger and edited by Karen Leon at https://www.jewishgen.org/yizkor/sarny/sar350.html.

Weinberg, Gerhard L. "Airpower in Partisan Warfare." In *Soviet Partisans in World War II*, edited by John A. Armstrong, 361–85. Madison: University of Wisconsin Press, 1964.

Weinberg, Tadeusz (Gadi T. Carmon). "Poland Is Not Yet Lost." In *Jewish Fate: Testimonies of the Living*, Vol. 2 [Polish], edited by Marian Turski, 5–13. Warsaw: Association of Jewish Veterans and Victims of World War II, 1999. Available online at https://zapispamieci.pl/tadeusz-weinberg/.

Werb, Bret. Liner notes to *Rise Up and Fight! Songs of Jewish Partisans*. Recorded 1995–1996. United States Holocaust Memorial Museum USHMM-02, 1996. CD.

Wörn, Achim. "Jews in Szczecin, 1945–50: At the Crossroad between Emigration and Assimilation." *Region: Regional Studies of Russia, Eastern Europe, and Central Asia* 6:1 (2017): 55–85.

Wulach, Jakob. "On the Road to Extinction." In *Korets (Volyn): In Memory of Our Community That Is No More* [Hebrew and Yiddish], edited by Eliezer Leoni, 361–65. Tel Aviv: Former Residents of Korets in Israel, 1959.

———. "The Orphanage." In *Korets (Volyn): In Memory of Our Community That Is No More* [Hebrew and Yiddish], edited by Eliezer Leoni, 170–72. Tel Aviv: Former Residents of Korets in Israel, 1959. Translated by Sara Mages at https://www.jewishgen.org/yizkor/korets/kor167.html.

Yad Vashem. "Motale's Violin." Posted December 8, 2021. YouTube video, 4:28. https://www.youtube.com/watch?v=ck_wlJWsRSc.

———. "Murder Story of Korzec Jews in the Kozak Forest." Untold Stories—Murder Sites of Jews in Occupied Territories of the USSR. https://collections.yadvashem.org/en/untold-stories/killing-site/14627900.

———. "Murder Story of Korzec Jews in Szytnia." Untold Stories—Murder Sites of Jews in Occupied Territories of the USSR. https://collections.yadvashem.org/en/untold-stories/killing-site/14627899.

———. "Murder Story of Korzec Jews in the Sukhovolya Forest." Untold Stories—Murder Sites of Jews in Occupied Territories of the USSR. https://collections.yadvashem.org/en/untold-stories/killing-site/14627898.

Zaluska (Fuchs), Batya. "In the Korets Ghetto and in the Woods." In *Korets (Volyn): In Memory of Our Community That Is No More* [Hebrew and

Yiddish], edited by Eliezer Leoni, 451–69. Tel Aviv: Former Residents of Korets in Israel, 1959.

Zawdi, Shraga. "The *Beth Midrashes* in Korets." In *Korets (Volyn): In Memory of Our Community That Is No More* [Hebrew and Yiddish], edited by Eliezer Leoni, 99–100. Tel Aviv: Former Residents of Korets in Israel, 1959.

Zayka, Avigdor. "The Massacre in the 'New Town.'" In *Korets (Volyn): In Memory of Our Community That Is No More* [Hebrew and Yiddish], edited by Eliezer Leoni, 408–12. Tel Aviv: Former Residents of Korets in Israel, 1959.

Zeltser, Arkadi. "How the Jewish Intelligentsia Created the Jewishness of the Jewish Hero." In Soviet Jews in World War II: Fighting, Witnessing, Remembering, edited by Harriet Murav and Gennady Estraikh, 104–28. Boston: Academic Studies Press, 2014.

Ziemke, Earl F. "Composition and Morale of the Partisan Movement." In *Soviet Partisans in World War II*, edited by John A. Armstrong, 141–196. Madison: University of Wisconsin Press, 1964.

Discussion Questions
for *Partisan Song*

1. Many members of the Jewish community in Moshe Gildenman's hometown of Korets, Ukraine, believed that the Germans would spare their lives, an optimism that seems naive with the benefit of hindsight. Do you believe that it is beneficial to maintain hope, even in the most desperate of situations? Why or why not?

2. The reactions of the Jews to the impending liquidation of the Korets ghetto varied, including denial, resignation, suicide, and, in Moshe Gildenman's case, vengeance. How have others, in history or in your own life, reacted in impossible situations?

3. When Moshe Gildenman escaped from the Korets ghetto, he took a revolver and his copy of the Yiddish songbook *Freedom's Songs*. What does his decision to safeguard a book of Yiddish songs say about his priorities? If you had to leave your home with only that which you could carry, what would you take? What does that say about you?

4. While the legendary Jewish partisan Tuvia Bielski felt, "It is more important to save Jews than to kill Germans," Moshe Gildenman prioritized killing as many Germans as he could, even if it meant leaving behind Jewish refugees who were unfit for combat. In your opinion, who made the better decision? Why?

5. Throughout their experiences with the Soviet partisans and the Red Army, Moshe Gildenman and his son, Simcha, had to overcome the antisemitic stereotype that Jews were too cowardly to be trusted in combat. Have you ever been in a position where someone made a poor assumption about you based on a stereotype? Were you able to change that misperception? If so, how?

6. The boy partisan Motele Schlein concealed his Jewish identity, even among Jews he trusted with his life. What aspects of your background have you concealed from people you otherwise trust? Why did you feel it was necessary to protect yourself in this way?

7. In the forest, the Jewish partisans sang Jewish songs and danced Jewish dances. What does this say about their desire to preserve Jewish culture? What aspects of your culture would you work hardest to maintain if you had to leave your community behind?

8. Moshe Gildenman's son, Simcha, compiled a book of songs as mementos of people he met during and after the war. What music would you preserve to remember your friends? Why would you choose those particular works?

9. Before the murders of his wife and daughter, Moshe Gildenman had never even held a weapon, but he was at times ruthlessly brutal as a partisan and officer in the Red Army. Do you think you would be capable of such violence in a similar situation? Why or why not?

10. Before reading *Partisan Song*, what was your understanding of the ways in which Jews resisted the Nazis during the Holocaust? How has that understanding changed, now that you have read the book?

Index